You don't need a weatherman
To know which way the wind blows

SUBTERRANEAN HOMESICK BLUES

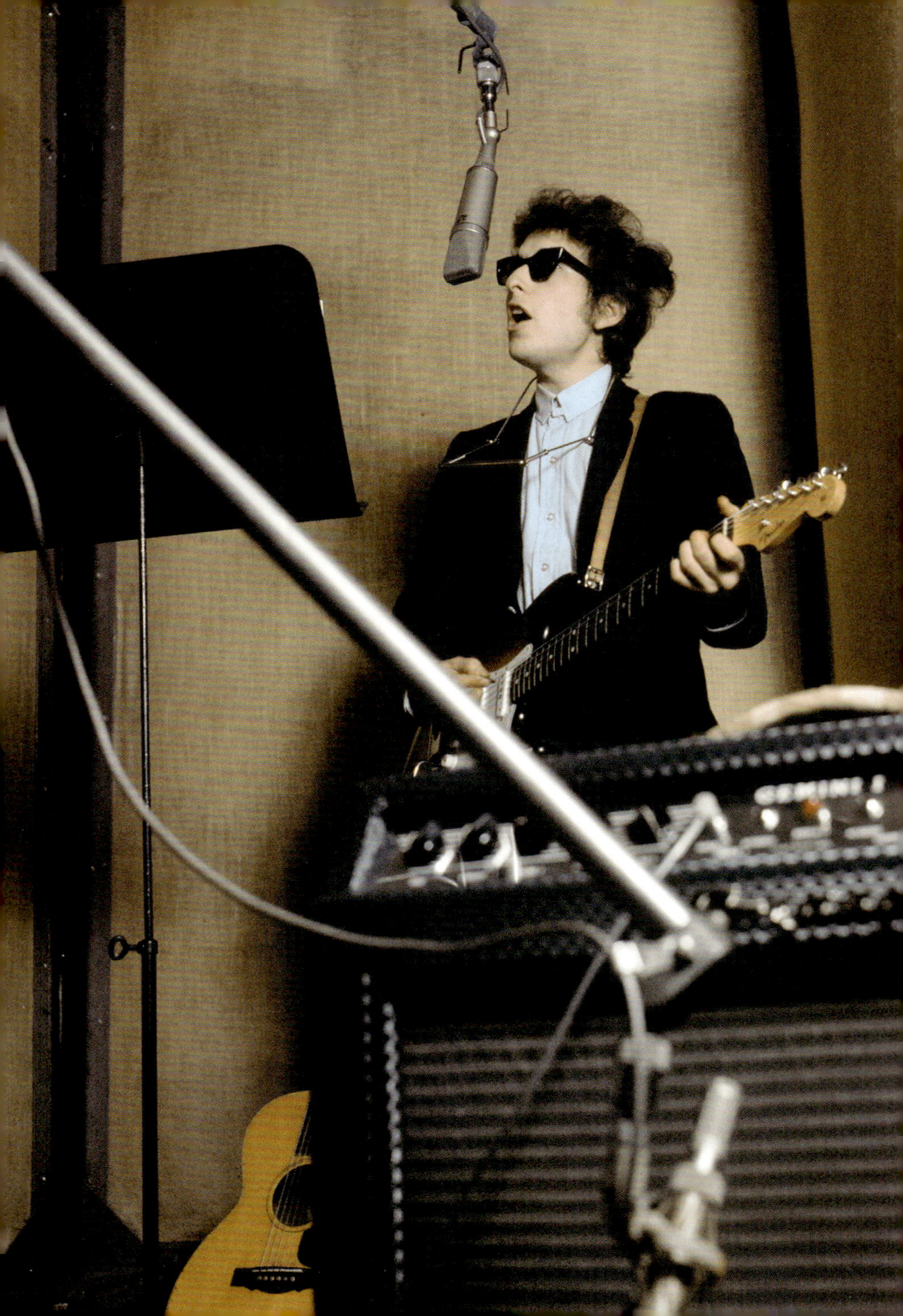

DANIEL KRAMER

Bob Dylan

A Year and A Day

TASCHEN

William Zanzinger killed poor Hattie Carroll
With a cane that he twirled around his diamond ring finger
At a Baltimore hotel society gath'rin'
And the cops were called in and his weapon took from him
As they rode him in custody down to the station
And booked William Zanzinger for first-degree murder
But you who philosophize disgrace and criticize all fears
Take the rag away from your face
Now ain't the time for your tears

William Zanzinger, who at twenty-four years
Owns a tobacco farm of six hundred acres
With rich wealthy parents who provide and protect him
And high office relations in the politics of Maryland
Reacted to his deed with a shrug of his shoulders
And swear words and sneering, and his tongue it was snarling
In a matter of minutes on bail was out walking
But you who philosophize disgrace and criticize all fears
Take the rag away from your face
Now ain't the time for your tears

Hattie Carroll was a maid of the kitchen
She was fifty-one years old and gave birth to ten children
Who carried the dishes and took out the garbage
And never sat once at the head of the table
And didn't even talk to the people at the table
Who just cleaned up all the food from the table
And emptied the ashtrays on a whole other level
Got killed by a blow, lay slain by a cane
That sailed through the air and came down through the room
Doomed and determined to destroy all the gentle
And she never done nothing to William Zanzinger
But you who philosophize disgrace and criticize all fears
Take the rag away from your face
Now ain't the time for your tears

In the courtroom of honor, the judge pounded his gavel
To show that all's equal and that the courts are on the level
And that the strings in the books ain't pulled and persuaded
And that even the nobles get properly handled
Once that the cops have chased after and caught 'em
And that the ladder of law has no top and no bottom
Stared at the person who killed for no reason
Who just happened to be feelin' that way without warnin'
And he spoke through his cloak, most deep and distinguished
And handed out strongly, for penalty and repentance
William Zanzinger with a six-month sentence
Oh, but you who philosophize disgrace and criticize all fears
Bury the rag deep in your face
For now's the time for your tears

THE LONESOME DEATH OF HATTIE CARROLL

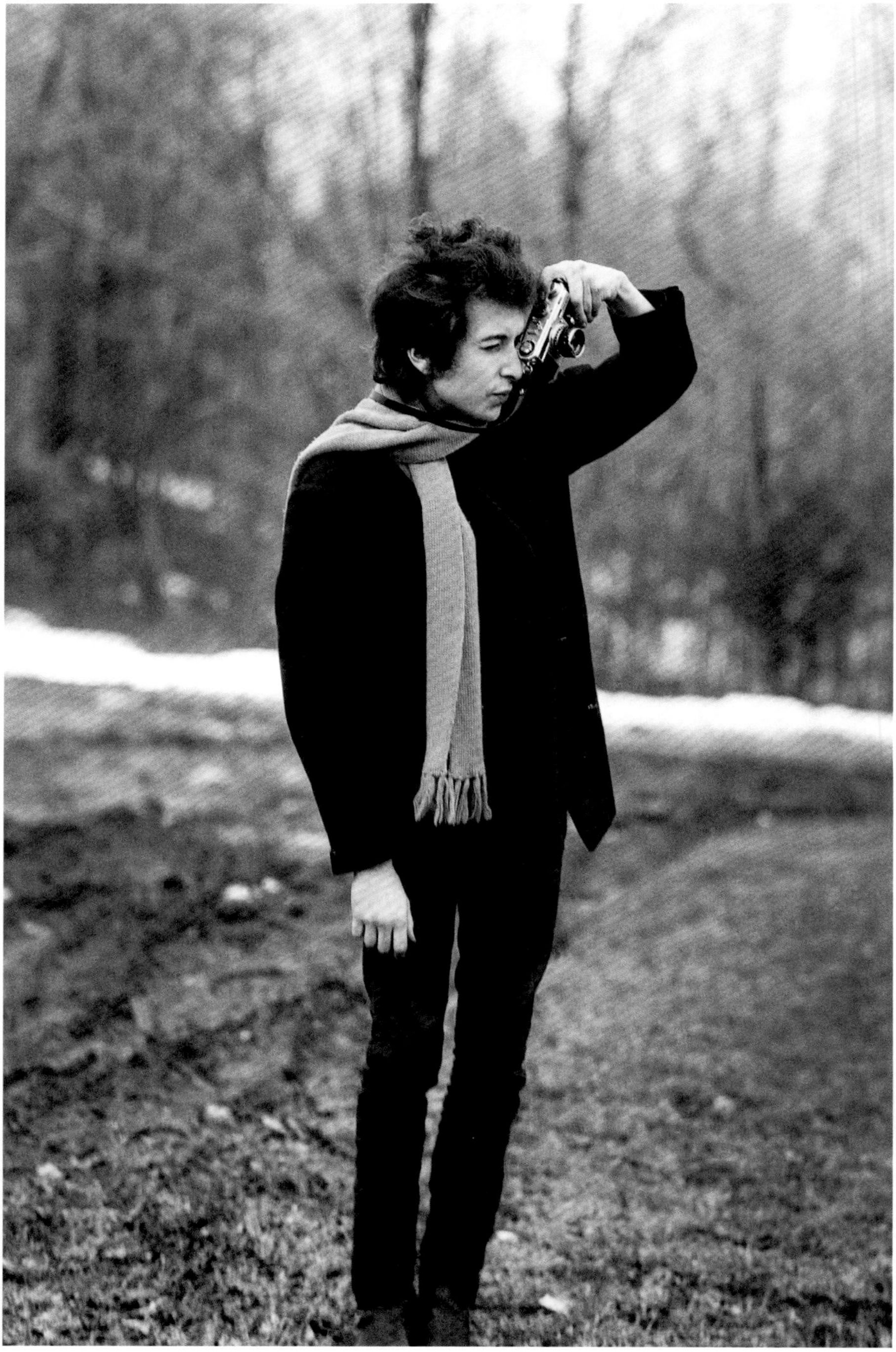

Preface

It all began in February 1964, when I happened to see a young performer on the popular Steve Allen variety TV show. That's how this story begins. That's when I saw Bob Dylan for the first time.

Alone under a spotlight with only his guitar, Bob Dylan's sound and forceful approach to his music immediately got my attention -- then I heard his lyrics! He was singing about the corruption of justice: the wanton slaying of an aging hotel barmaid by a wealthy and influential guest at a Baltimore dinner party. A newspaper account of the woman's murder was the true-life inspiration for "The Lonesome Death of Hattie Carroll," which concludes by describing the woefully inadequate punishment for this public murder -- a six-month sentence. Six months! It was poetry, poetry as good as any I had ever read, and I thought he was very brave to be saying such things on a widely seen popular mainstream TV show.

From time to time, Dylan added to the overall effect by leaving his lyric and playing the harmonica he wore in a wire holder around his neck. The music, the harmonica, and the guitar playing were strong and emphasized urgency and enabled me to feel the tragedy more (completely) deeply. He got me, although hearing his voice would have been enough to do that. It was the kind of sound I always liked. It reminded me of a voice from the hills. It was an old voice, it seemed craggy and weather-beaten, like a voice that had been left out in the rain and rusted. I attributed veracity to this voice, but what I didn't know then is that Mr. Dylan is a singer of many voices.

Later, after seeing Bob Dylan on the TV, I was still aware of his tapping on my shoulder. I was taken by what this man had done and how he had done it. With simple, basic tools he drove his message home, and certainly what he was saying about the corruption of justice was very brave. I sensed an important talent and thought that I should photograph him.

Before the summer of 1964 I didn't know very much about folk music. If I were asked to name a folk song, I probably would have said, "On Top of Old Smokey." If I were asked to name a folksinger, I probably would have been at a loss. At the age of 12, when I spent two weeks at a Boy Scouts camp, we sang songs about blue tail flies, herring boxes without tops, girls with long flaxen hair, mountain ranges, and little dogies who were getting along, and every now and then I would go through a few stanzas of "Streets of Laredo" around the campfire, or hum along with "Home on the Range." I never gave it much thought. I guess I was just Frank Sinatra all the way.

I tracked down the name of Bob Dylan's management company and made a phone call. Naturally I was told Mr. Dylan was not available. And so it went. I would call and they would say no. Eventually they asked me to put my request in writing--I did and it did me no good. After months of calling I happened, one day, to call after business hours, and, as luck would have it, Albert Grossman, Bob Dylan's manager, picked up the phone. By this time he knew why I was calling. Still, once again, I quickly explained that I wanted just one hour for a portrait session with his client and convinced him that I was a reasonable, completely sane, published, professional photographer. I was caught by surprise when his almost immediate answer was, "Okay, come up to Woodstock next Thursday. You can have an hour--call my secretary for details." Just like that...just like that!

The day I met Bob Dylan started with a two-hour drive to Woodstock, New York. Just beyond the town, set off from the public road by an unmarked driveway, and concealed from view by an expanse of grounds covered with trees and heavy foliage, was the home of Albert Grossman. A sign posted on a tree along the driveway read: "IF YOU HAVE NOT TELEPHONED, YOU ARE TRESPASSING." Here Dylan spent a good deal of his time when he was not on the road or in the city. More than a hideout, the large house was a peaceful retreat. There was a pool behind the house, and two smaller buildings were used as a garage and guesthouse. Everything was bright and still on this warm August morning.

Dylan was not there when I arrived, and I passed the time waiting at the pool. Then, the roar of a motorcycle in the driveway broke the quiet. It disappeared into the garage, and moments later a thin, gangly young man dressed in jeans, boots, and a rumpled work shirt walked toward me. Ringlets of hair protruded from under his motorcycle rider's cap. His pale complexion and slight frame made him appear younger than his 23 years. As we greeted each other, we shook hands, and I was surprised at how gentle his handshake was (yet he was so strong when he performed). I've since decided it was his way of being polite and not giving me too much on our first meeting. Knowing him now, he was probably being cautious. We talked about what I wanted to do, and I told him I wanted to make a portrait and that it would not take too long. He invited me to do what I needed to do to get some pictures and disappeared into the house. I followed and found him sitting at a dining booth in the kitchen reading a newspaper. He turned the pages of the paper and never acknowledged my presence. This set the pace. Apparently he was not going to do anything, especially for my camera. It was not that he wasn't cooperating. Actually, he was being reasonably available and in a short while he accepted that I would photograph and select my own pictures as long as they derived from what was happening.

Hours later as I drove back to New York, I thought about the hours spent with Bob Dylan. They seemed to reveal some essential part of his personality. It was evident that he was a man who set his own marks and resisted being manipulated. He knew what he wanted to do and what he wanted to produce. Later I would see this part of his personality when he was recording or performing.

A few years earlier I had returned home from my time in the army and decided not to immediately go back to school, where I had planned to study law. I wasn't certain that I wanted to continue on that path, and I decided to take a year to look around. I had begun taking pictures when I was about 14 years old but never really thought of photography as a profession; still, to earn some money I set out to work as a photographer's assistant in New York City. I was lucky and got a job as an assistant at the studio of the fashion photographer Allan Arbus. His wife, Diane Arbus, also did her darkroom work there. It turned out to be more than just a job. From Allan I learned to manage a studio, work with models, and run the business--and from Diane I learned to open my eyes a bit wider, to think about my pictures in new ways. My next job was that of assistant to Philippe Halsman, who photographed more _Life_ magazine covers than any other photographer and was considered to be one of the great portrait photographers. From Philippe I learned how to make light do your bidding, instead of the other way around, and how to choose a decent wine--and that photography could be a great adventure and a pathway to the whole world. It was also the start of a lifelong friendship with him and the entire Halsman family.

Armed, so to speak, with this experience, education, and some professional skills, I cautiously went into business in the spring of 1964 and opened a studio just off Fifth Avenue. Not much later I chanced to meet W. Eugene Smith, one of the 20th century's most important photographers and a personal hero. We became good friends, and he mentored me through some of the work I did with my Bob Dylan project. He even helped to bring the pictures to the attention of magazine editors. Before I knew it, the pictures were being published regularly.

I didn't know when I began working with Bob Dylan that my association with him would become a long one. I didn't

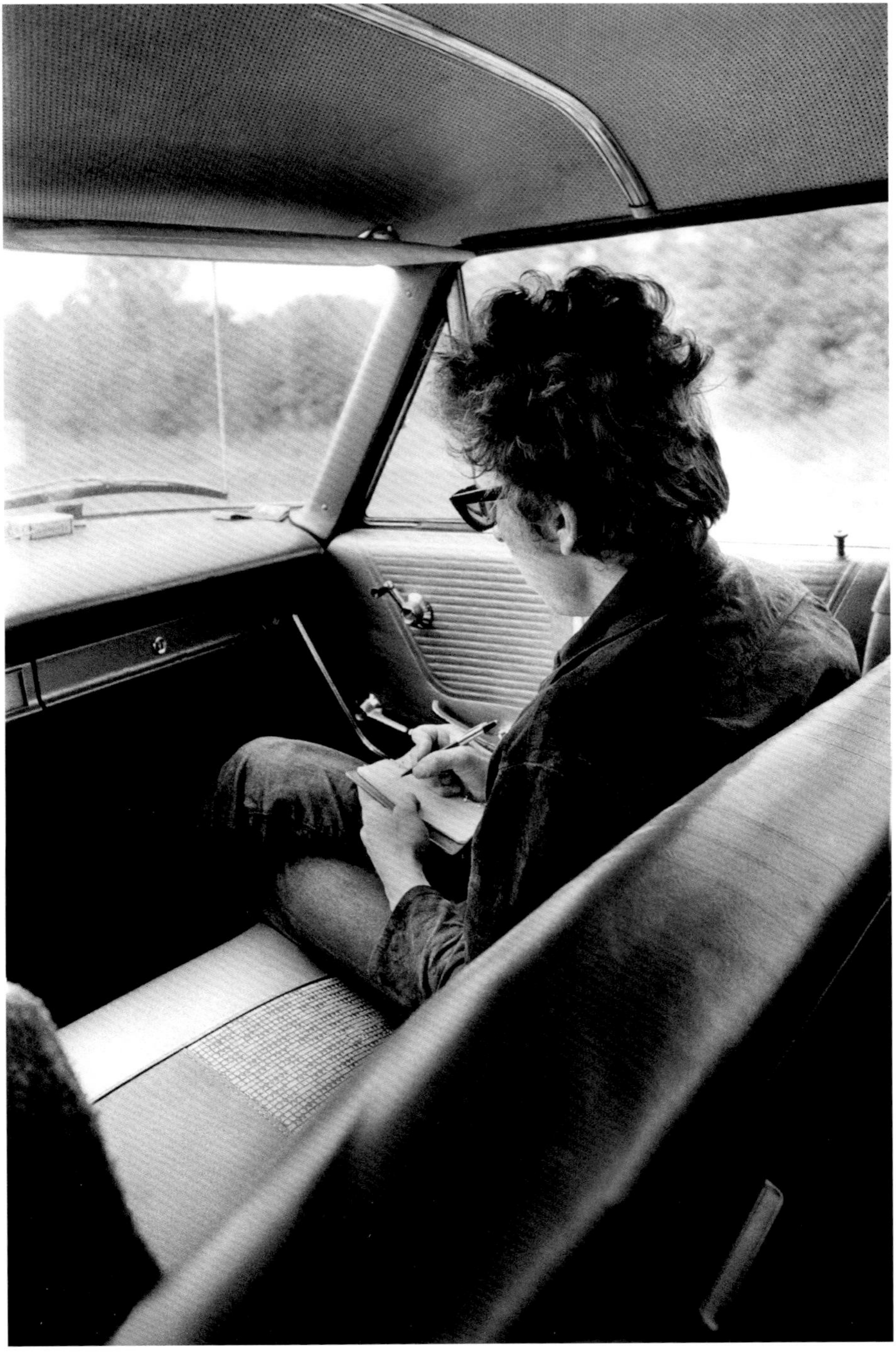

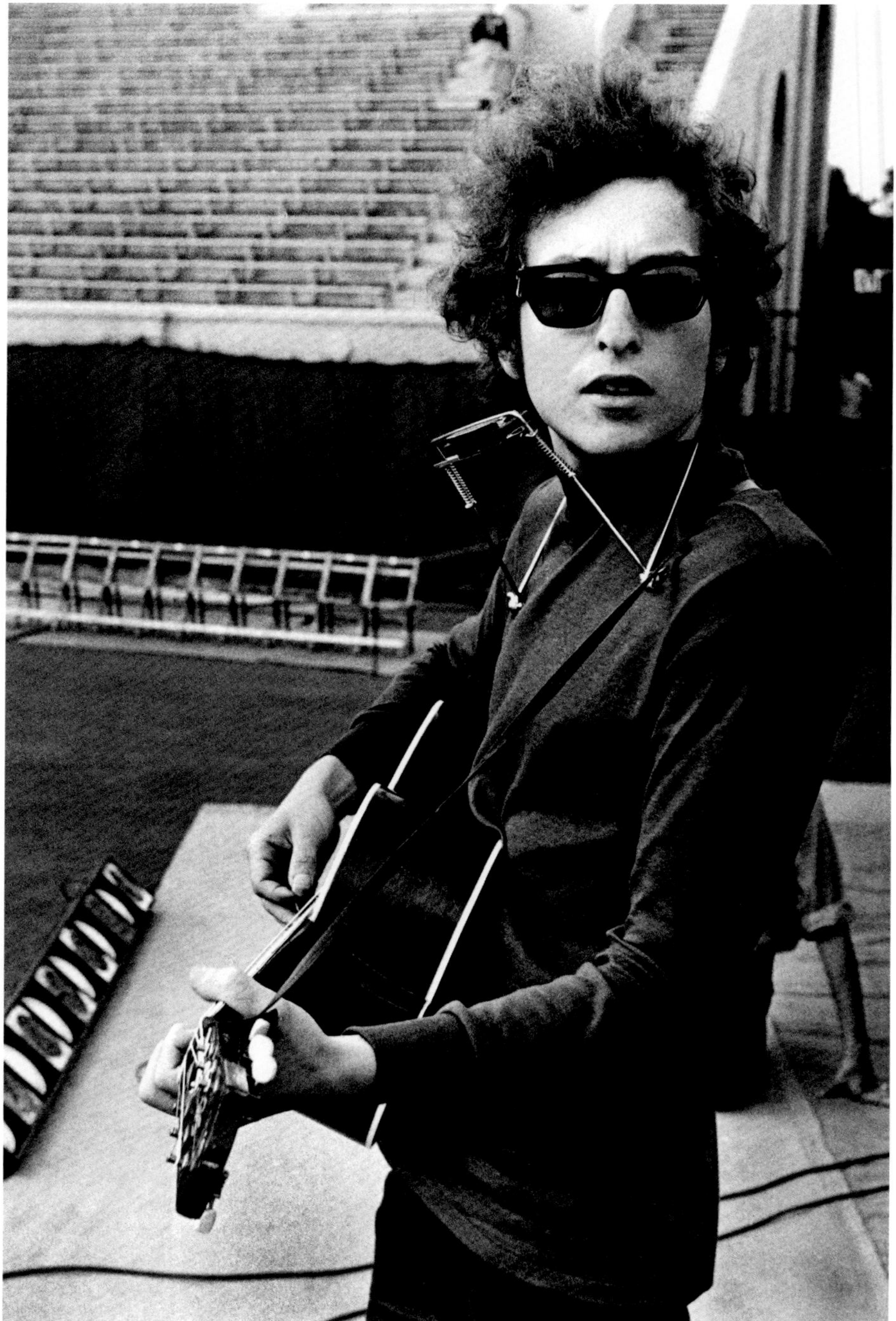

know that I would photograph him many times for more than a year--that I would have the opportunity to document many facets of his professional life and to produce three important album covers, and so much more. I thought that after a few sessions it would be over, but instead I learned that Bob Dylan was a more interesting and complex subject than I expected. Bob was in a constant state of creative evolution. In the one year in which I photographed him, his music and his appearance changed radically. The single performer with his guitar and harmonica was now the leader of a band, requiring truckloads of equipment (as at his now famous Forest Hills concert in 1965). He also went electric--not at the Newport Folk Festival, and not at Forest Hills, but, as far as I'm concerned, in January 1965 at Columbia Records Studio A in New York City when he recorded Bringing It All Back Home. One side of the record was acoustic, the other side featured Bob on an electric guitar with a band. The record was released on March 22, 1965, and in late July of that year, with the release of "Like a Rolling Stone," six-minutes-plus of brooding lyrical verse dropped in a sea of three-minute love songs, he changed the way singles could and would be played on the radio.

Everything with Bob got bigger. At the outset I had no idea that the pictures would include, among others, Joan Baez, Allen Ginsberg, Peter Yarrow, Odetta, Johnny Cash, Les Crane, and Albert and Sally Grossman. Or that after the now-legendary Forest Hills concert I would hide Bob under a blanket in a blue Ford station wagon, concealing him from an exuberant crowd in hot pursuit, while his road manager Victor Maymudes inched the car through the crowd.

All in all there were about 30 photo sessions, starting with Woodstock, usually with little advance notice. We continued as we started--sometimes the sessions were for a few hours, sometimes the day, and sometimes longer. And, because these events happened quite some time ago, I have included throughout this book some of my earlier writings describing those moments, from both my previous book, originally published in 1967, and other writings.

Although I attended many Dylan concerts, and heard many of the songs again and again, the commitment with which he performed always gave them a new life. Sometimes I felt I was hearing and seeing a brand-new Bob Dylan. I was also seeing a brand-new me, for I had to remake myself from a mostly studio photographer to an I-can-shoot-anything-anywhere photographer who could make camera settings and change film in darkened theaters. I was shooting with 35mm cameras at a time when automation was rare. No autofocus, no motor advance, and, more important, no auto exposure. (Almost all of the black-and-white pictures were made with Kodak Tri-X, developed in D-76.) And one other small matter: I had to learn to shoot when the sound of the music or Bob's voice would cover the click of the shutter and not when there was a breath or a space in Bob's phrasing. The camera shutter was like a hammer blow in a quiet theater or recording studio designed to amplify and carry every sound.

I was fortunate to be shooting during this special "big bang" year when Bob Dylan made two of his greatest albums, when he changed music and the music business, and when he went from a young man ready to go to someone who went all the way and then some -- someone who has won, among many other awards, 11 Grammys, the Kennedy Center Honors, an Oscar, a Pulitzer Prize, and been awarded doctorate degrees. It was the year I photographed three Dylan album covers that have become iconic. It was a terrific year, and now, thanks to a wonderful publisher and editor, there is this book.

-- Daniel Kramer, New York City

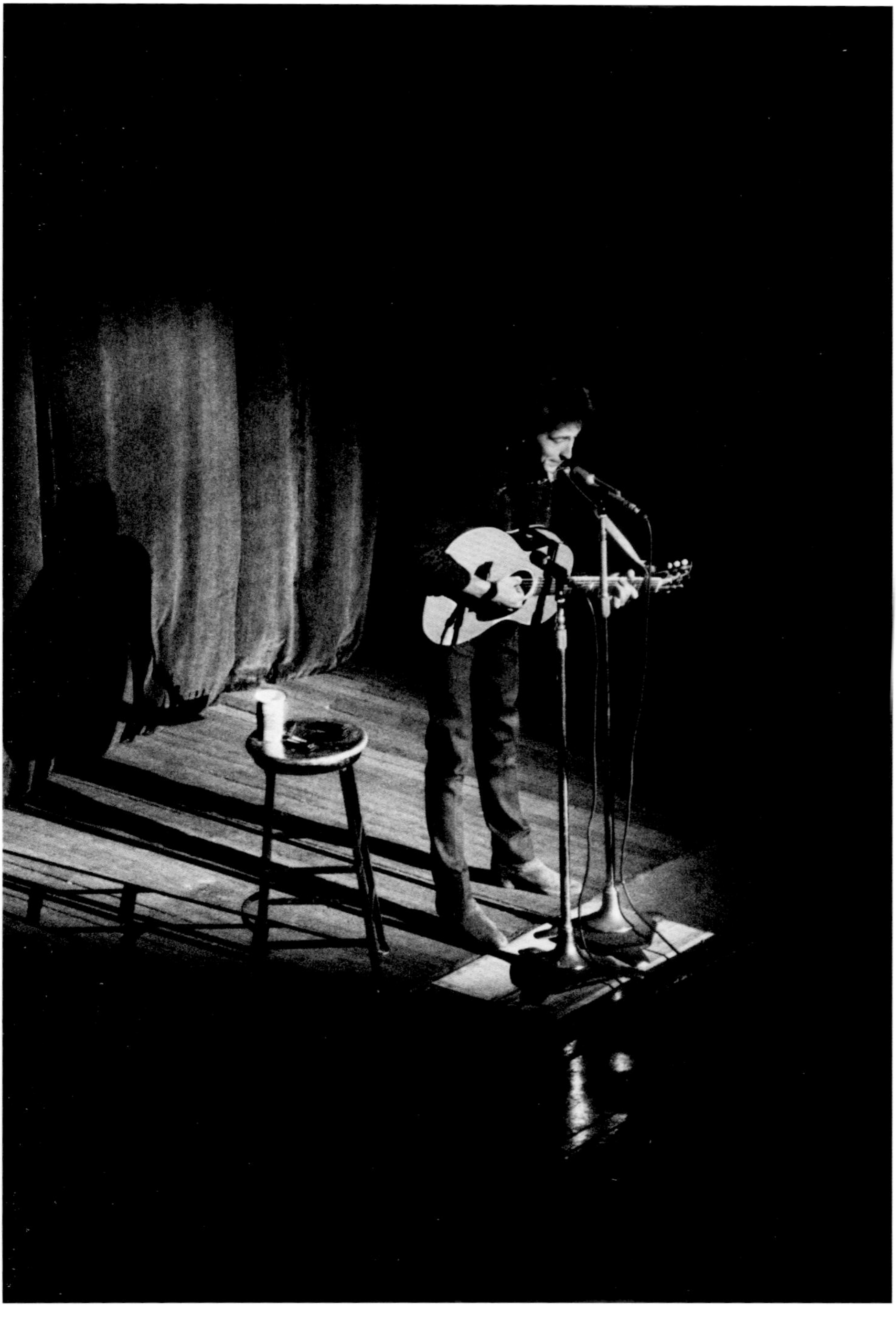

Come writers and critics
who prophesize with your pen

And keep your eyes wide
the chance won't come again

And don't speak too soon
for the wheel's still in spin

And there's no tellin' who that it's namin'

For the loser now will be later to win

For the times they are a-changin'

THE TIMES THEY ARE A-CHANGIN'

Chapter One

Wood-stock

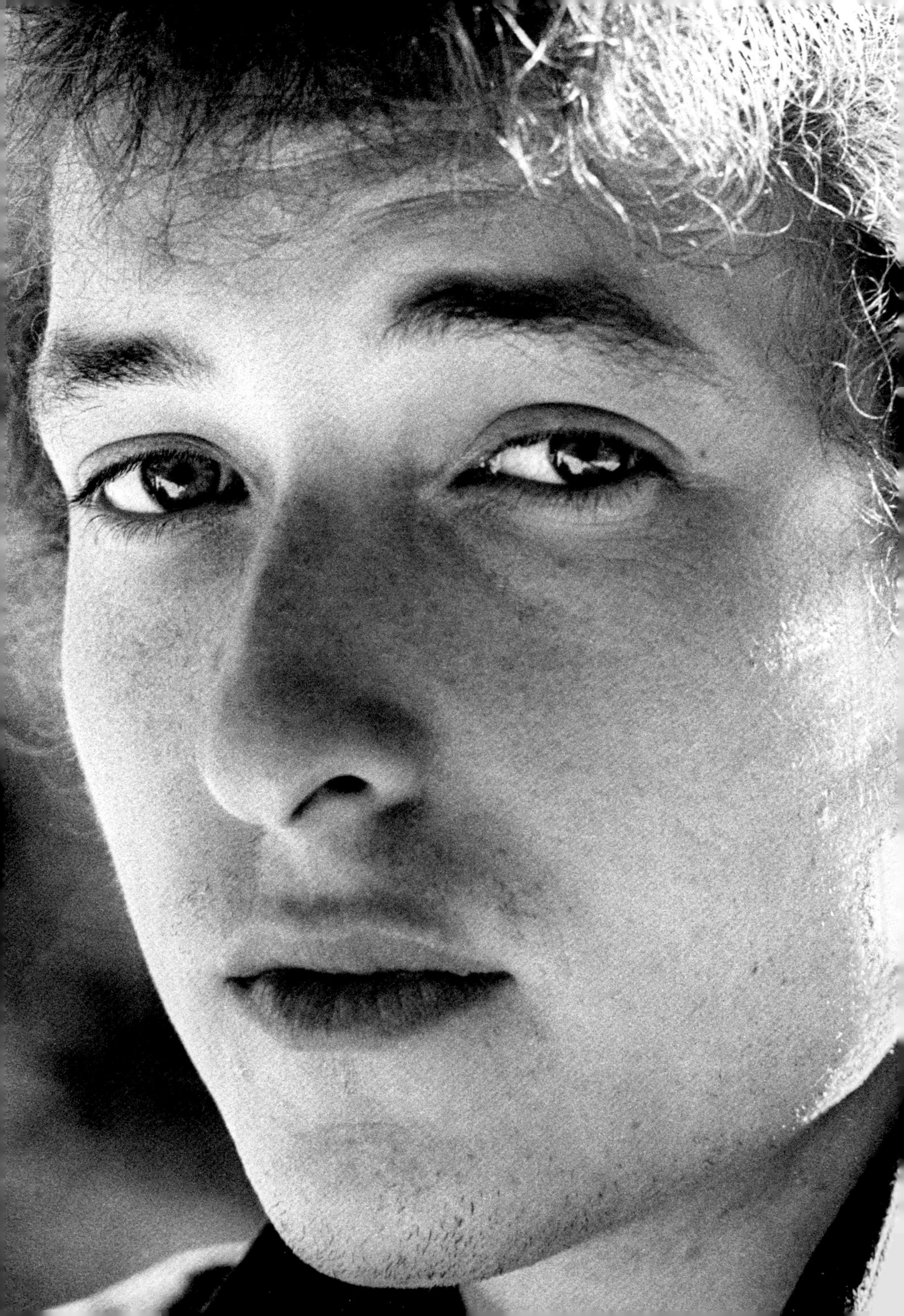

I drove to Woodstock with two bags of camera equipment on August 27, 1964, the day I was to have my long-awaited meeting and photo session with Bob Dylan at the home of his manager, Albert Grossman. I was greeted by Sally Grossman, Albert's wife, and a friend of hers, Sara, and was told that Bob would be along soon. They invited me to wait with them at the pool. Sally's friend was Sara Lownds, who would later become Bob's wife. After quite a while, Bob Dylan arrived on a motorcycle.

Although he was polite and friendly, Bob Dylan didn't seem to have much enthusiasm for a photo session. After we exchanged some words of greeting, I explained that I came to make his portrait. That I hoped to make a visual statement to complement the feeling I had when I heard him sing "Hattie Carroll." As we spoke, he shuffled his feet and bobbed his head up and down somewhat impatiently, as though preoccupied.

He told me he would be about the house and I should feel free to photograph him. He was not very enthusiastic about my plan for just a portrait, preferring to do the things he normally would be doing. People are usually eager to place themselves at the disposal of the photographer in order to make the pictures as effective as possible. They want to know how they can be helpful, asking where the photographer would like to work or what they should wear. They are willing to construct artificial situations. Bob Dylan did not offer any of this.

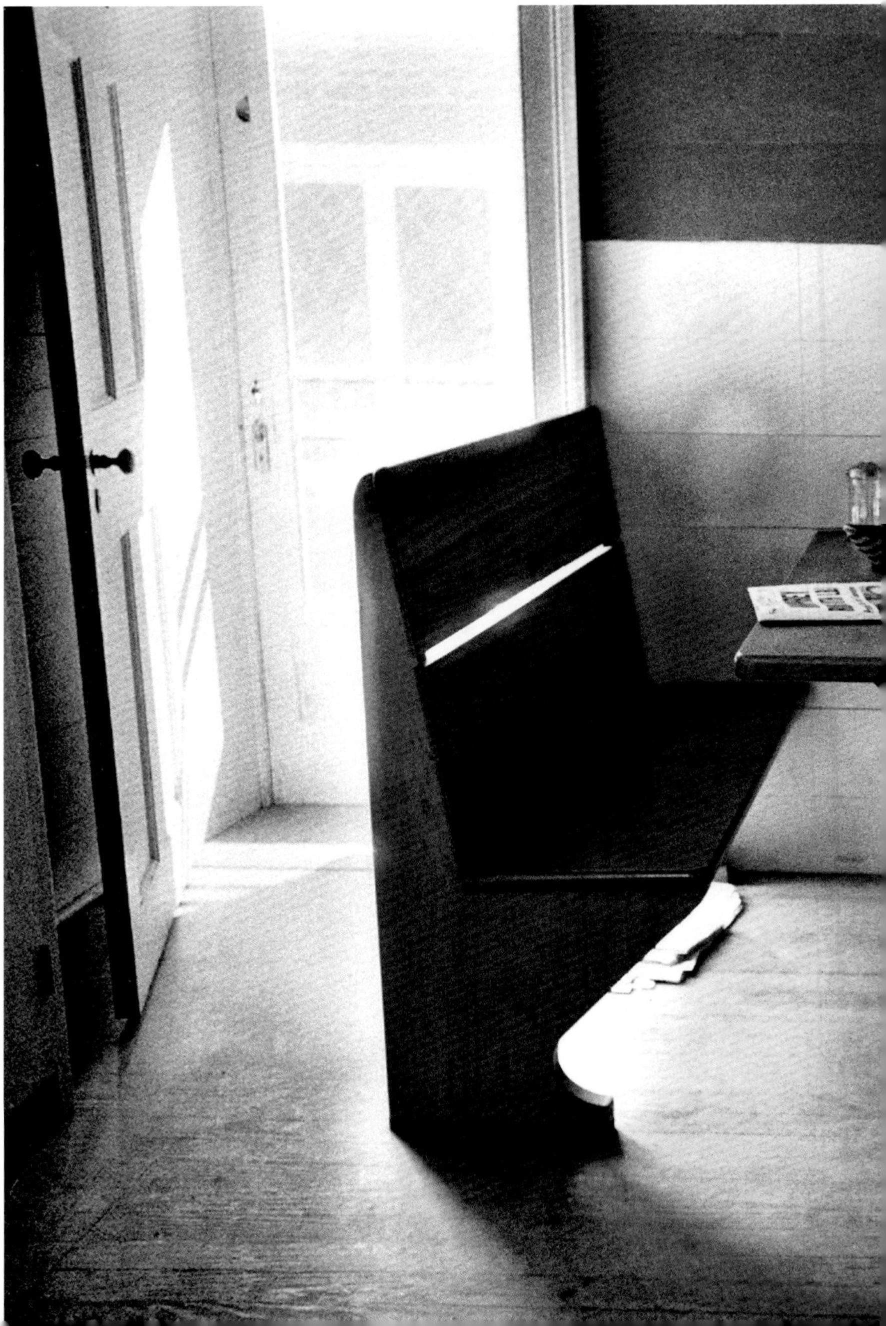

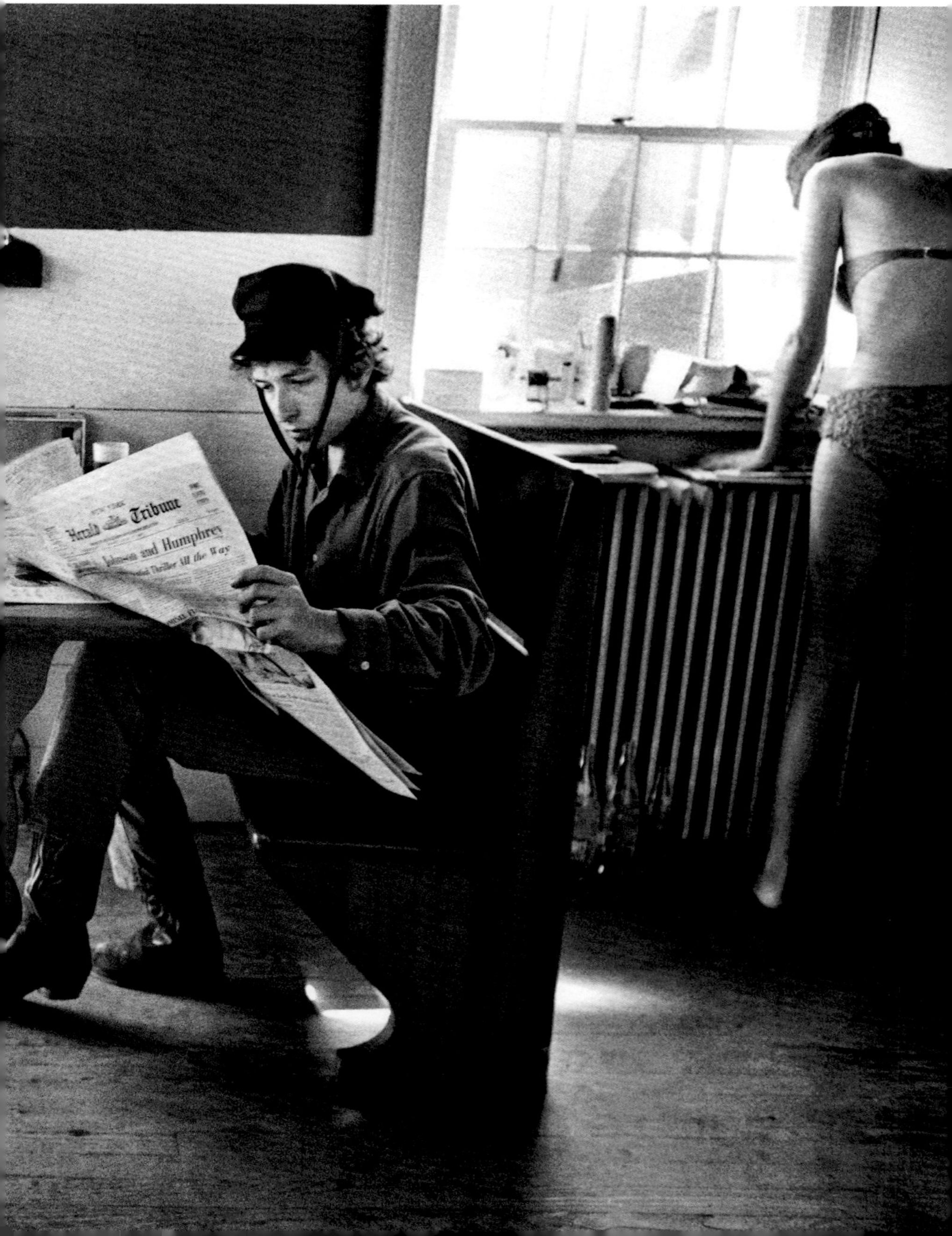
Herald Tribune
Johnson and Humphrey

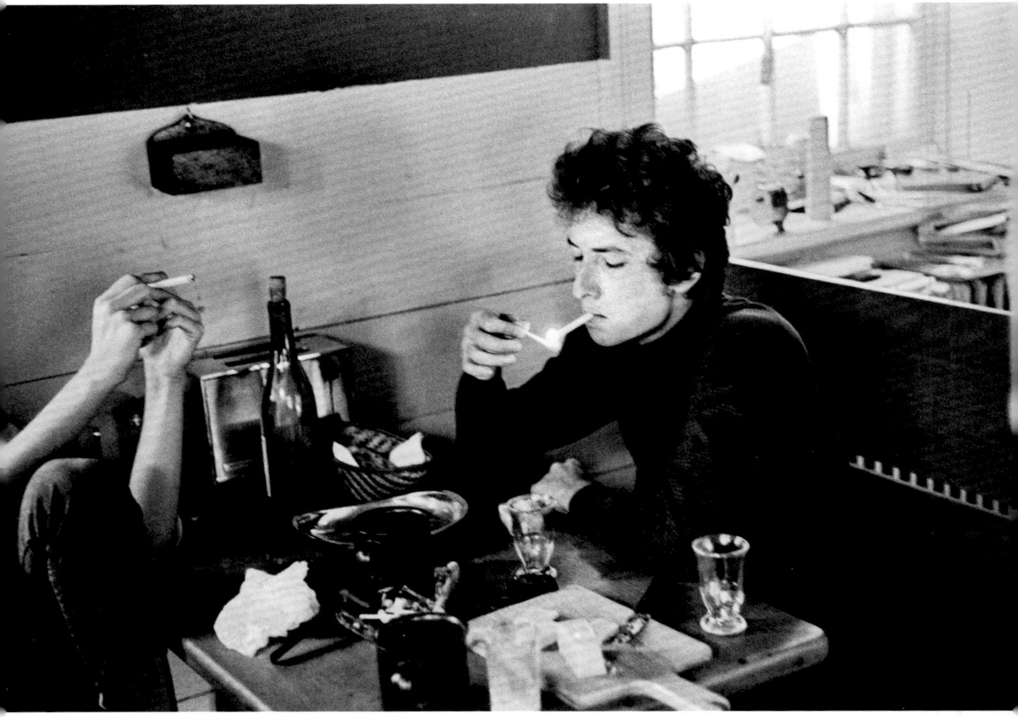

At that time most of my work was based on creating a picture, a portrait with a particular lighting or set to tell a story. It was usually something I controlled. Now it was catch-me-if-you-can, forcing me to hone some skills I had not used in a while. The session went well. My one hour was stretched into several and Bob didn't rush me. At one point, after I had worked for a while and made a number of pictures, I suggested we go out to the front porch where the light was very good. I asked him to sit in a rocking chair, which he did, but after a few exposures he stood up, telling me this was not the way he would like to be photographed.

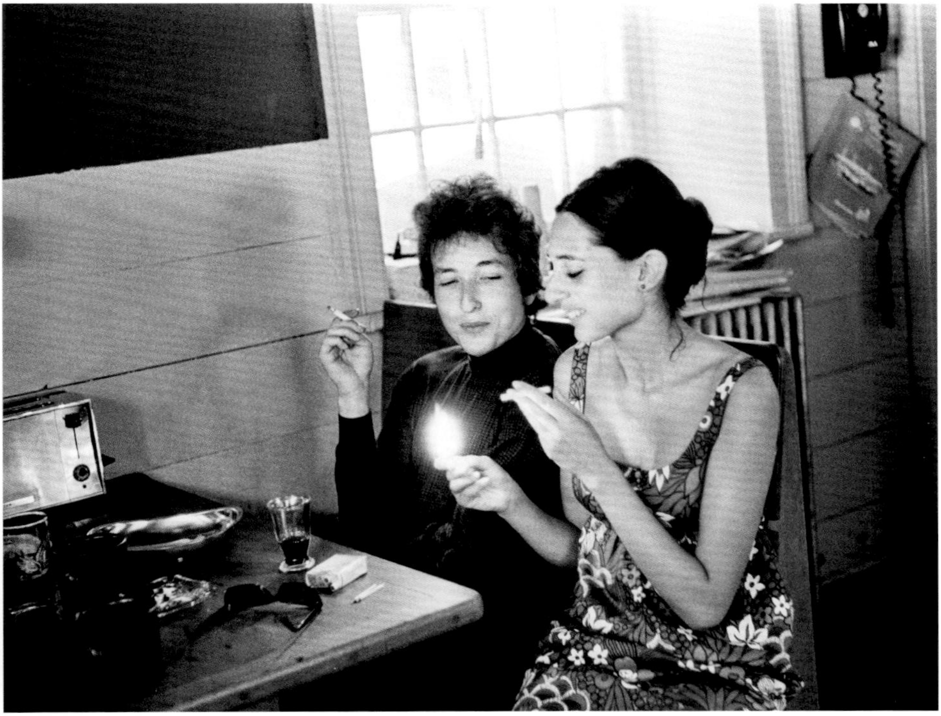

Albert Grossman's House
Woodstock, New York
August 27, 1964

"Fine," I said, and switched to plan B. Actually there was no plan B. I stopped shooting and, there on the porch, explained what it was I wanted to do. I told him what I had felt, the first time I saw him perform on the television screen half a year earlier. He let me know he understood this and that he was willing to cooperate, but that he wanted the pictures to come from the things he did, and not from things we would arrange for him to do. So I suggested photographing him doing the things that seemed most natural for him--working, writing music, or playing the guitar.

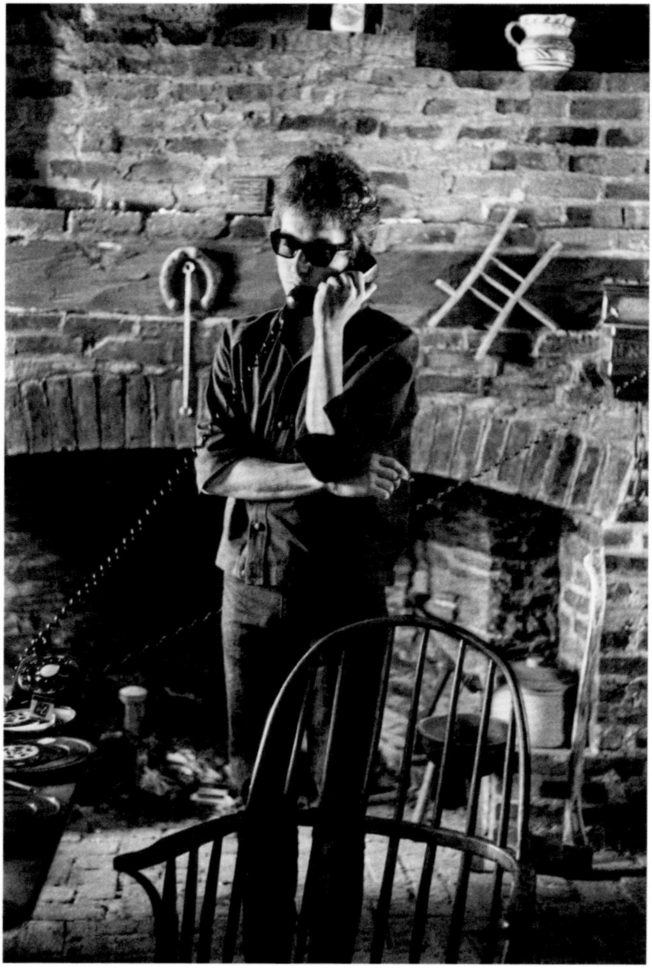

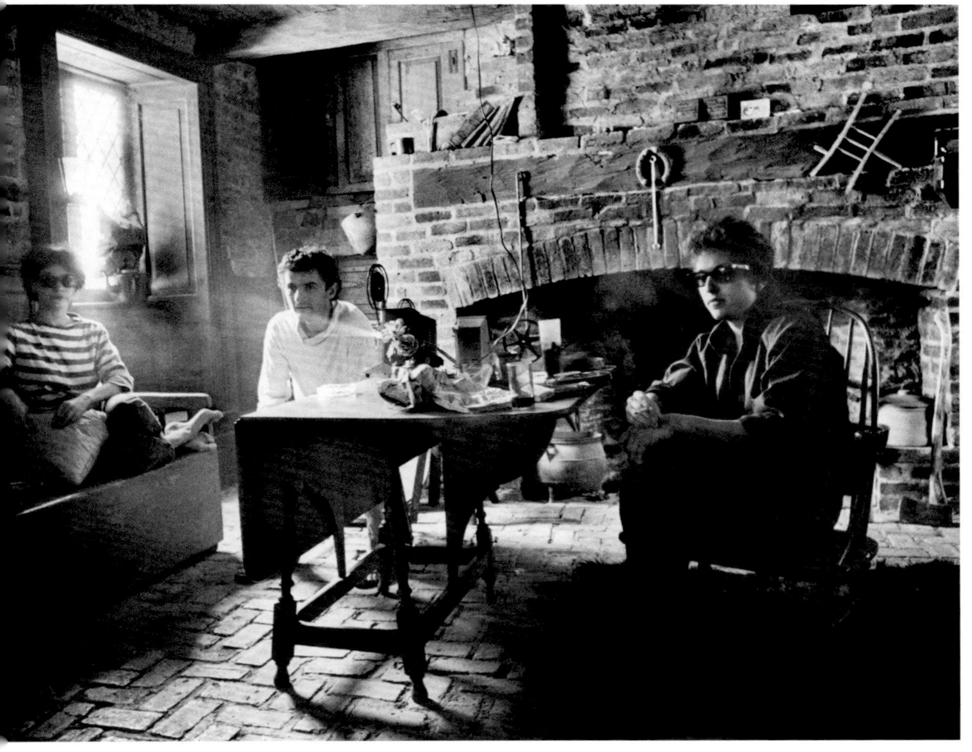

Dylan told me that the pictures I wanted wouldn't work out, since he was always alone when he wrote and that it would be silly to make a picture of him posing at the typewriter. As for the guitar, he almost never played, except when performing, and he didn't like pictures with the instrument. Instead, he suggested I photograph him on the swing. His mood changed when he stood up and he pumped the swing higher and higher. He smiled--a rare thing, I learned, for Dylan to do for the camera. I felt I was being challenged and decided to meet that challenge by not forcing the situation.

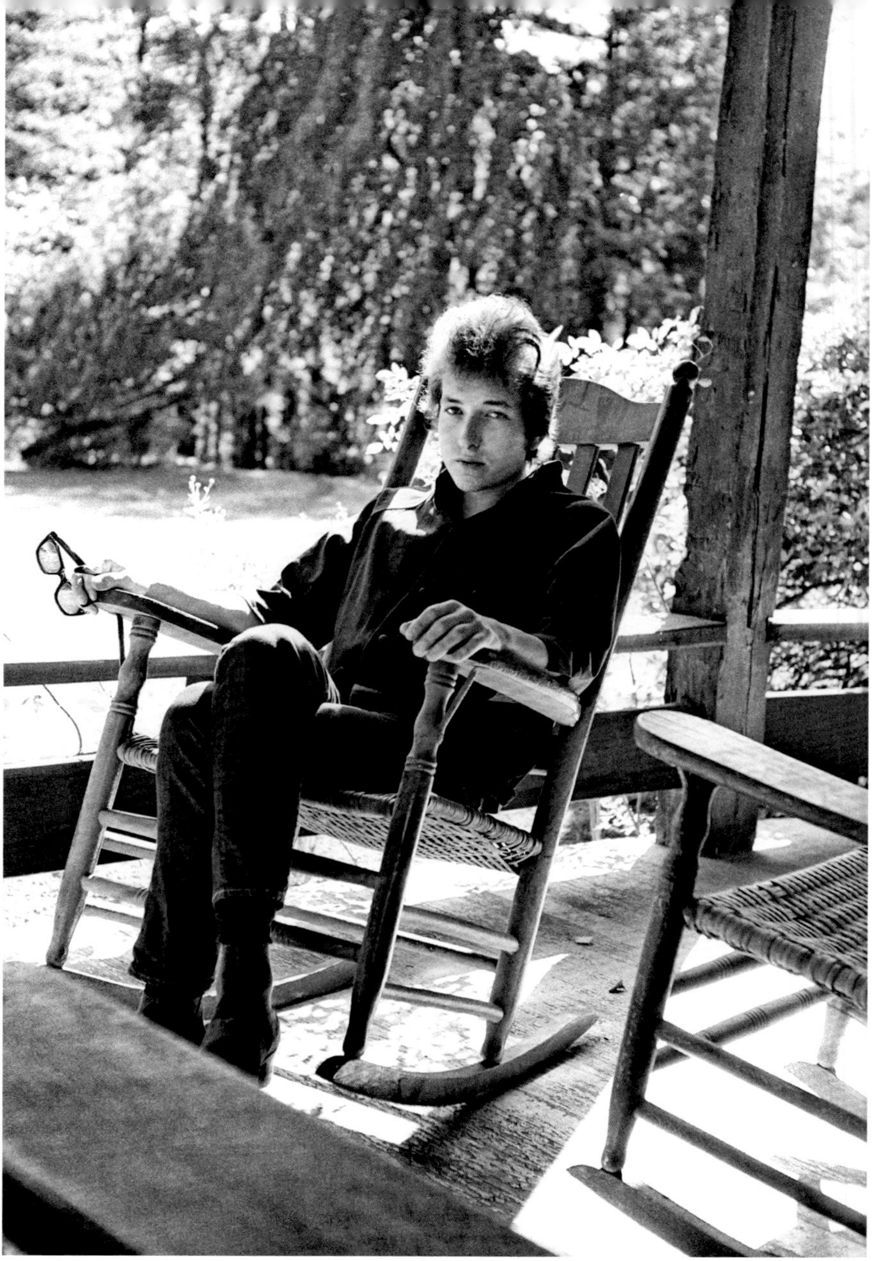

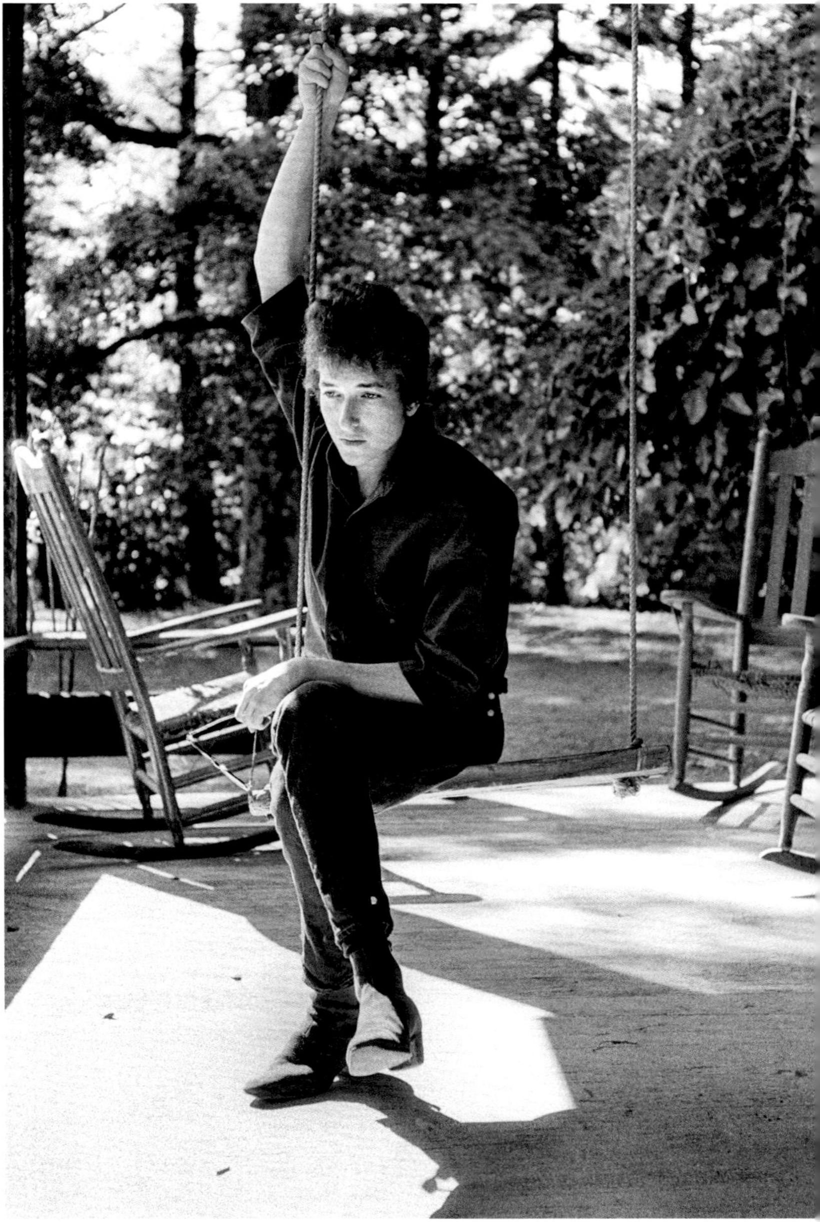

This, I would learn, is characteristic of Dylan, especially when he has to wait or sit for any length of time. At least that was the Bob Dylan I met in 1964. If standing, he would often bend and straighten one leg to a steady pulsation, as if he needed an outlet for his energy. His restlessness keeps him on the move. This is an extension of the man himself. Dylan is always in flux, constantly looking for new things and new ideas, and when he finds them, he bends them into a shape that is uniquely his own.

So I photographed Dylan as he climbed trees, watched home movies, and lounged in the kitchen reading the newspaper. While we were shooting at Albert's house, we were joined by Victor Maymudes, Dylan's road manager, a tall, dark-haired man with a strong face of a type that I had seen many times in paintings from the Italian Renaissance. Victor was a quiet man who was acutely aware of everything around him. His job was to accompany Bob to his concerts and manage the affairs of the road and the performances. More than this, he was Bob's friend, and the two men often spent time together when they were not working.

When we returned to the house, Bob and Victor spent some time practicing with bullwhips. I was surprised to see Dylan wielding his whip with great facility, cracking it in the air with an authority equal to Victor's, although Victor was a much larger man. I began to question the mild handshake I received as a greeting.

Dylan was certainly not a weakling; on the contrary, he impressed me as being a strong, quick, active person. He was always on the move; even when sitting he was not still--there would usually be some movement: one foot beating time in the air or a leg jiggling nervously.

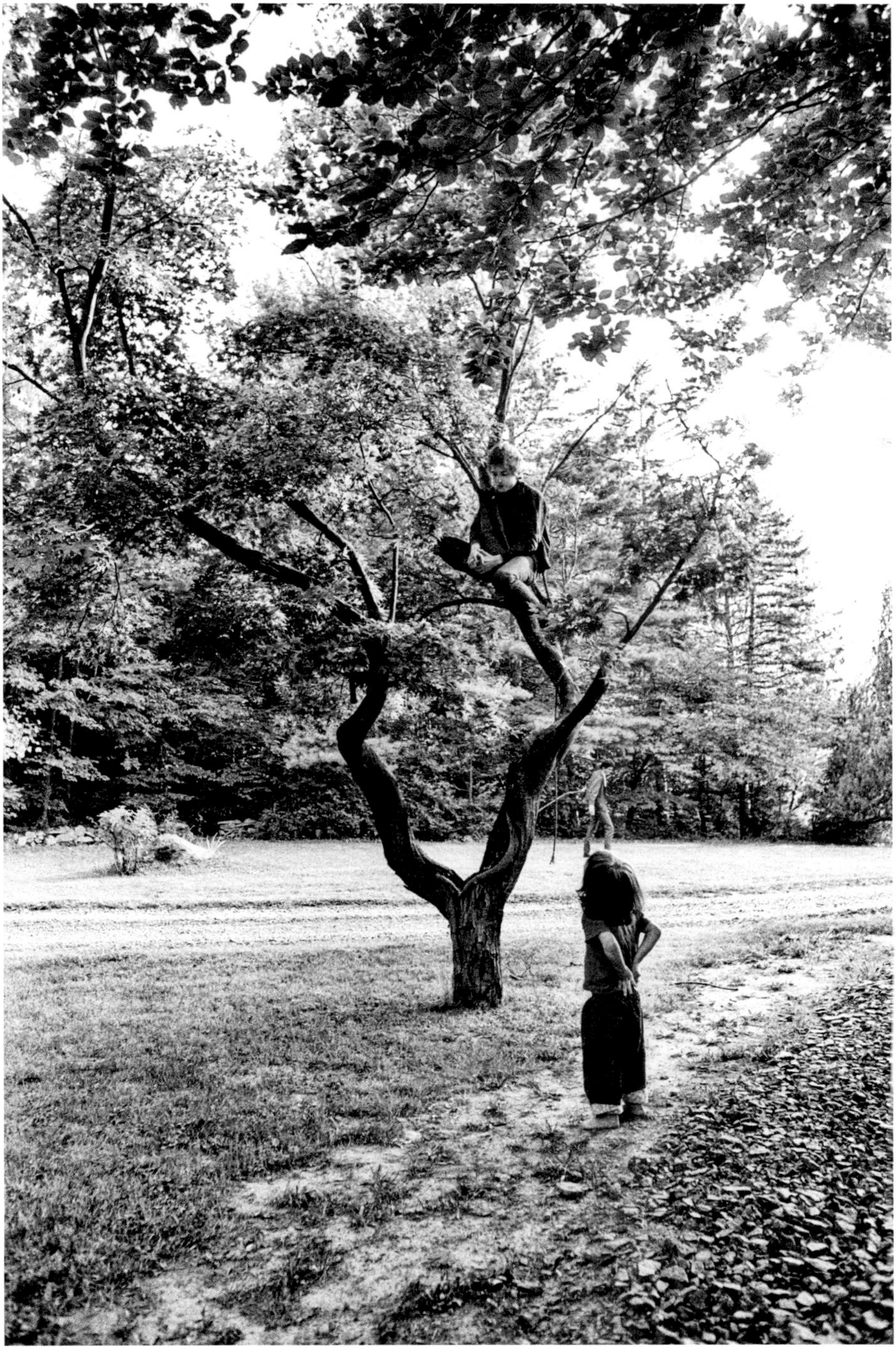

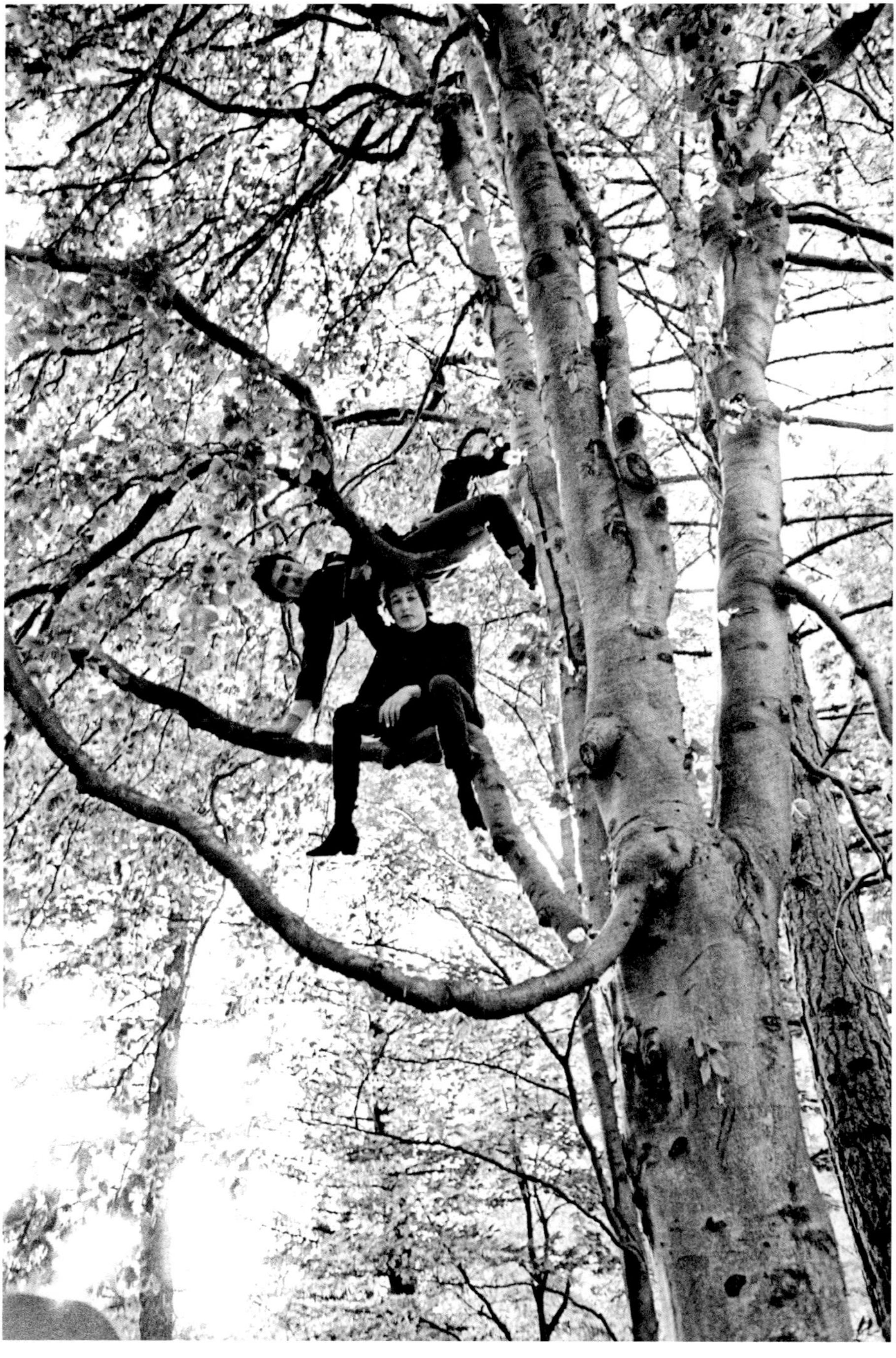

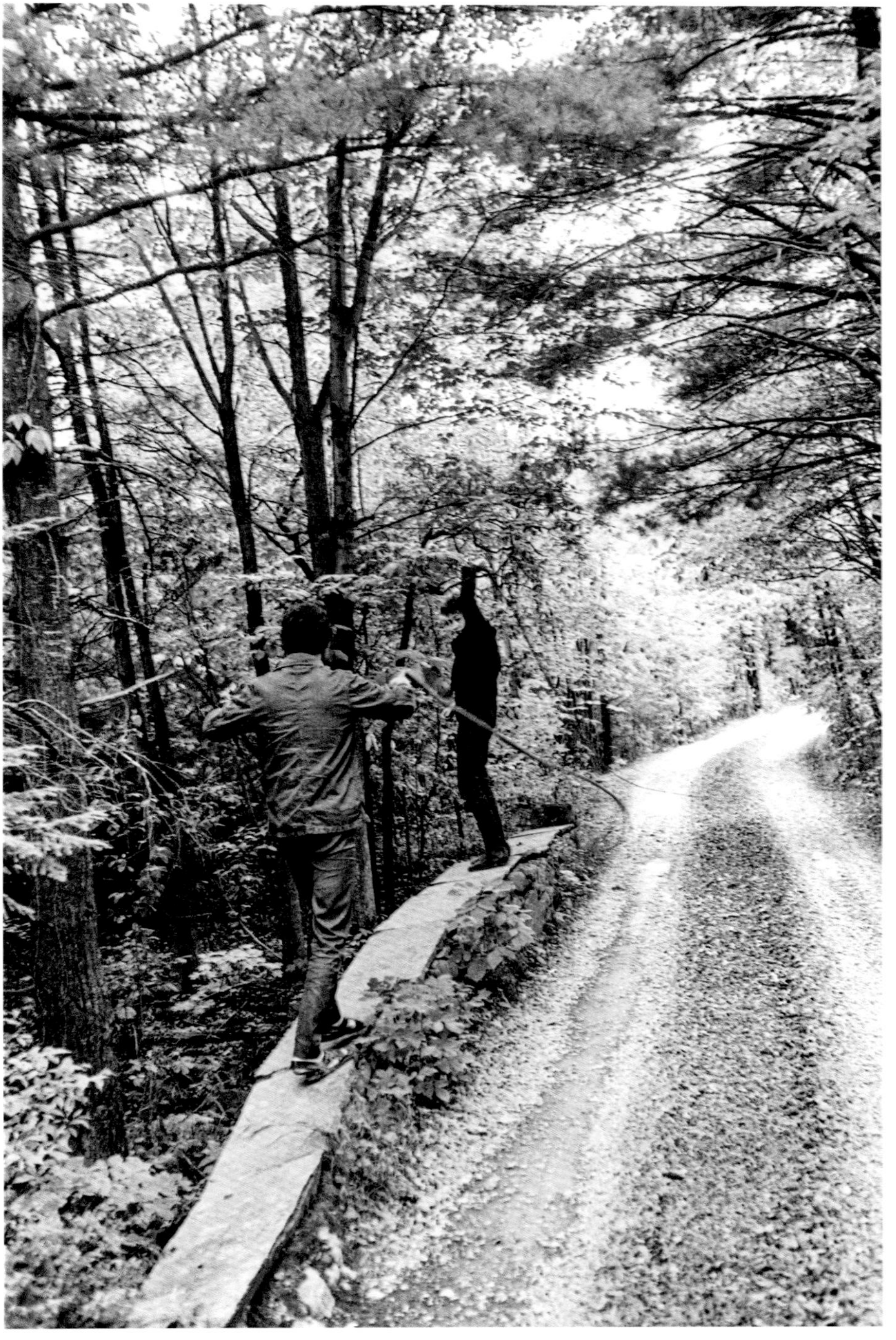

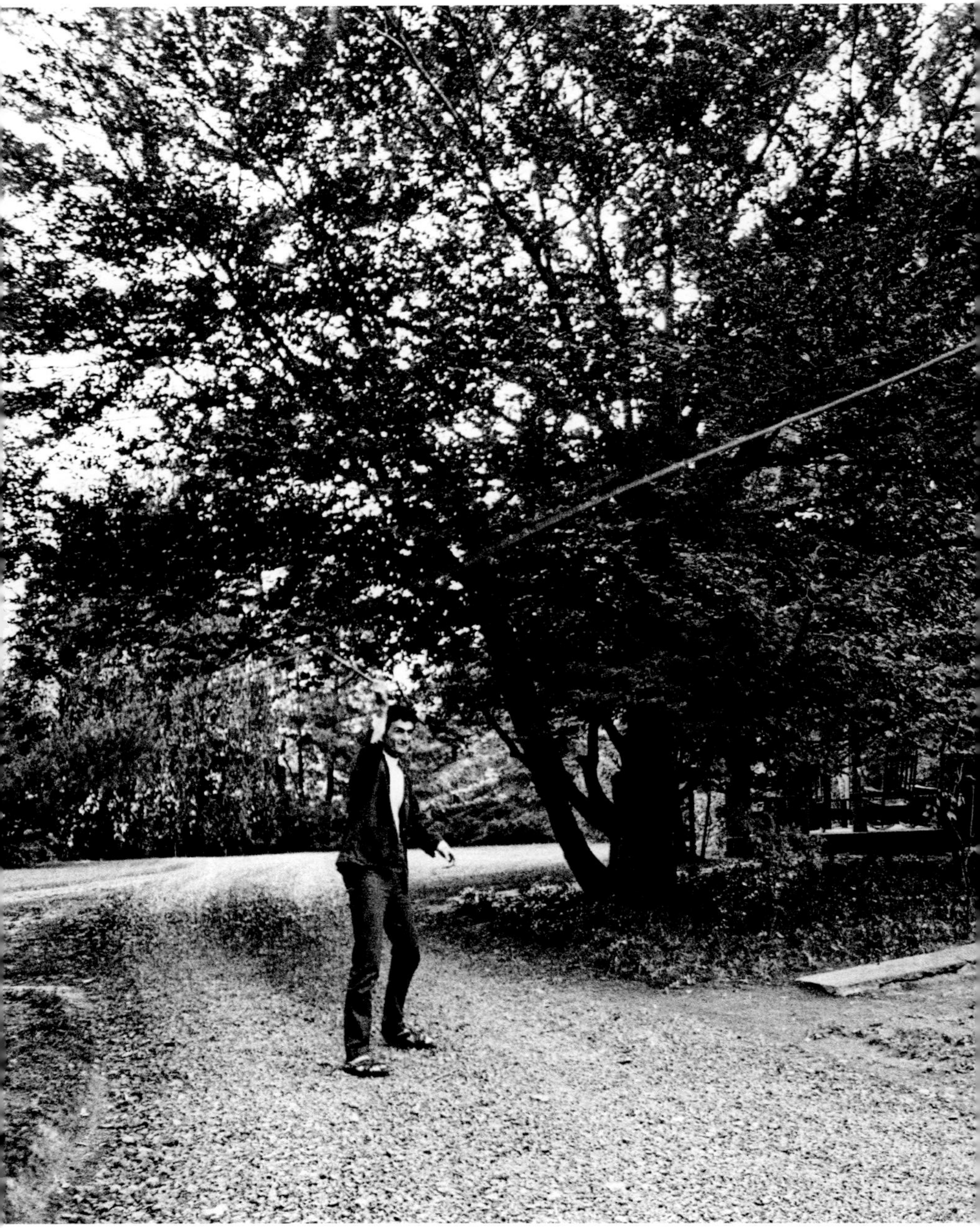

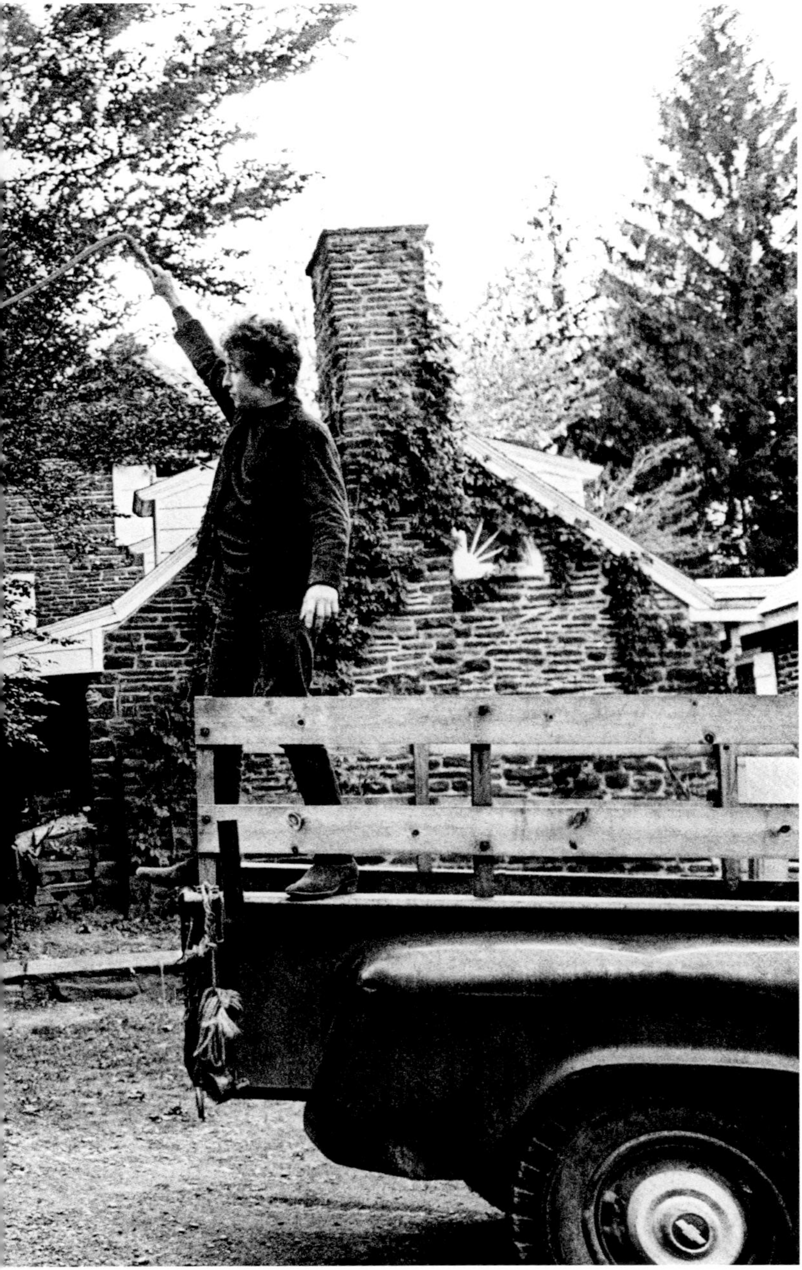

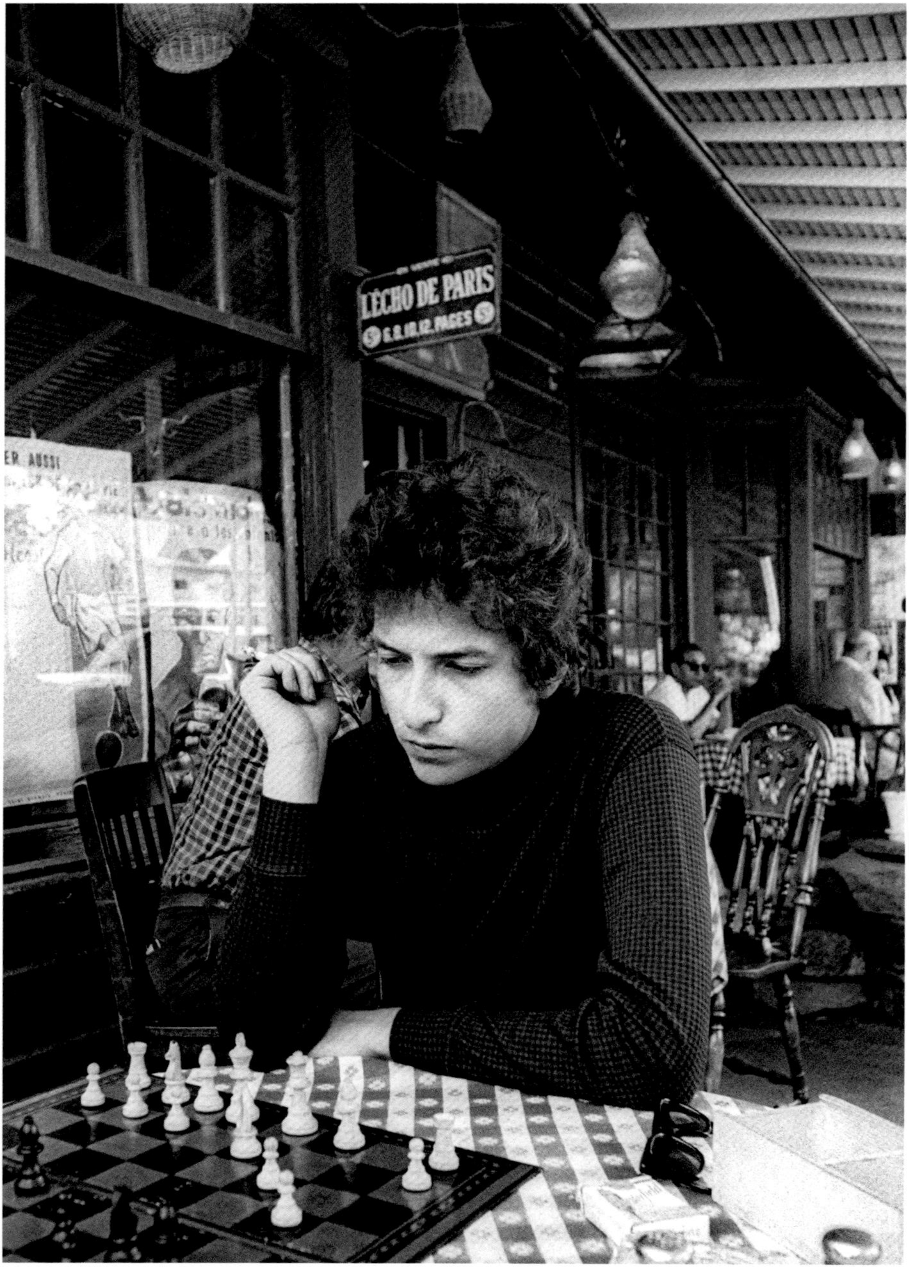
L'ECHO DE PARIS
6.8.10.12. PAGES

After a while Bob suggested we go to town to eat, which was just fine with me, a chance for more situations to photograph. We ended up at an outdoor table at Bernard's Café Espresso. The red-and-white-checked tablecloths, some wine and cheese, the two men relaxing, made me feel we had all been transported to the local café of some quiet French village. Bob and Victor played chess at a table shaded from the sun by an overhanging roof. I realized early on that the chess game was not a gimmick--Bob and Victor enjoyed what they were doing. After a while we were joined by some friends from the neighborhood who decided to hang out with the chess players.

Bernard's Café was a wonderful place--a combination coffeehouse-restaurant-café. It had the qualities and charm of all three, and on that day I met Bernard Paturel, the restaurant owner, a large man with a large mustache. At one point during lunch, Bob picked up one of my cameras and photographed me. He enjoyed the camera, and some months later we would have a terrific "shoot out" photographing each other. Eventually, the sun began to fade. It was getting late and we decided to call it quits. Bob walked me to my car in the late light at day's end. He asked me to let him know when the pictures could be seen. We shook hands, and I couldn't help noticing that this handshake was firmer and warmer than the one with which he greeted me.

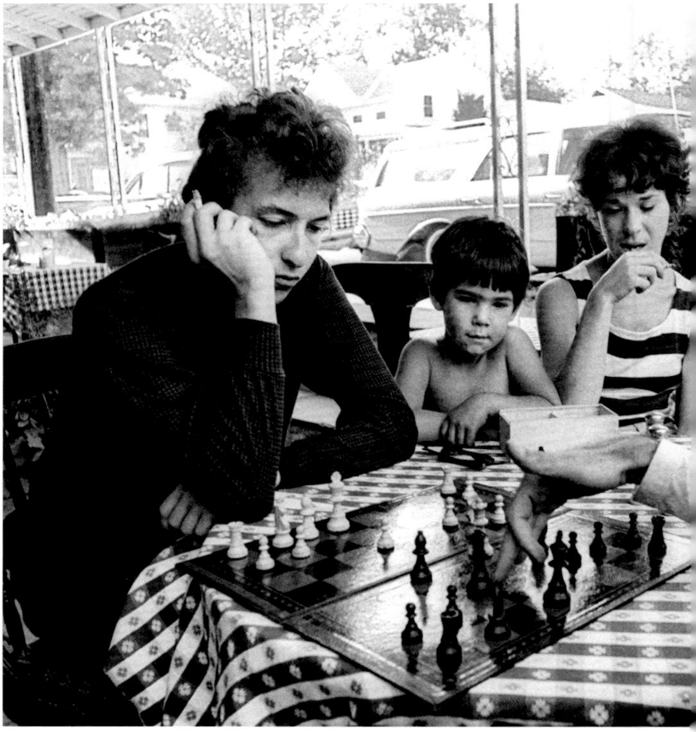

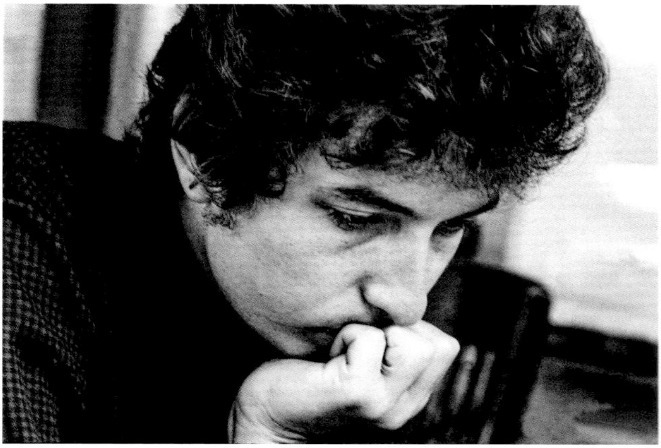

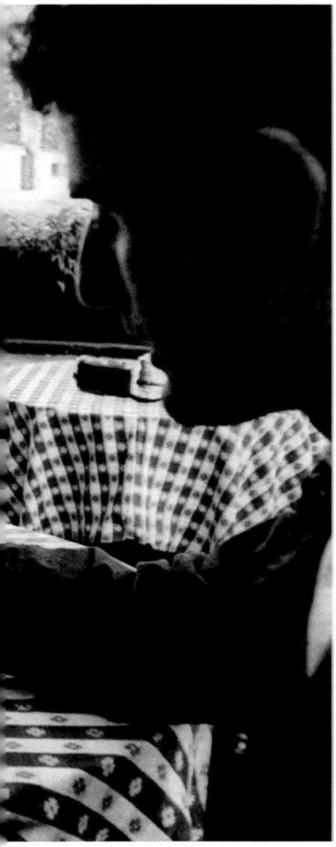

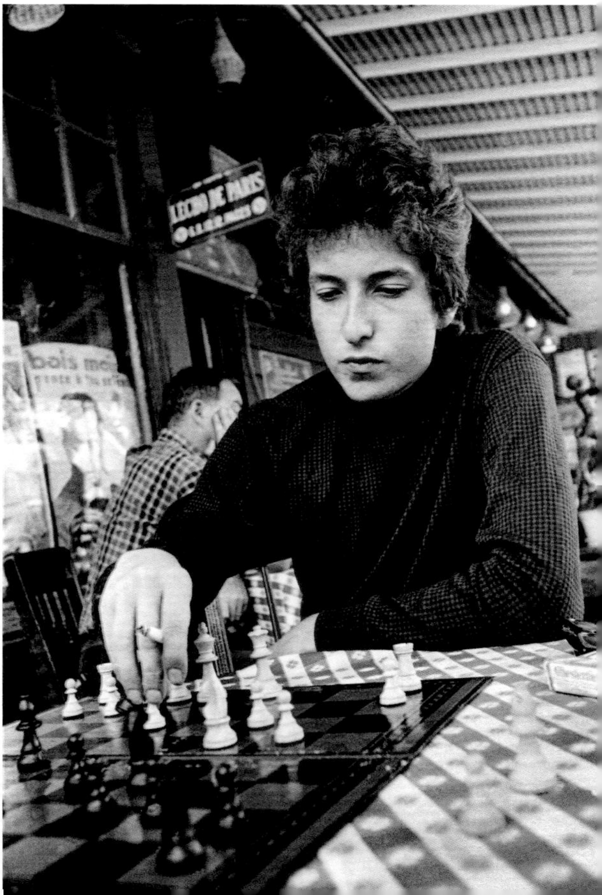
L'ECHO DE PARIS

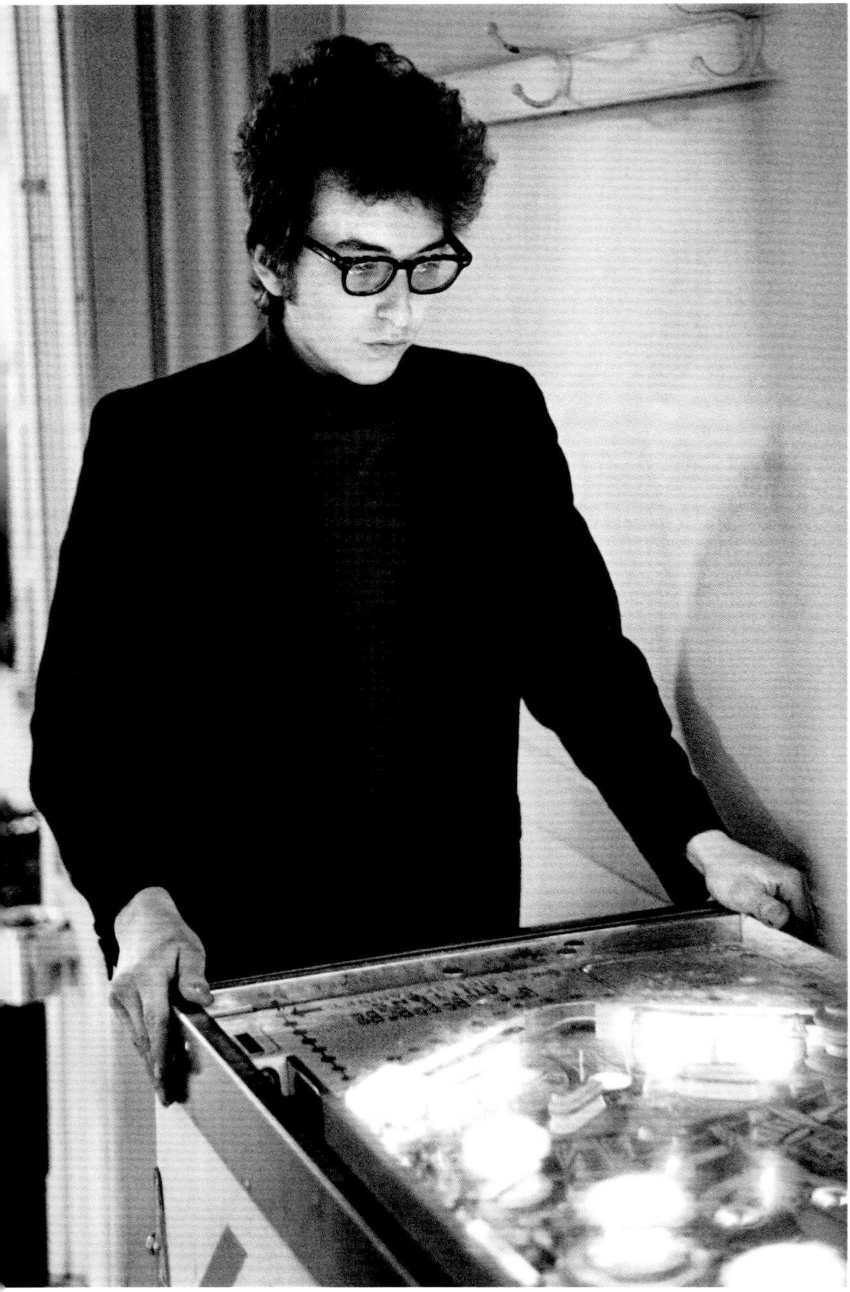

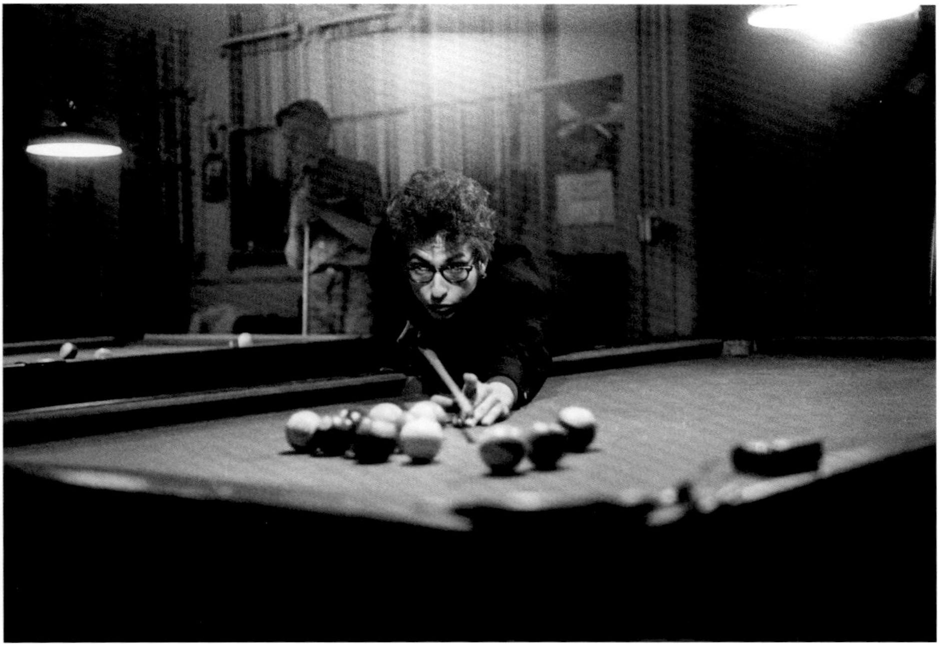

Pool Hall Near Bernard's
Kingston, New York
December 11, 1964

A few months after our first meeting, the four of us--Bob, Victor, Bernard, and I--were together again and decided to make the short trip to a pool hall in Kingston, New York. I don't remember how the games worked out, but Bob and Bernard turned out to be decent players,and I really enjoyed the shoot. Bernard was a good friend of Bob's and helped out when Bob was healing in Woodstock after his motorcycle accident. Bernard and I became friends too, and remained so for many years. He and Victor are no longer with us, but Bernard's Café is now the home of the Center for Photography in Woodstock.

Take me on a trip upon your magic swirlin' ship

My senses have been stripped,
my hands can't feel to grip

My toes too numb to step

Wait only for my boot heels to be wanderin'

I'm ready to go anywhere,
I'm ready for to fade

Into my own parade

Cast your dancing spell my way

I promise to go under it

MR. TAMBOURINE MAN

Chapter Two

Town Hall

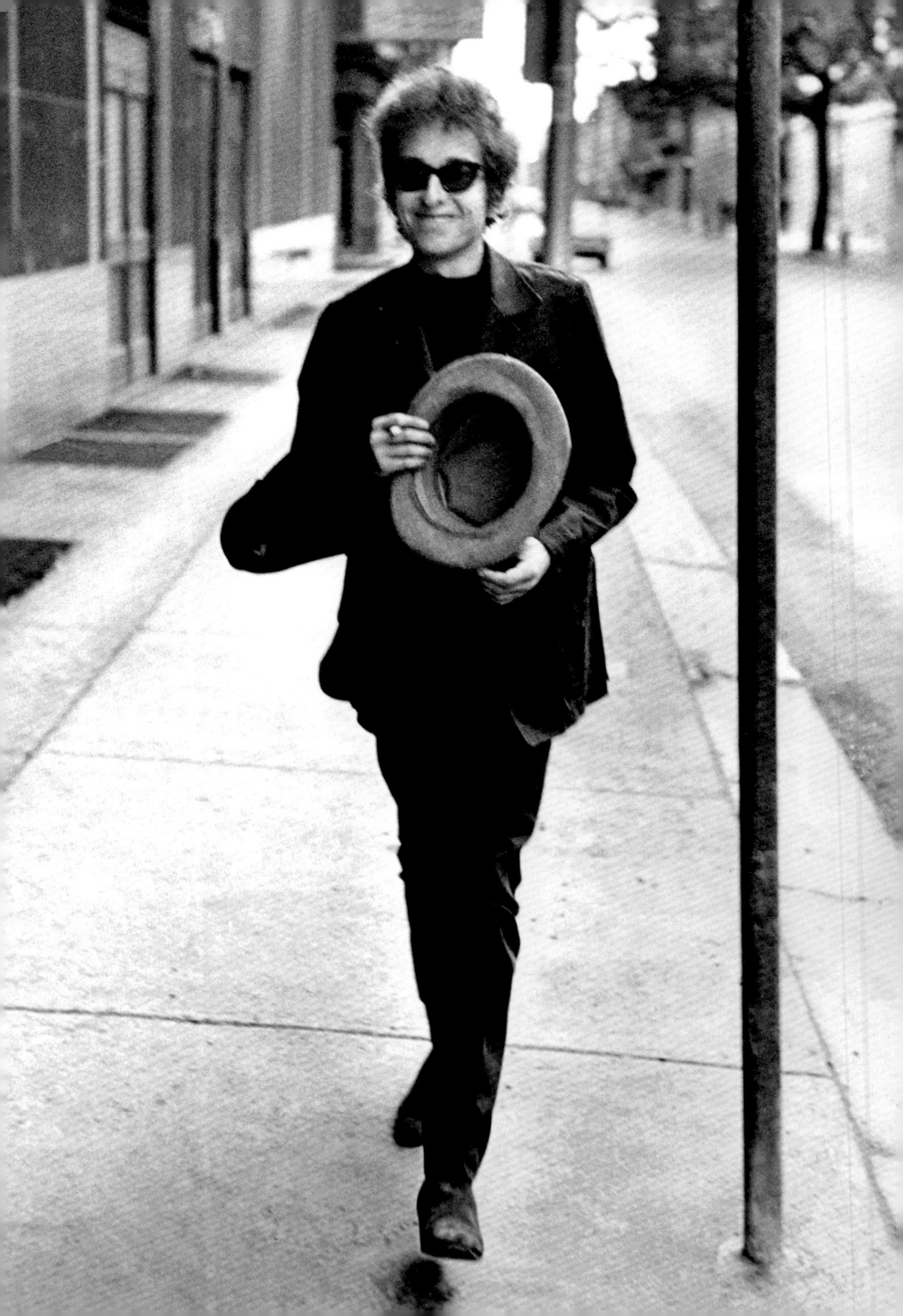

A portfolio of prints under my arm, I visited Bob at Albert Grossman's office in New York a few weeks after the Woodstock session. I spread the prints out on a conference table and waited. Bob and Albert pored over the pictures and liked them. Bob got a big kick out of one of him sitting in a tree, perched on a branch, looking as if he belonged there. Bob jokingly told Albert he should sing from a tree at his next concert. Grossman, without cracking a smile, convinced Bob that the problem of transporting it would present too many complications. While Bob and Albert walked around the conference table looking at the pictures, Bob surprised me by saying, "I'm going to Philadelphia next week--would you like to come?" The right answer seemed to be "yes."

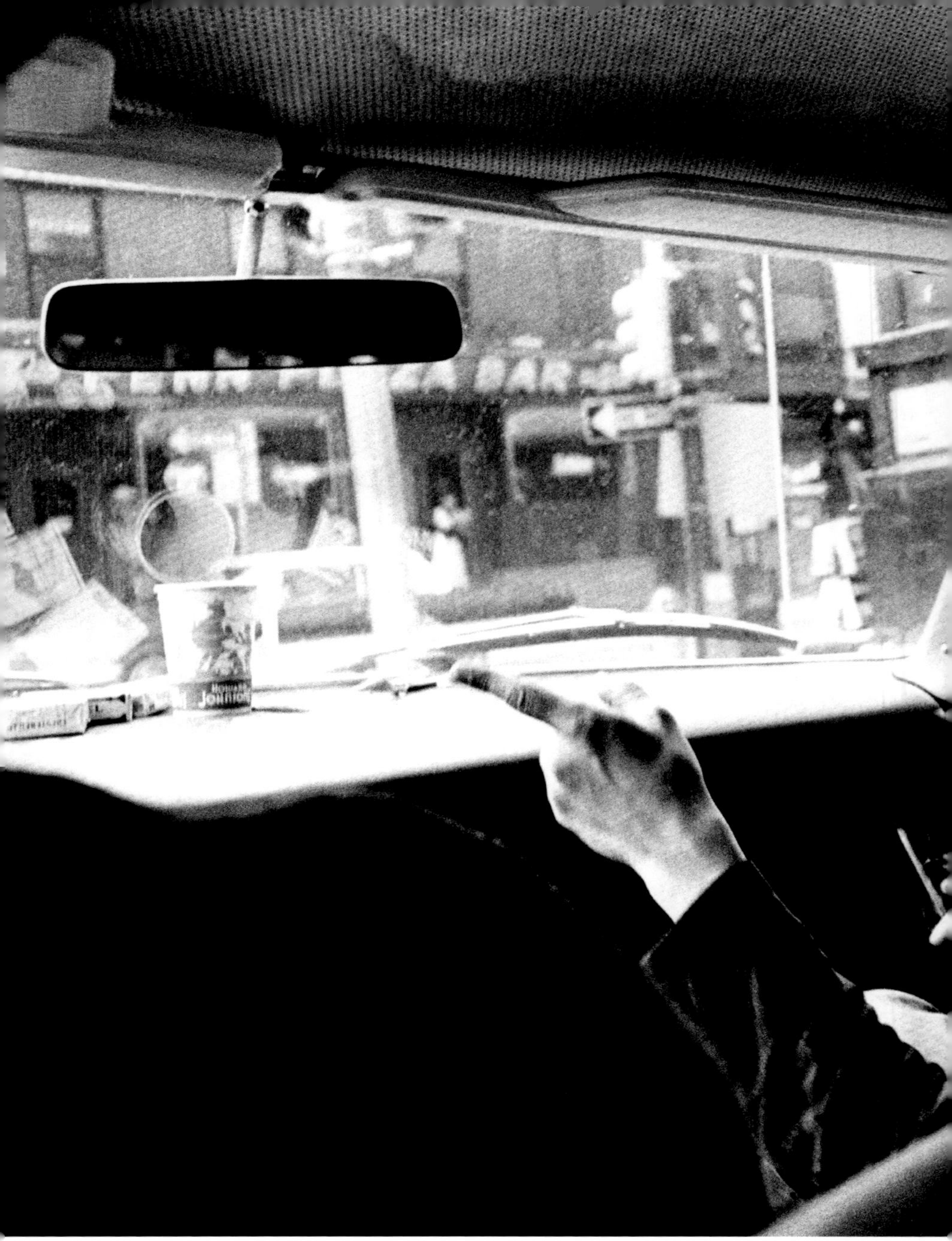

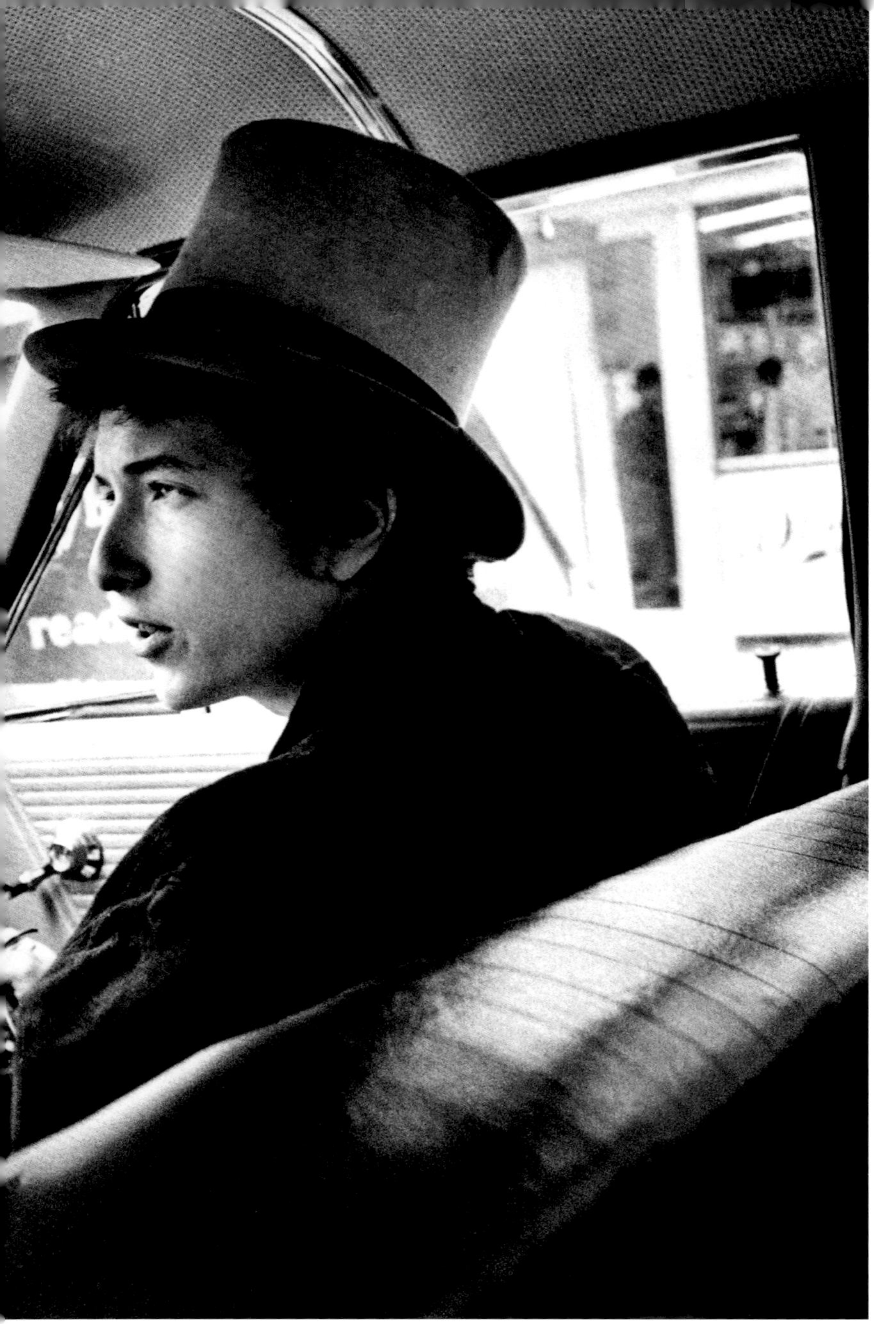

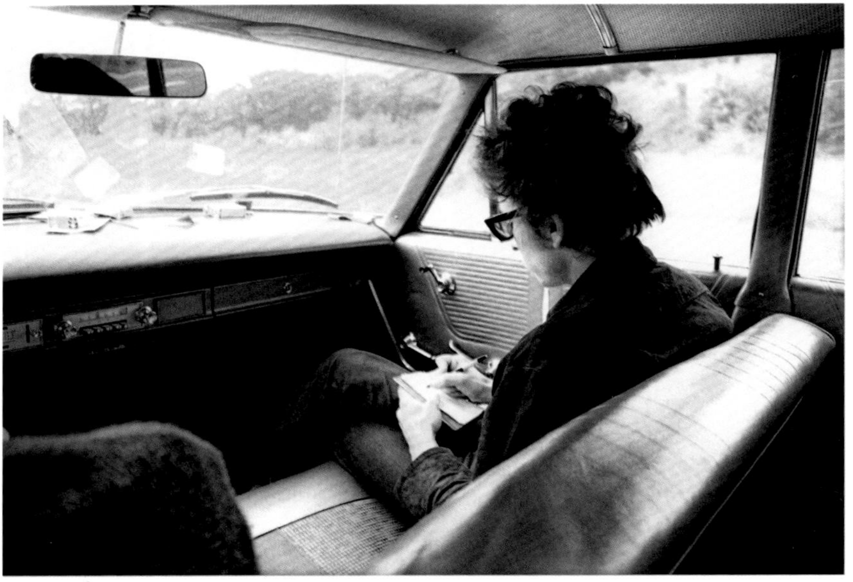

"Victor and I are driving," Bob said. "We can pick you up." The two-and-a-half-hour ride to Philadelphia in the Ford station wagon was the perfect time for us to get to know each other. Victor drove, and the three of us talked mostly about nothing in particular, until I mentioned that I had worked on a photographic shoot with Salvador Dalí. Bob became very interested, not just in the artist but in his "showmanship," and the way Dalí was always finding ways to catch the public's attention.

What was becoming obvious about Bob Dylan was his ability to make the best use of almost any time he could extract from his busy day. Often he would write in his small black notebook as he did for a while during the car trip to Philadelphia. Or he would read newspapers.

He would grab at moments that were available to him. He would interrupt something in order to glimpse a TV screen to see another performer. I photographed him when for just a few minutes he played with some melodies on a backstage piano while someone was out locating the key to his dressing room. He spent a great deal of time writing new material. At this, he seemed to be prolific. In retrospect, it's clear that Bob was in the process of winding up a very large spring. I didn't know then how much of that spring would be let loose in the coming months.

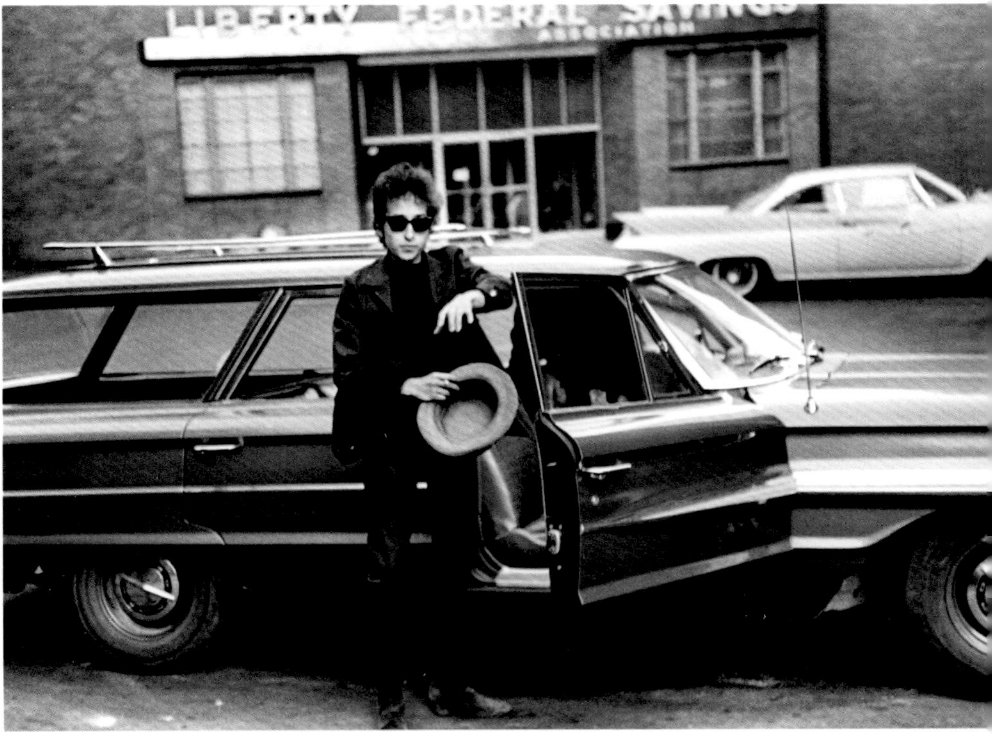

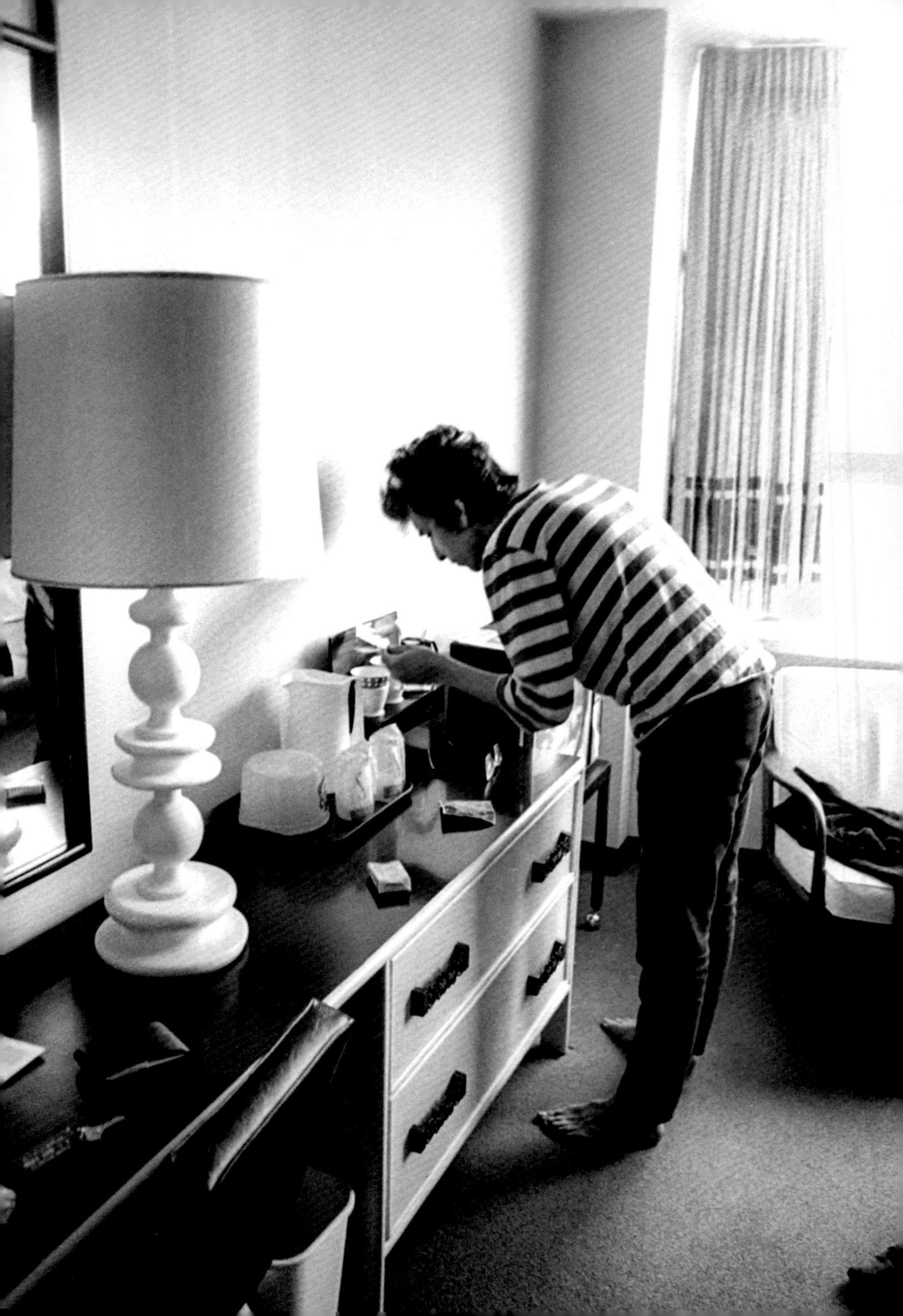

Bob was always busy, but although so many things consumed a great deal of his time, he tried hard to reserve some time to do the things he felt like doing. He told me that one of the ways he managed to be punctual and accomplish things was to commit himself only to one or two things a day. In this way, he was able to meet the demands he placed upon himself. If he told me he would call on Thursday, I was pretty sure that I would get that call. In all such regards, he was reliable if he had agreed to a schedule. On the other hand, if he didn't want to be found, you couldn't find Bob Dylan.

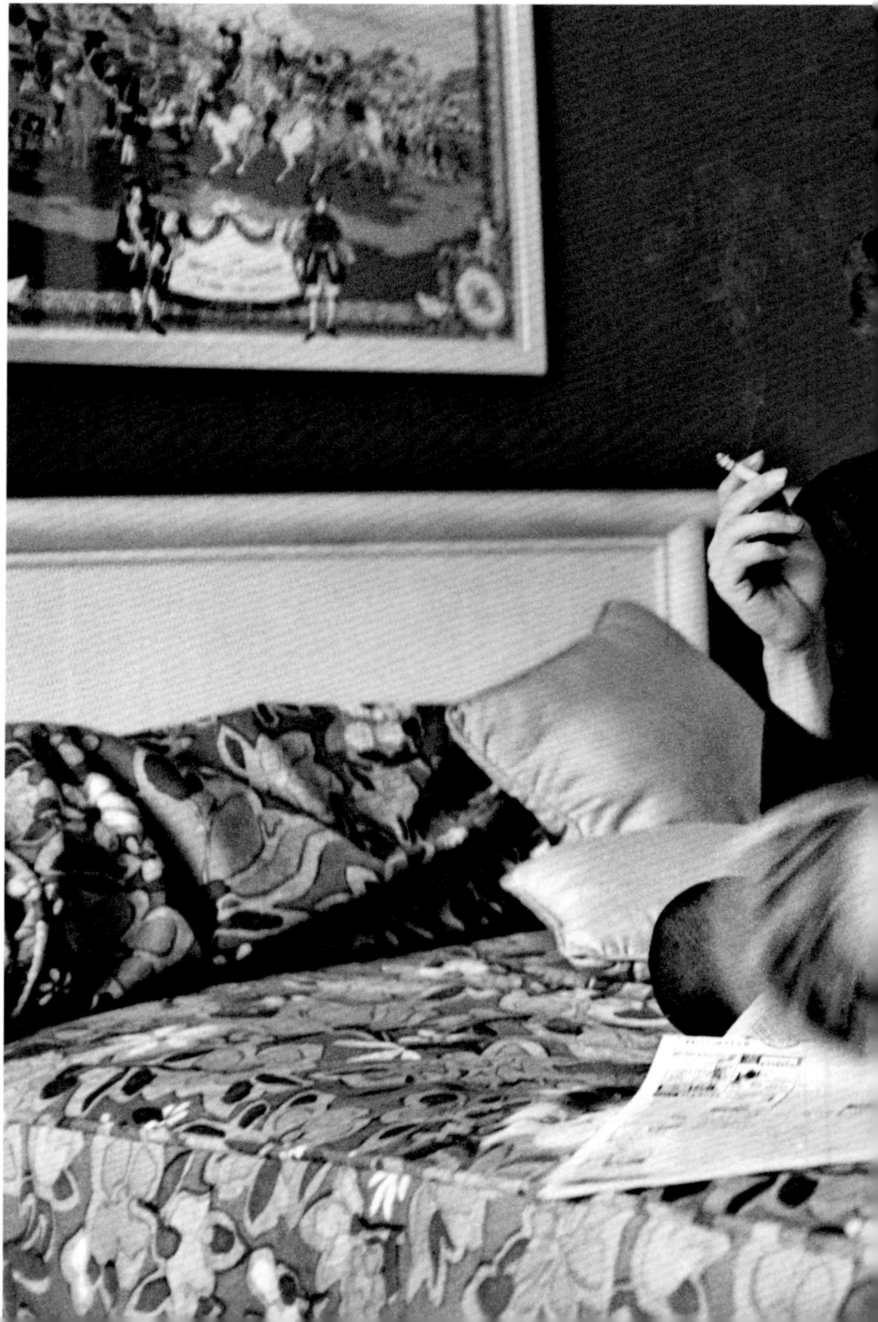

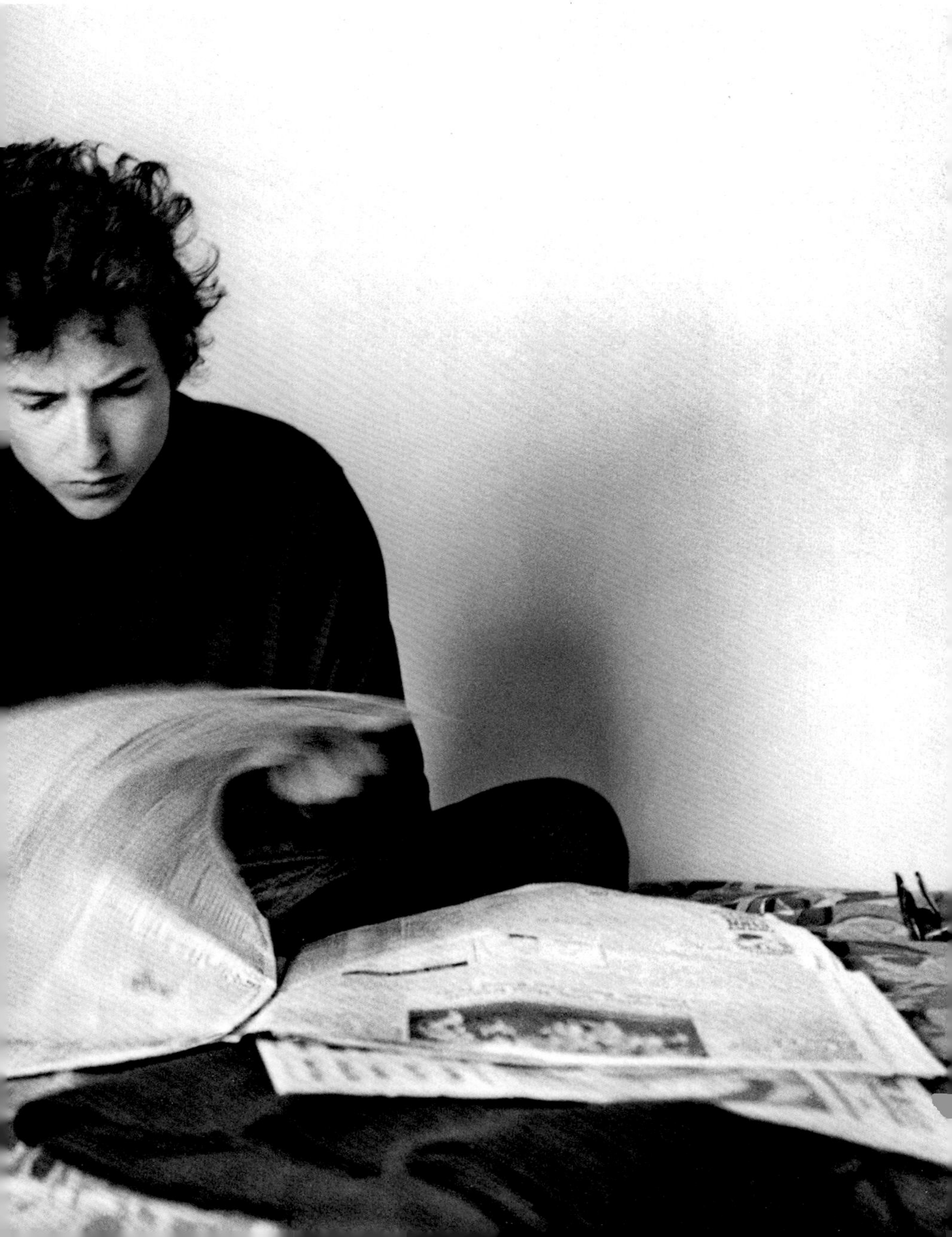

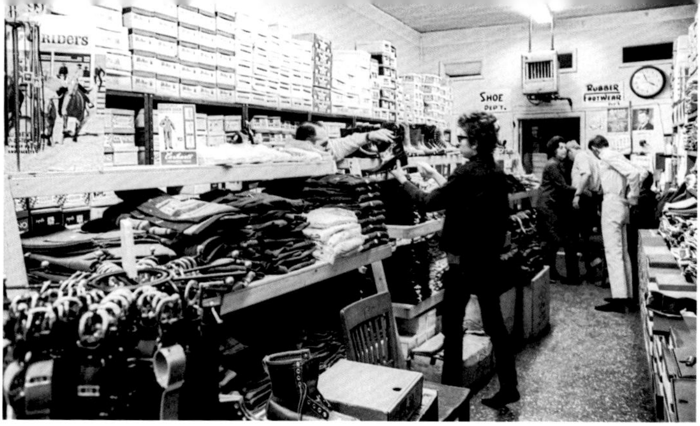
RIDERS
SHOE
DEP'T.
RUBBER
FOOTWEAR

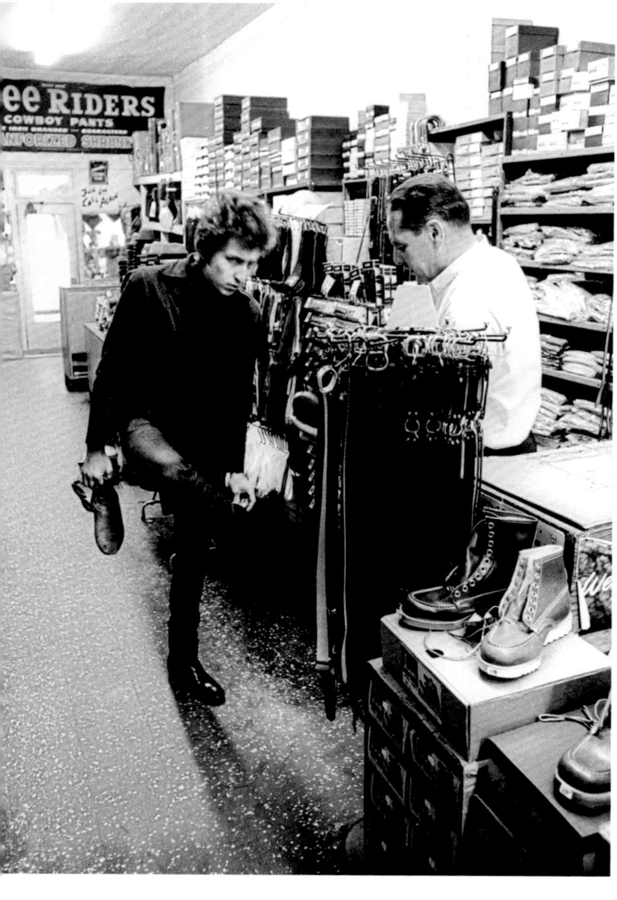
ee RIDERS
COWBOY PANTS

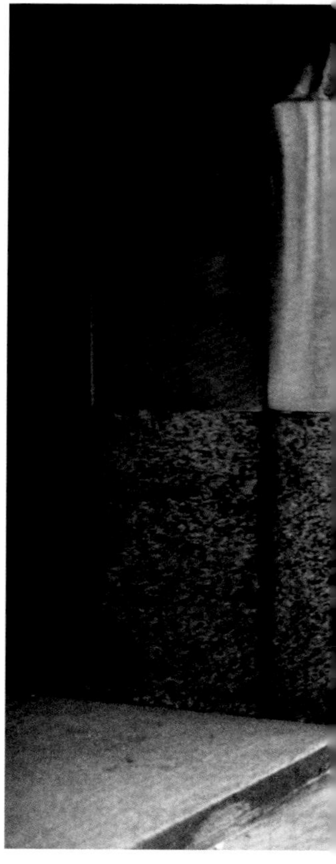

We had a few hours in Philadelphia before going to the Town Hall. I was able to make some pictures of Bob buying boots at an army and navy store and more pictures back in the hotel room. Dylan's appearance, his casual dress, the pile of hair on his head, and the legend of the folksinger as a free spirit led me to believe that his life was similarly carefree. Observing the process of putting everything together to perform in a new place with changing audiences quickly taught me that my impression was wrong.

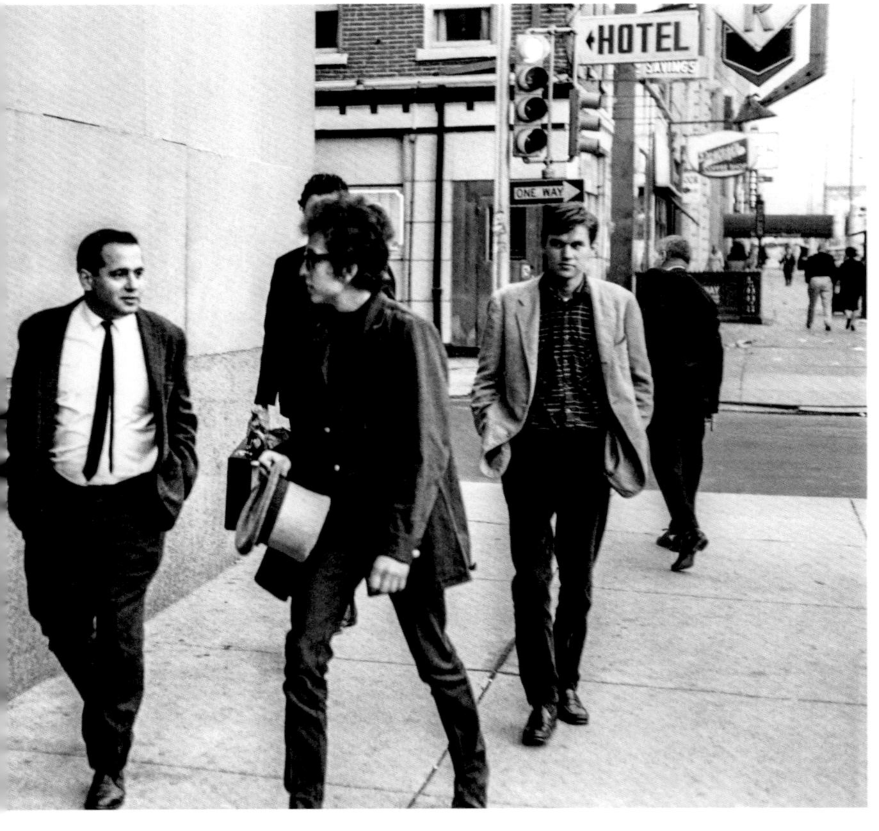

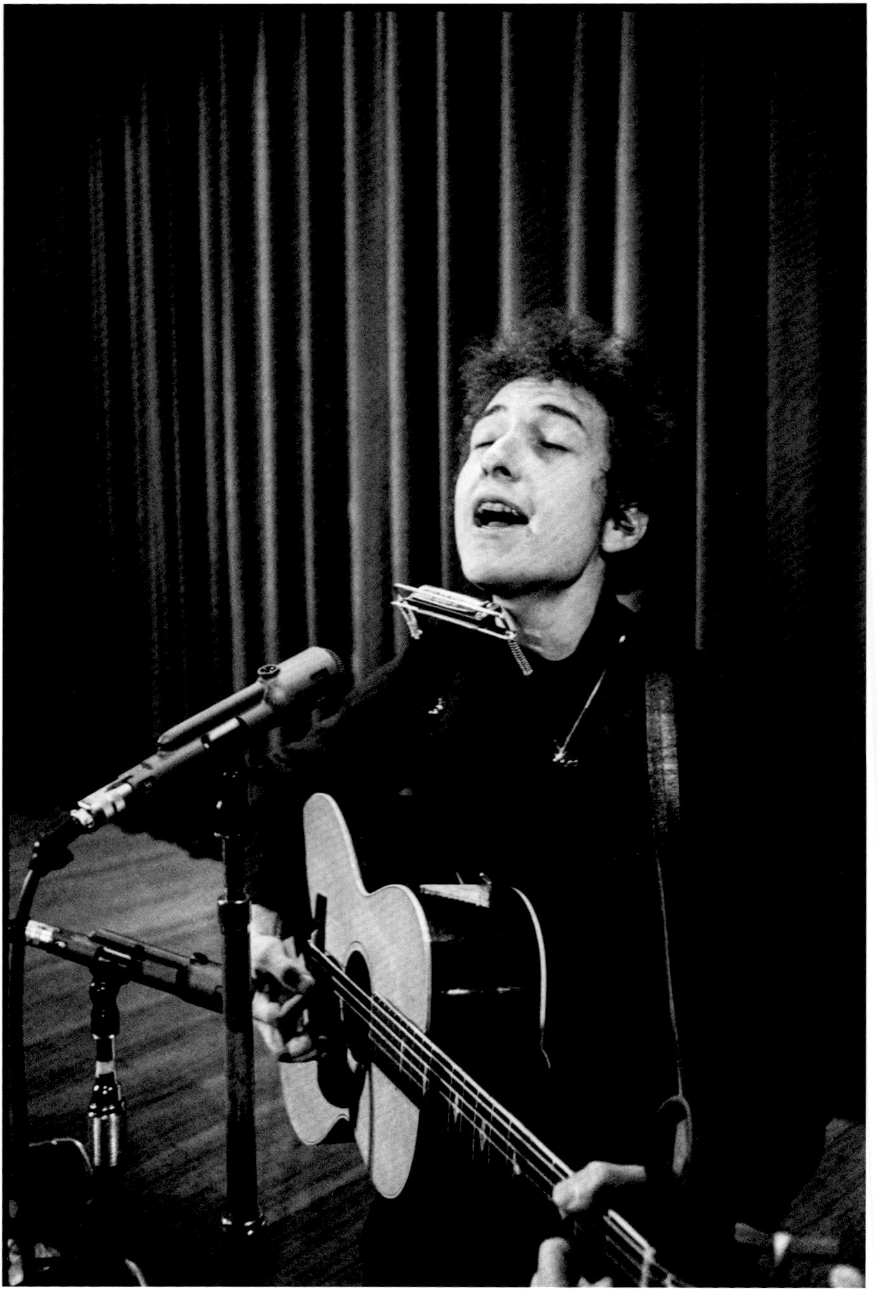

Standing in the darkness behind Bob at Town Hall, I was able to feel the lonesome task he had every time he faced an audience. He would usually spend some time alone before a performance would start, but he never asked me to leave or asked me not to photograph. He never inhibited my working. There were times when I went out on the stage and photographed him from behind while he was performing, in order to get back shots rim-lit by the spotlight. Once, after I had been photographing his concerts for a while, I asked if it was disturbing when I photographed him from nearby when he was performing. (I would crouch down in the aisle, sneak up in front of the stage, and come within a few feet of him with my camera.) He said it didn't bother him because he couldn't see anything out there anyway, the spotlight was almost blinding.

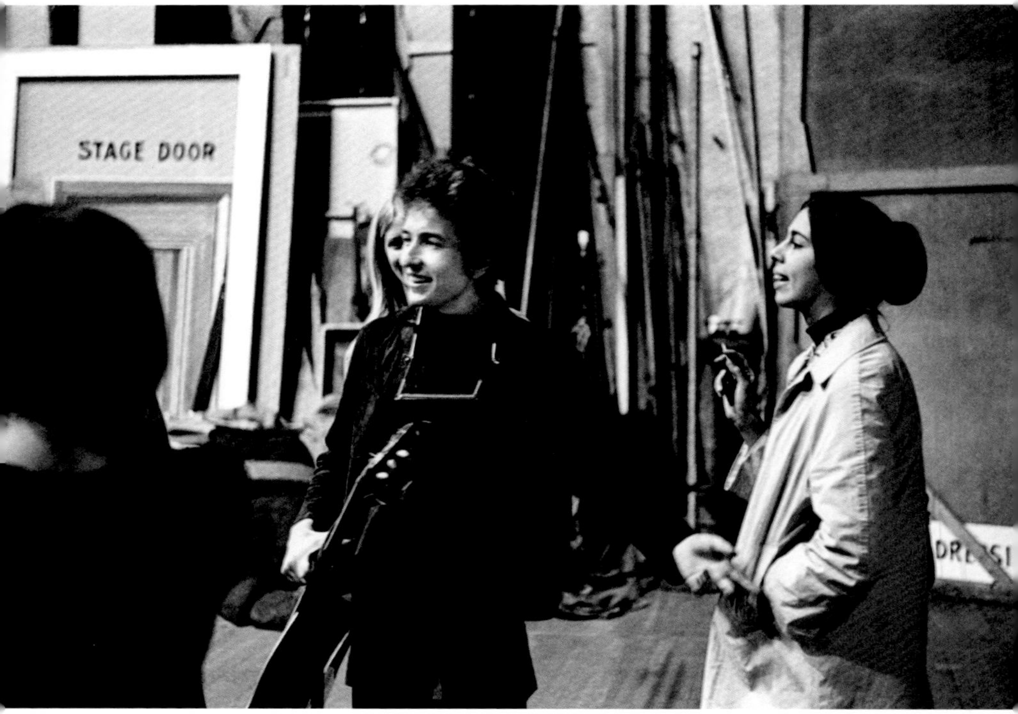

Bob never seemed to be ruffled or worried and always approached the concert as the "thing" he was doing, and it appeared very natural when he was doing that thing. I came to realize that no two audiences are the same, and each and every performance is a new and special happening that requires the artist to provide a new and special moment.

Frequently, friends would drop by the dressing room. After the equipment was tested, Bob would change into his performing clothes, which at the time consisted of suede boots, pressed denim jeans, usually a turtleneck shirt, and a favorite old suede jacket that was worn and stained.

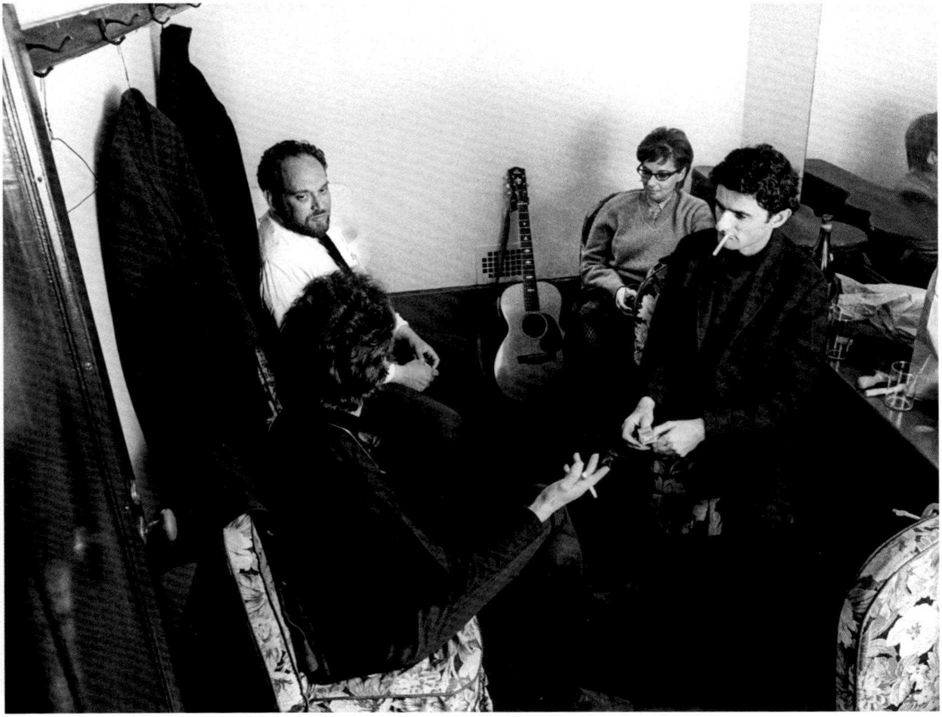

The traveling, the inconveniences, the waiting, the time spent and energy involved had one main objective--the concert. It would begin with Dylan waiting in the darkness of the wings for the cue to go on. He would stride out to the microphone and, almost before he took his first steps, be met by the spotlight that escorted him to center stage. He started strumming his guitar before he reached the mike, as if he couldn't contain himself. This set the pace and created a feeling of urgency, as if to say there's hardly enough time--there's hardly enough time to get it all said, to get it all out.

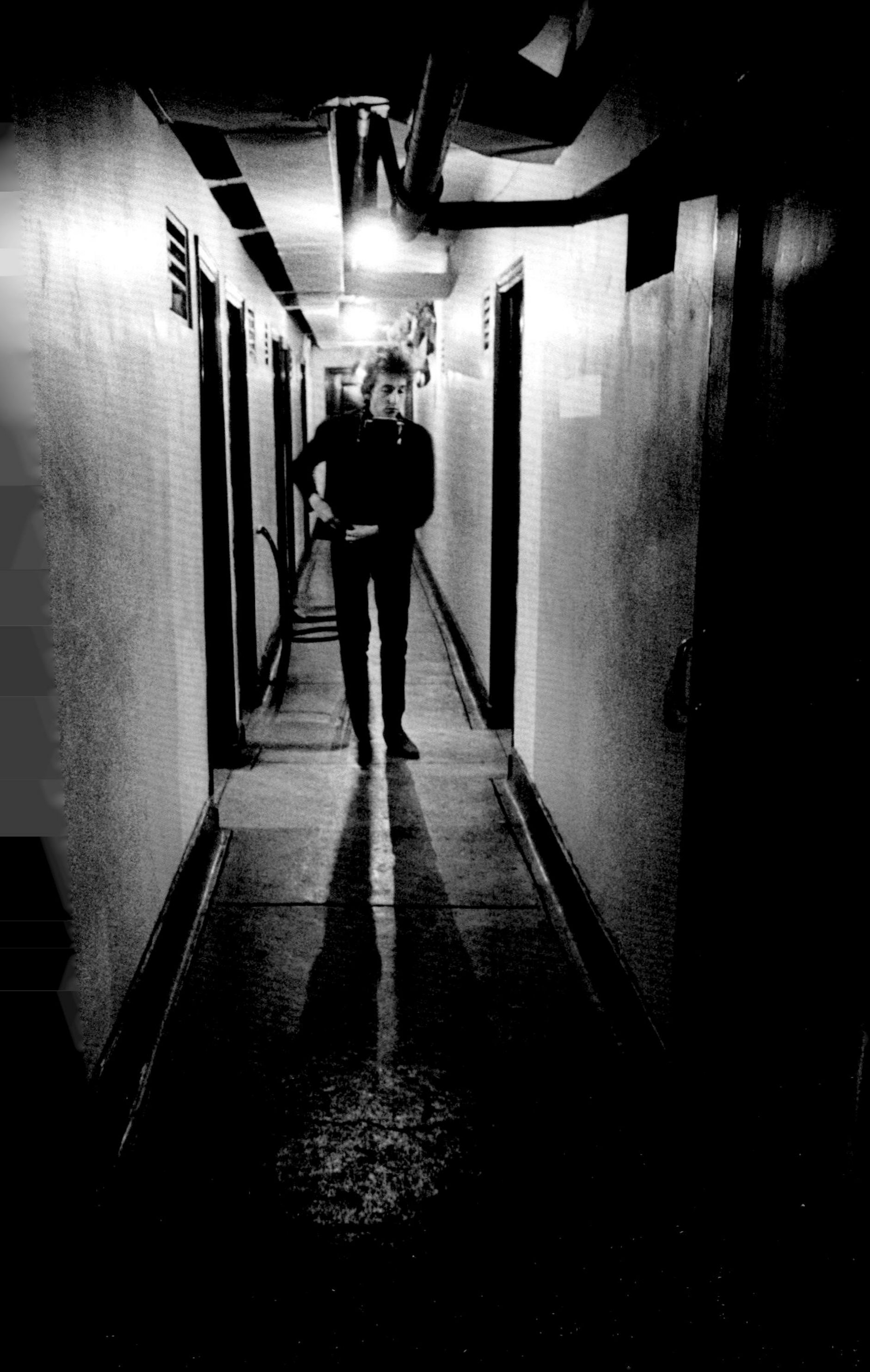

Performance At Town Hall
Philadelphia, Pennsylvania
October 10, 1964

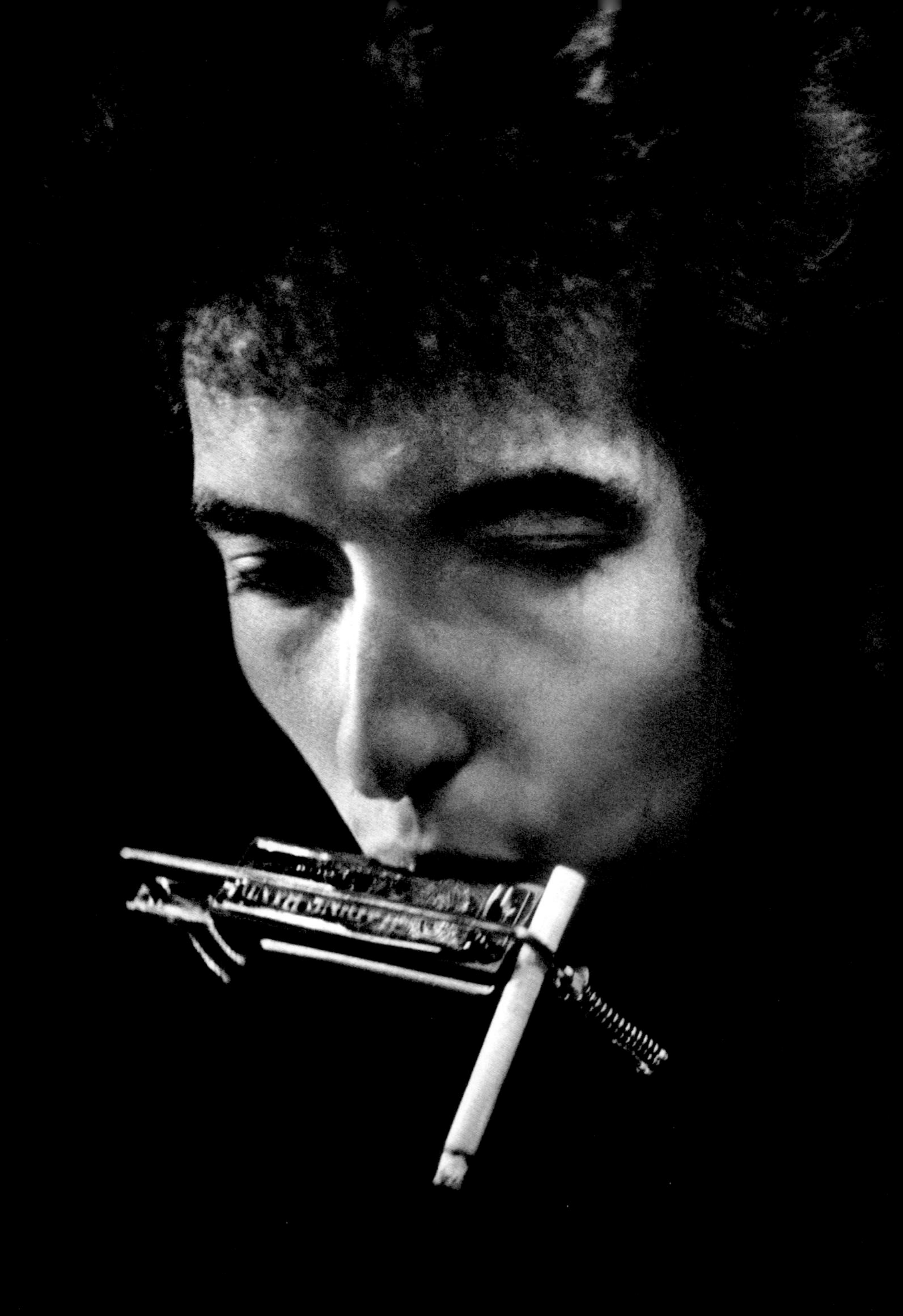

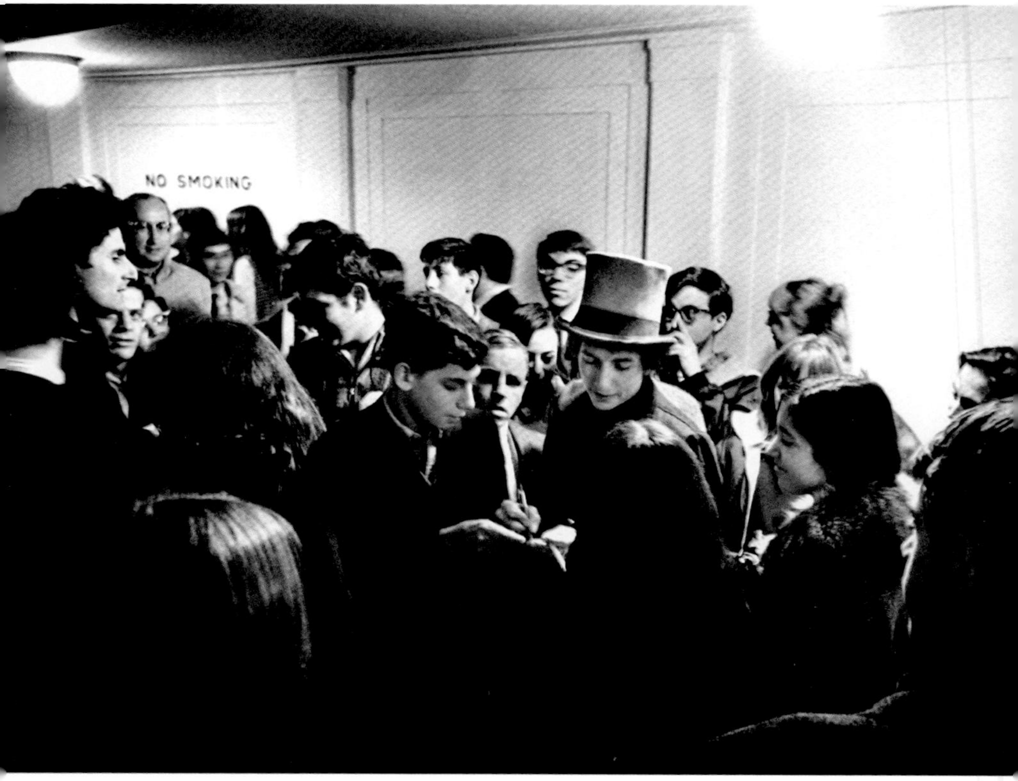
NO SMOKING

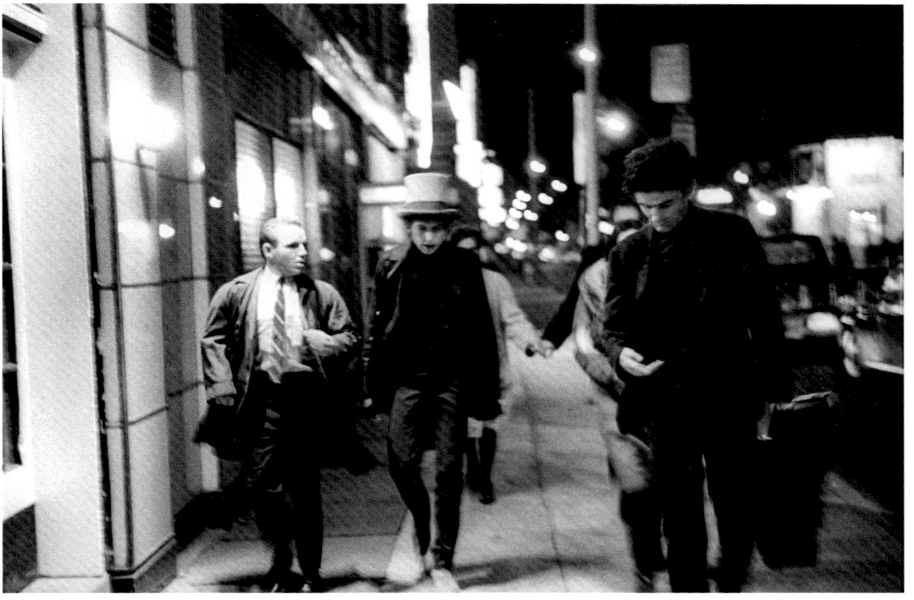

That first concert in Philadelphia was, for me, an unexpected surprise. I had only heard Bob sing one song on TV. Now live and onstage he was more than I had realized. It was a terrific performance and I had a great time. When I asked him which songs he was going to sing, he said the problem was not which ones to perform but which ones to leave out. I found myself getting deeper into the music and very much enjoying making the pictures.

When the performances were over, there was usually a wait in the dressing room while the crowds filed out so that not more than a few dozen fans would stay for autographs, to talk with him, to touch him. Bob was playful with his fans and made it possible for them to get close. Little did I know that this kind of friendliness would end soon. The crowds were going to get too big to handle in such a friendly way.

I ain't gonna work on Maggie's farm no more

No, I ain't gonna work on Maggie's
farm no more

Well, I wake in the morning

Fold my hands and pray for rain

I got a head full of ideas

That are drivin' me insane

It's a shame the way she makes me
scrub the floor

I ain't gonna work on Maggie's farm no more

MAGGIE'S FARM

Chapter Three

In the Studio

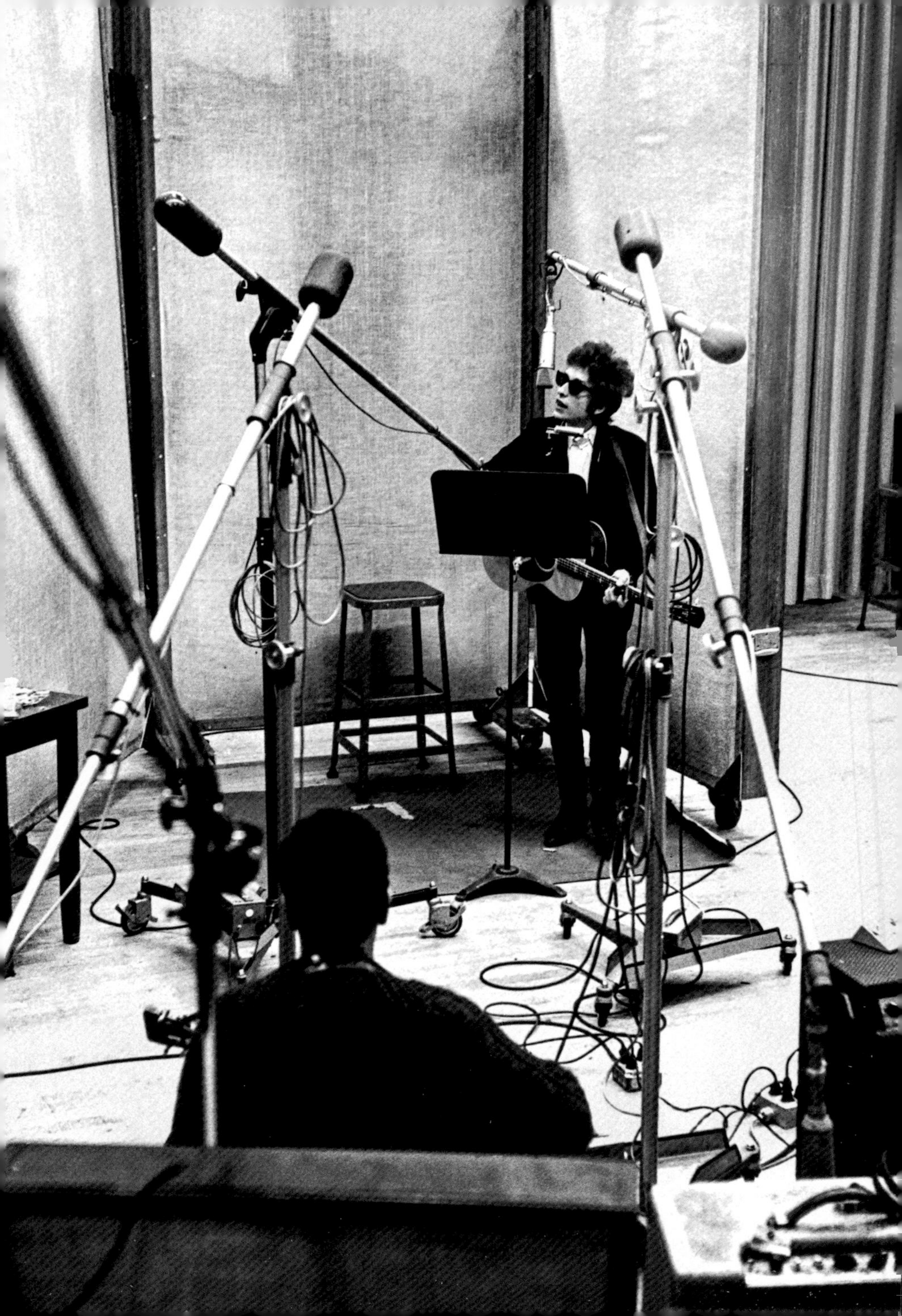

When I first heard the "electric" version of "Maggie's Farm" burst through the speakers in Studio A in the Columbia Records building at 799 Seventh Avenue in New York City in January 1965, I got another big suprise--the music had changed. It was all new, all different. Bob was there recording the album eventually titled _Bringing It All Back Home_. He had worked for several weeks writing some of the new material in Woodstock.

I was welcomed to photograph the sessions. I had no idea what was in store for me, but neither did the musicians hired for the sessions. Bob quickly began working with individual players--he seemed to be everywhere, hopping around from musician to musician--in an effort to bring what was in his mind to fruition.

For this album he seemed to be striking out in a completely new direction. Except for "Corrina, Corrina" on the _Freewheelin' Bob Dylan_ album, and perhaps another rare occasion, Bob had always recorded alone. Now he was going for something altogether new. Tom Wilson, his producer, searched for musicians who could work with Bob and bring his new sound to life. It was crucial to use musicians who could really meet the challenge and accommodate Dylan's needs. As a matter of fact, some musicians were replaced after the first day. Watching the band come together and watching Bob orchestrate what was happening, I was not just surprised--I was impressed. Tom Wilson told me sometime later, "If Bob appeared in the studio one day with a violin and began to play, it wouldn't surprise me at all."

<u>Bringing It All Back Home</u>
Columbia Records, Studio A
New York City
January 13–15, 1965

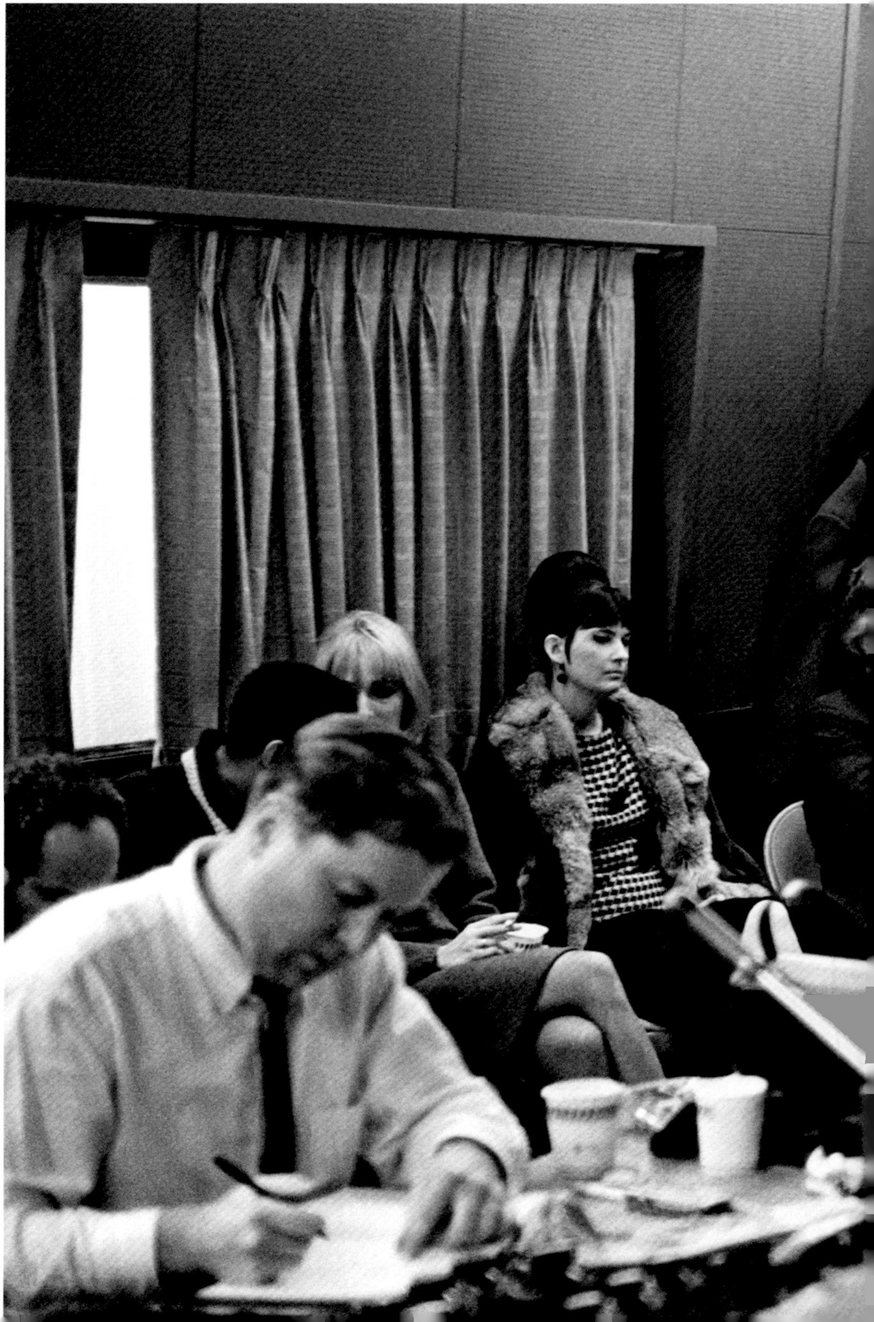

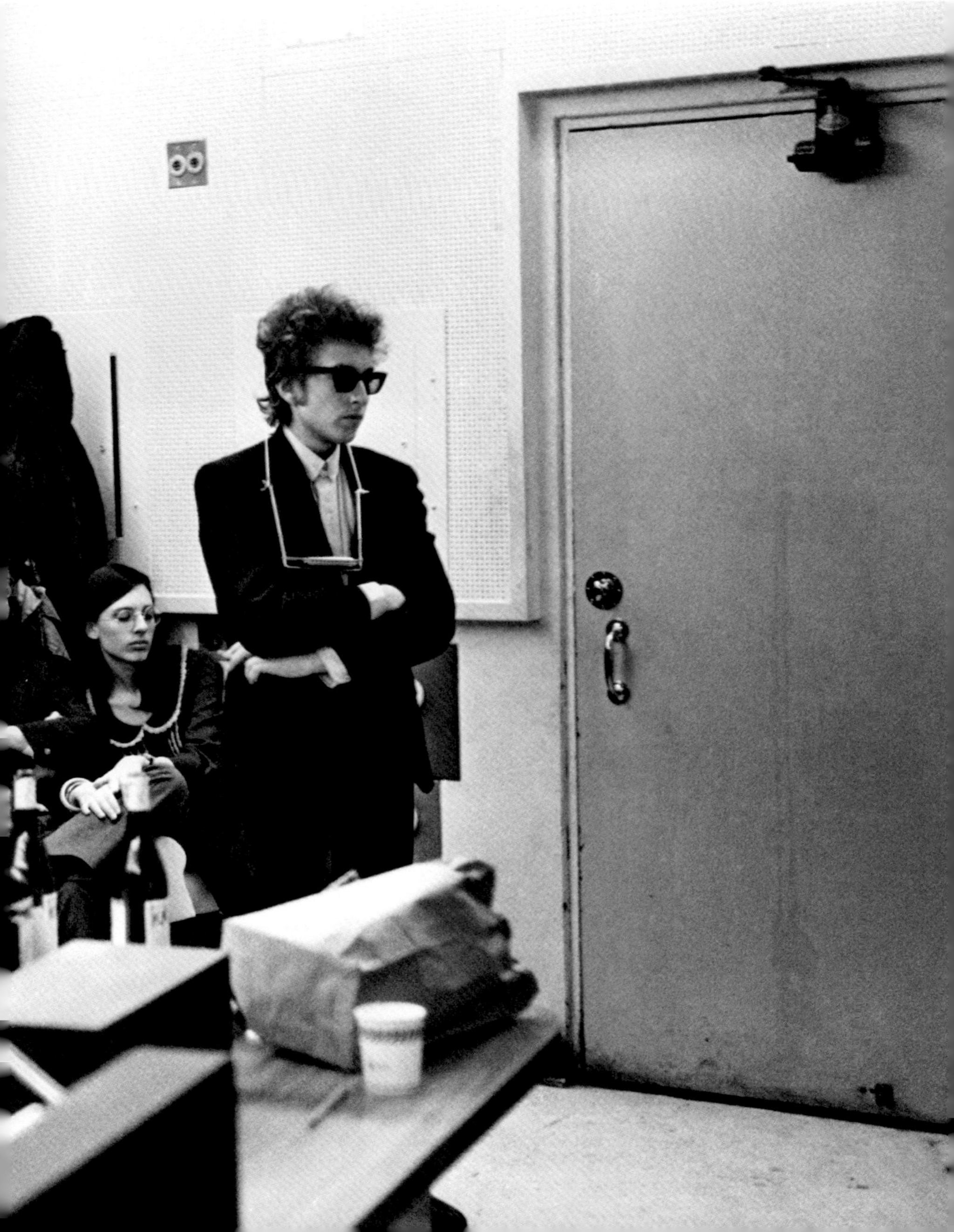

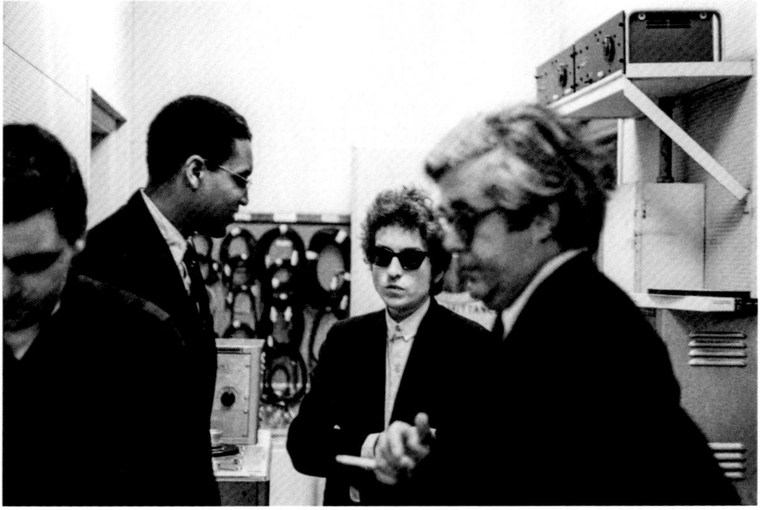

Musicians not used to playing with Bob had to adjust to his particular style and method of delivery. Playing alone, Dylan could have great impact, but it was difficult for other musicians to anticipate what he was going to do. Not only did they need to be experienced players, they had to be sensitive and flexible, and open to changing or abandoning an idea quickly.

At one point Bob lost his temper. He had been asked to sing into a microphone that was placed in front of three baffle panels arranged by the engineers to control the sound quality. Without his knowledge, around the mike area Tom Wilson was setting up an "obstacle course" consisting of music stands, mike stands, and other paraphernalia, all placed in such a way as to inhibit Dylan from moving around the studio or wandering off and leaving the microphone area. This wall of equipment finally got on his nerves; he felt closed in and distracted by it.

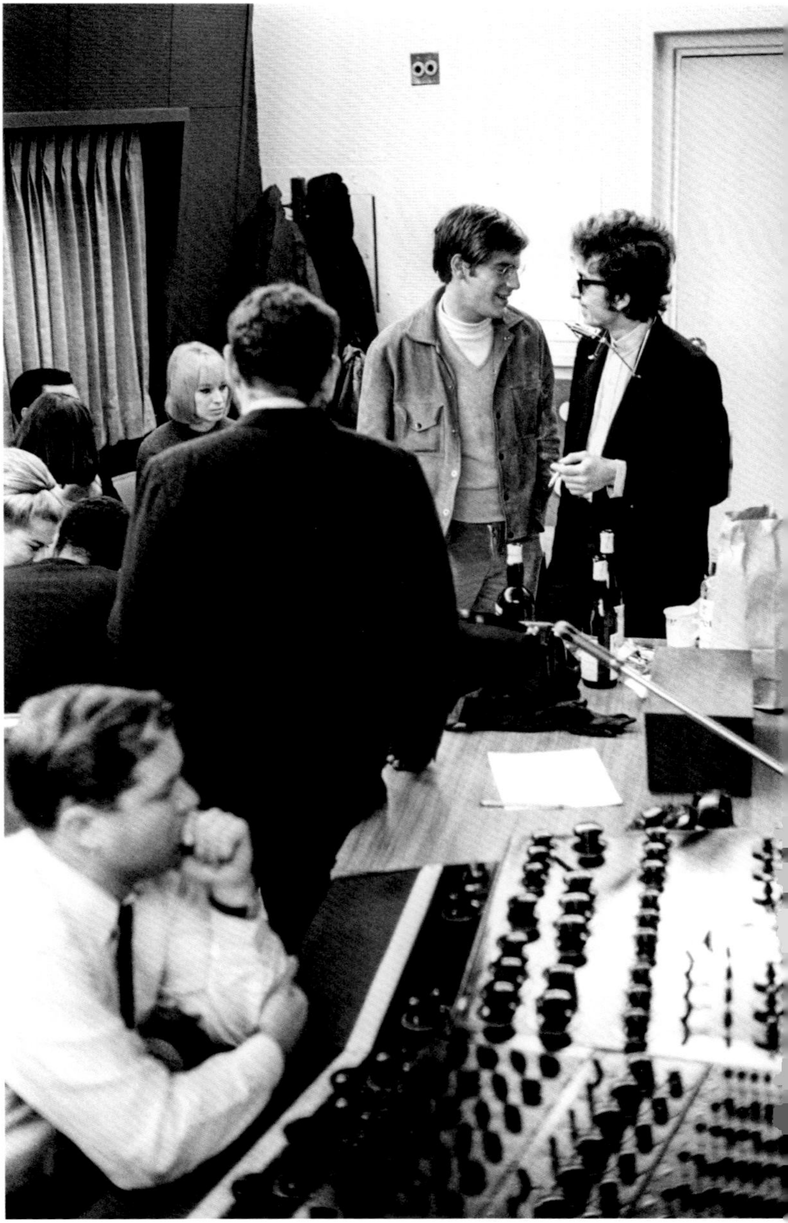

He suddenly stopped singing and bellowed over the microphone, "Can't we get rid of some of these things? Let's start with this," and he grabbed a chair a few feet in front of him, lifted it, and ran halfway across the studio with it. After putting it down, he turned toward the control booth, smiled, and then broke into a laugh, realizing it was not necessary to be upset. All he needed to do was ask to have the floor cleared. He did, and it was.

When recording "Bob Dylan's 115th Dream," the plan was for Bob to start playing the acoustic guitar and, at a certain point, the other musicians would join in. For some reason, the other players missed their cue and Dylan started singing anyway, almost as if he was not used to the idea that other instruments would accompany his.

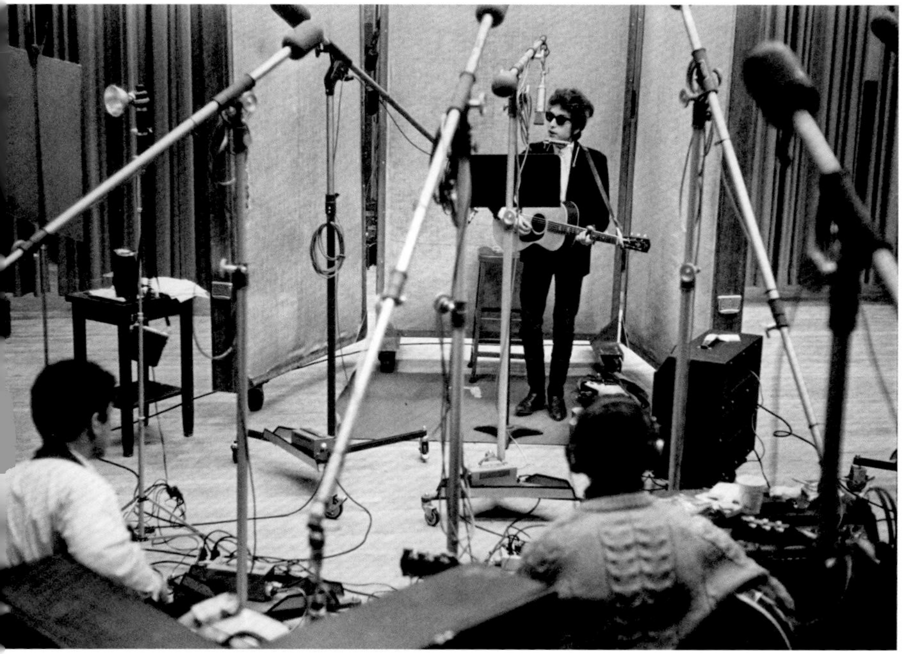

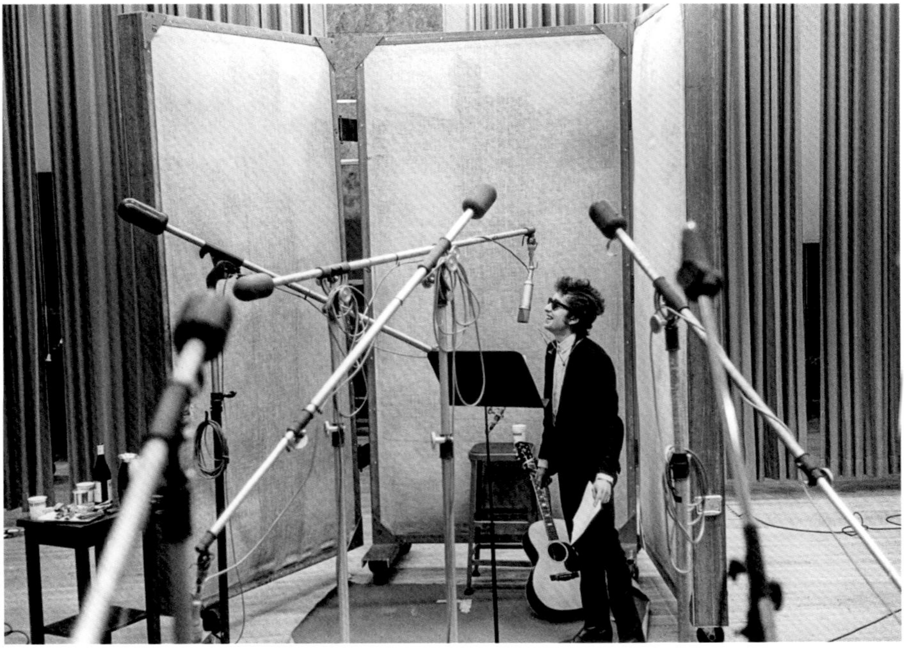

He kept playing. He was doing what he always did. It took him a moment to realize they had not come in with him and he had gone on ahead. Dylan began to laugh. Tom Wilson broke up in hysterical laughter, and soon everyone in the studio was caught up in it. Bob insisted that this laughter be kept on the final track for the release of the album. He shouted out to Wilson that he would "even be willing to pay for it!" The laughter was kept on the recording, and Wilson later told me that after the album's release a number of recording groups kept a "live" microphone on all the time during their sessions, hoping to get a planned "spontaneous" happening like this one.

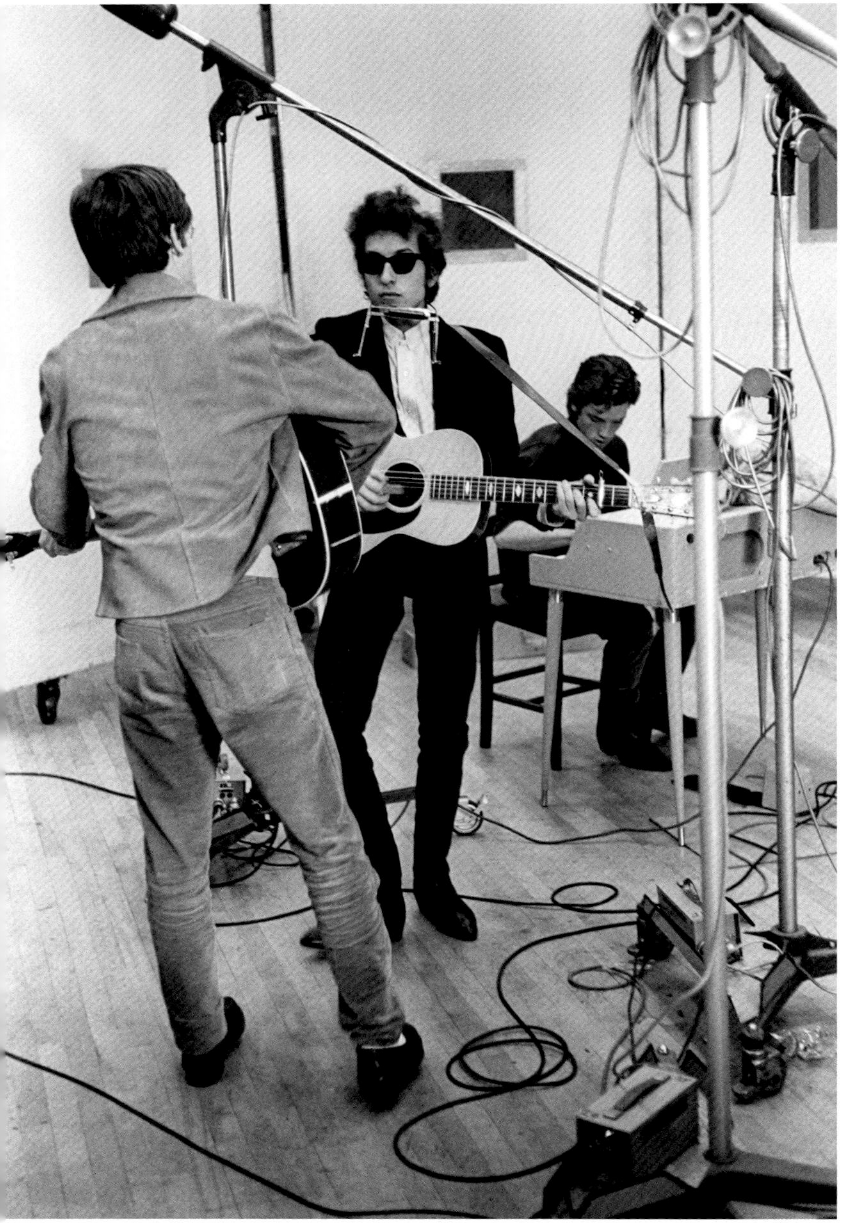

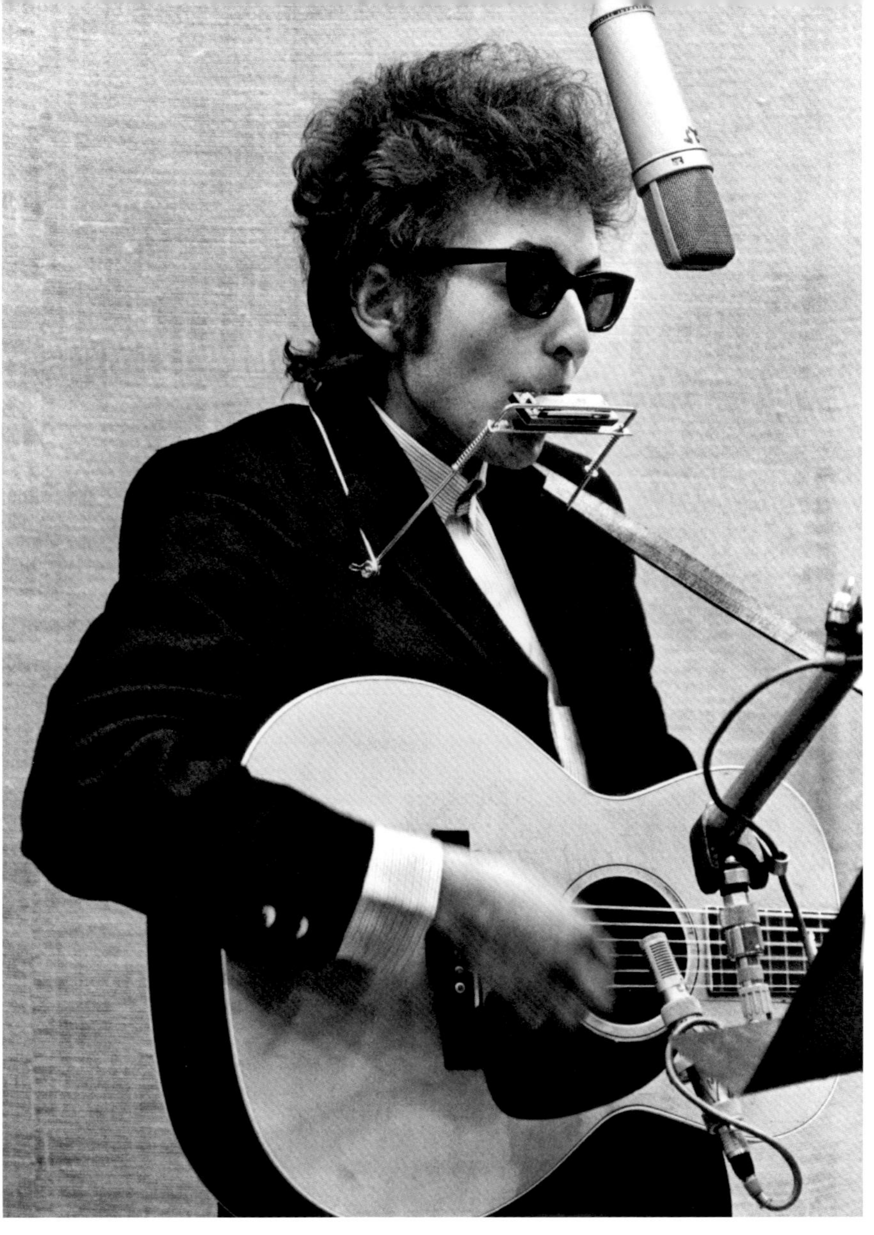

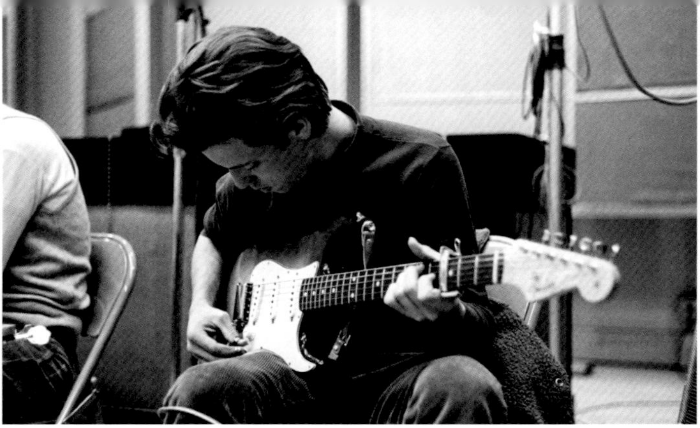

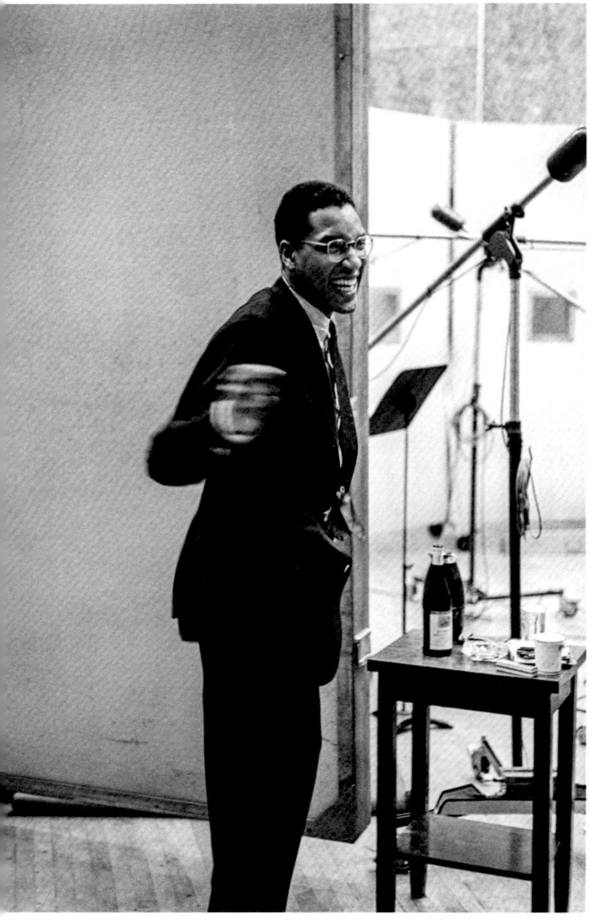

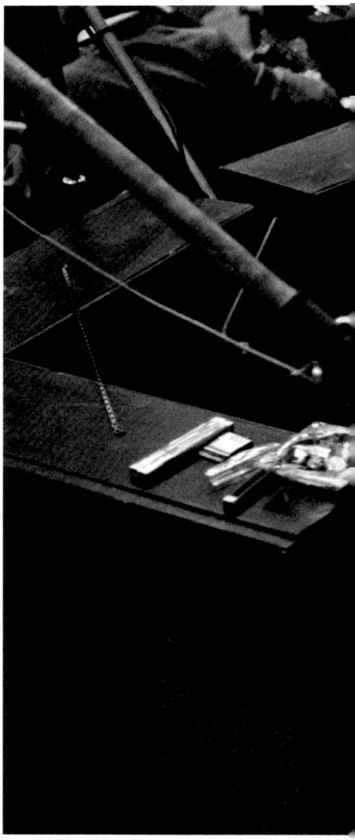

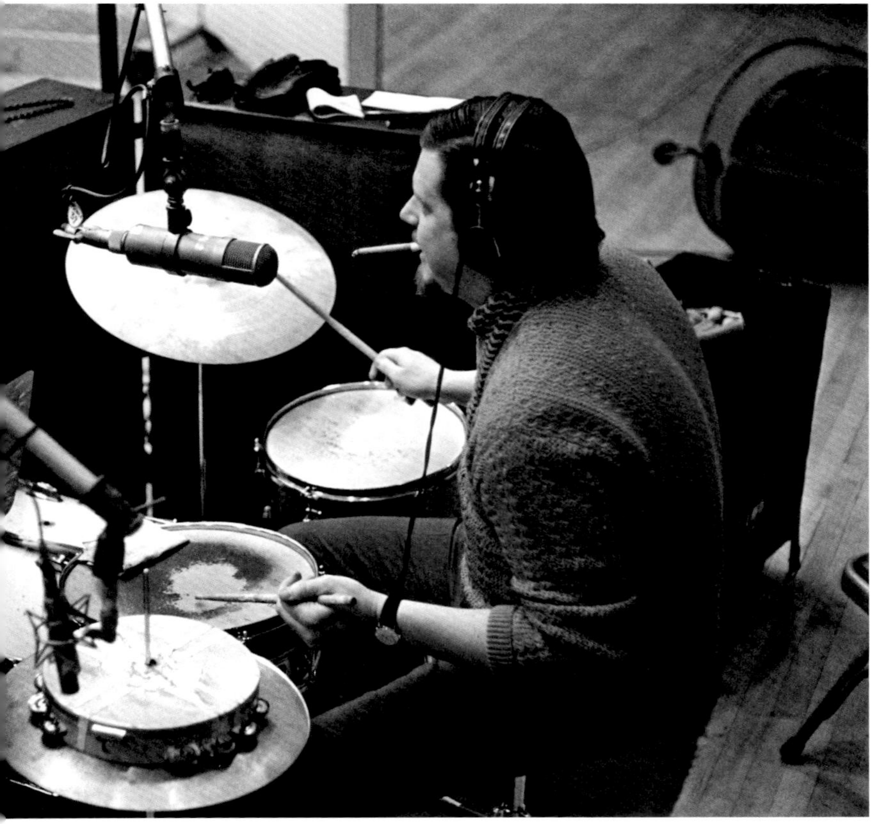

It was obvious from the very beginning of the recording sessions that something exciting was happening. At the next-to-last session, Dylan recorded "Tambourine Man," "It's Alright, Ma," and "Gates of Eden" one after the other, without hearing a playback. He had tried "Tambourine Man" a day earlier but set it aside because it didn't work out. This day he announced that he didn't want the engineering booth to goof--these were long numbers and he didn't want to do them more than once. They were recorded just that way, in one take. When the playback of "Maggie's Farm" was heard over the studio speakers, we were all elated. There was no question about it--it was terrific, it was happy, and it made everyone feel good.

Some days before the recording sessions began, Bob told me that he had written 18 songs for the album, but that he was only admitting to having done 12 and asked me not to tell anyone. He explained that he was holding six for next time. "How do I know I can do it again?" he said.

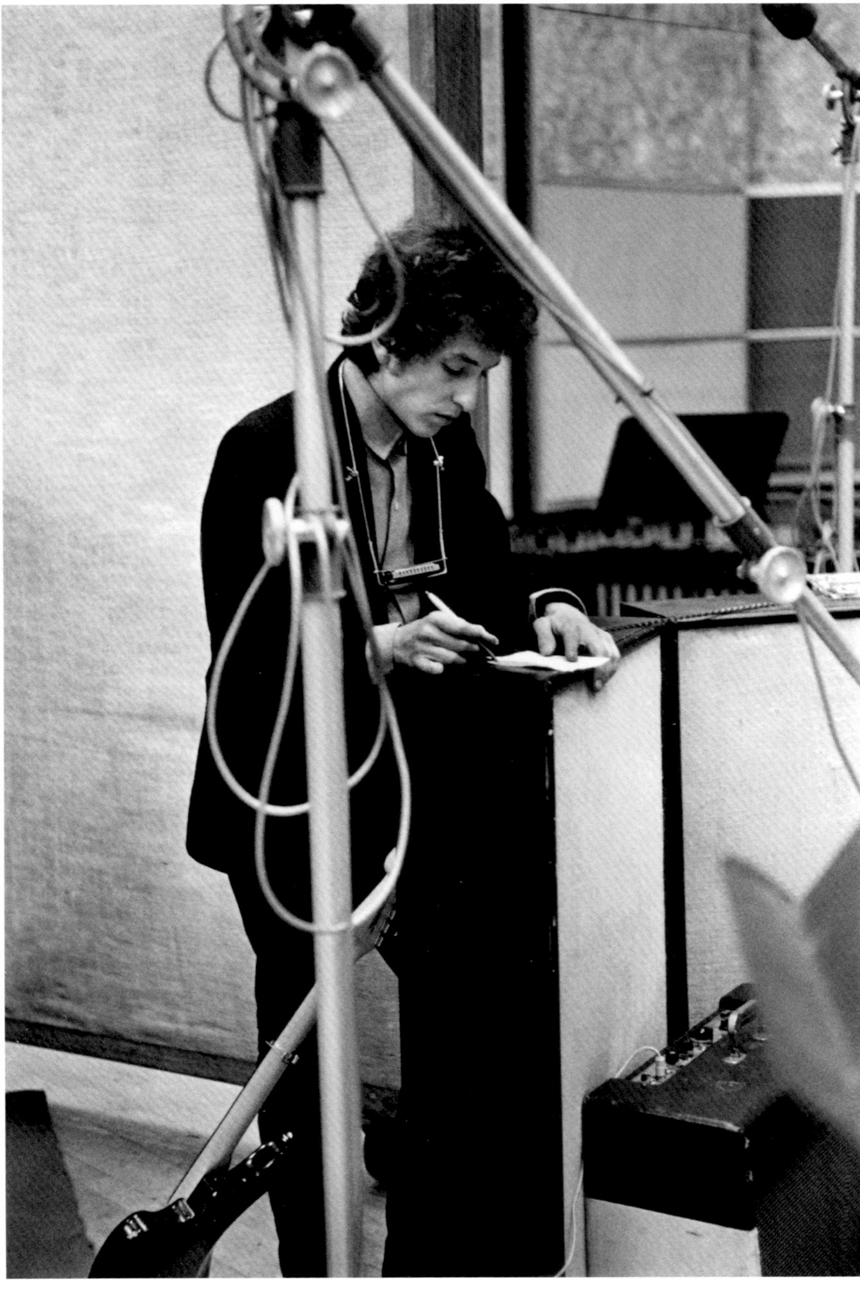

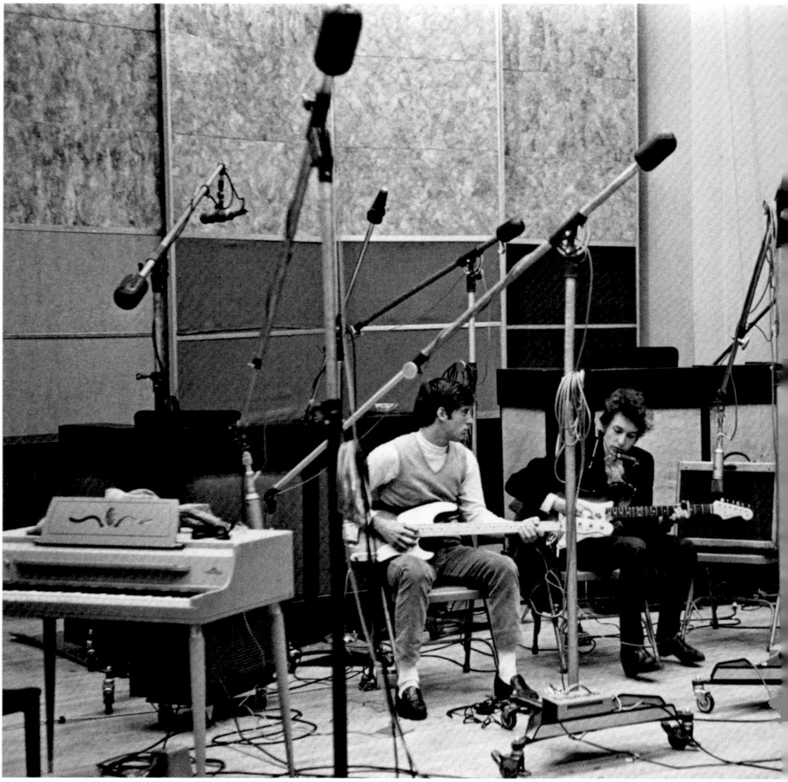

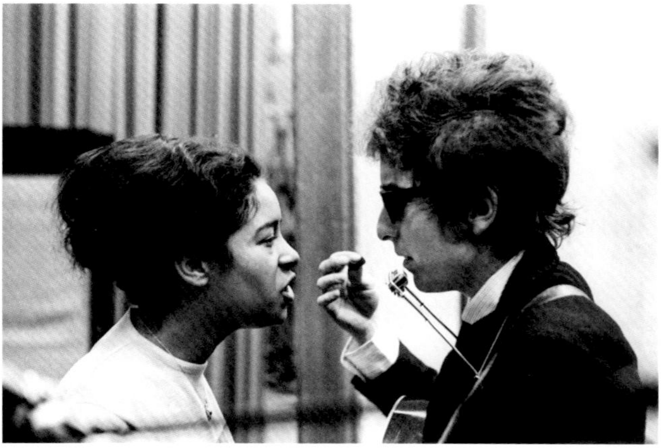

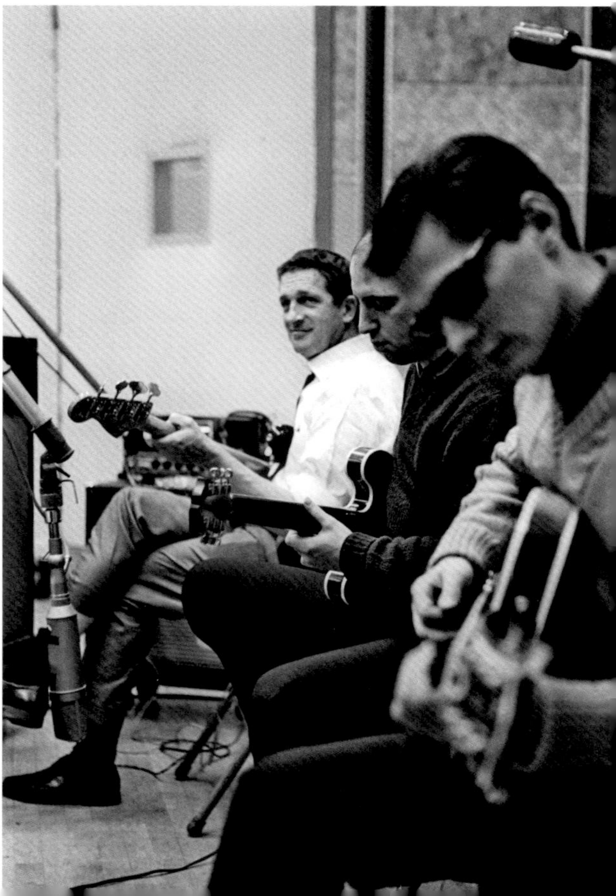

Bob moved through the sessions with enthusiasm, calculating, dealing with the ideas, exchanging his concepts with the other players. They all gave to the creation, communicating and contributing their individual talents. I discovered that Dylan is a much better musician than he usually allows people to realize.
In order to meet the challenges that grew out of the recording session, I saw him call more and more upon his musical ability and his technical knowledge, and this helped him win respect and cooperation from everyone in the studio.

Between takes, Bob would work individually with musicians until he was satisfied with what was happening. He was patient with them and they were patient with him. His method of working, the certainty of what he wanted, kept things moving. He would listen to the playbacks in the control booth, discuss what was happening with Tom Wilson, and move on to the next number. If he tried something that didn't go well, he would put it off for another session. In this way, he never got bogged down--he just kept on going.

Something new, created out of old parts, was being born in Studio A. Later it would be called folk rock, and it would permeate the entire world of popular music, with many other performers pursuing their own versions. The spring, having been tightened, now seemed ready to uncoil with the release of this album. As the music was created, word seeped out, and more and more people began to visit during the sessions. At times the control room looked like a commuter train packed with people watching the trees go by. It was a party of sound and music--there was wine, sandwiches, and a lot of hard work. Then there was the album cover. . . .

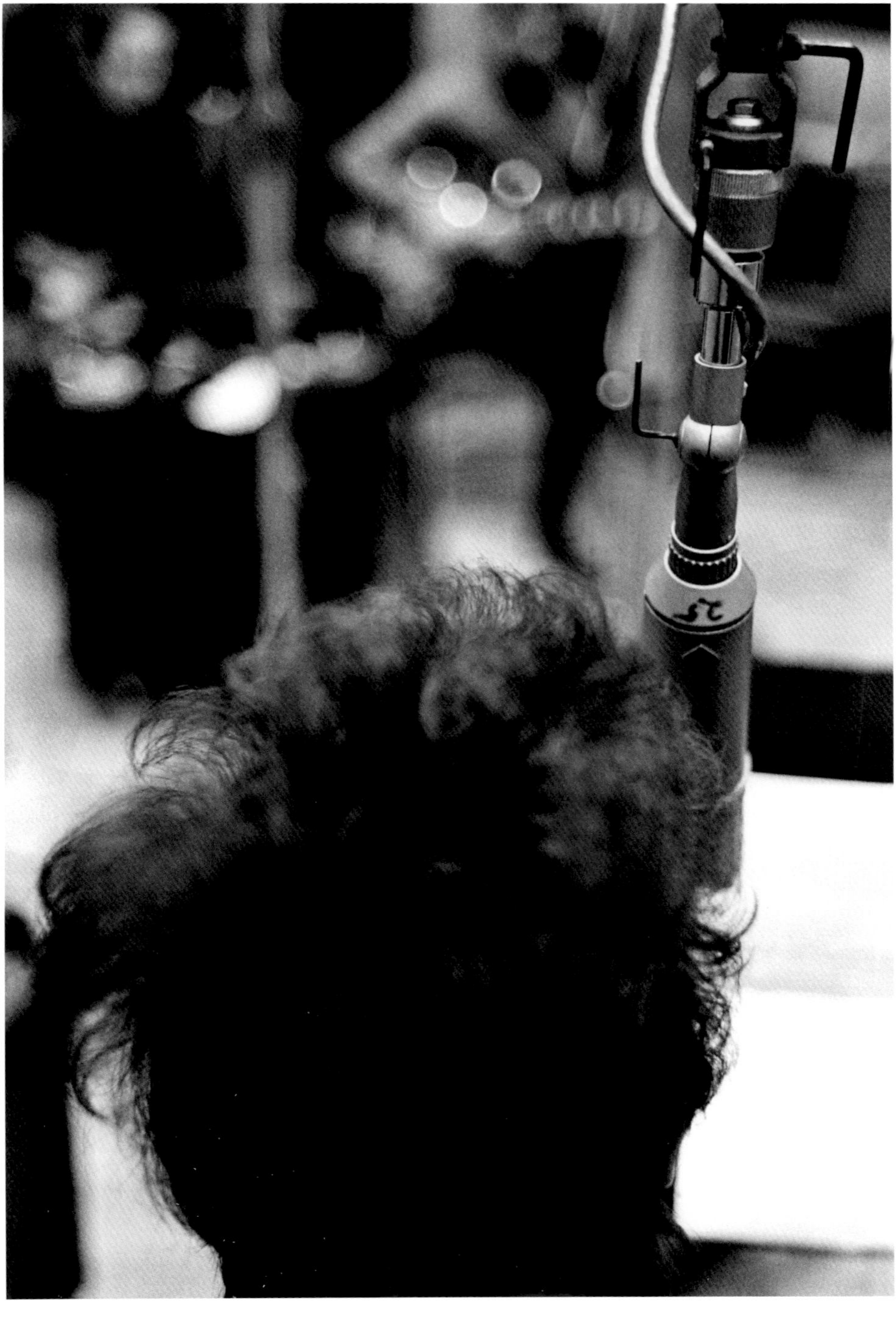

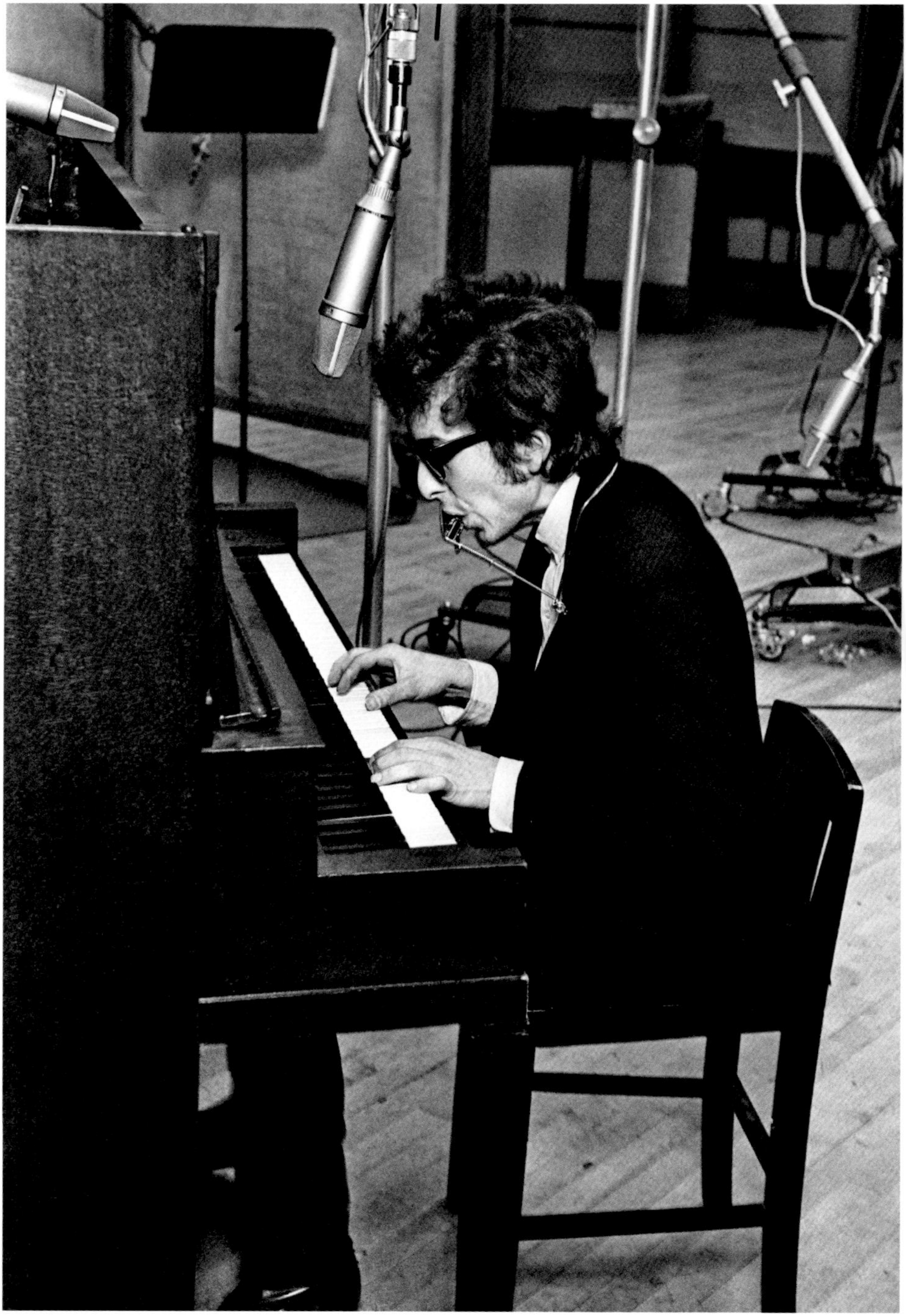

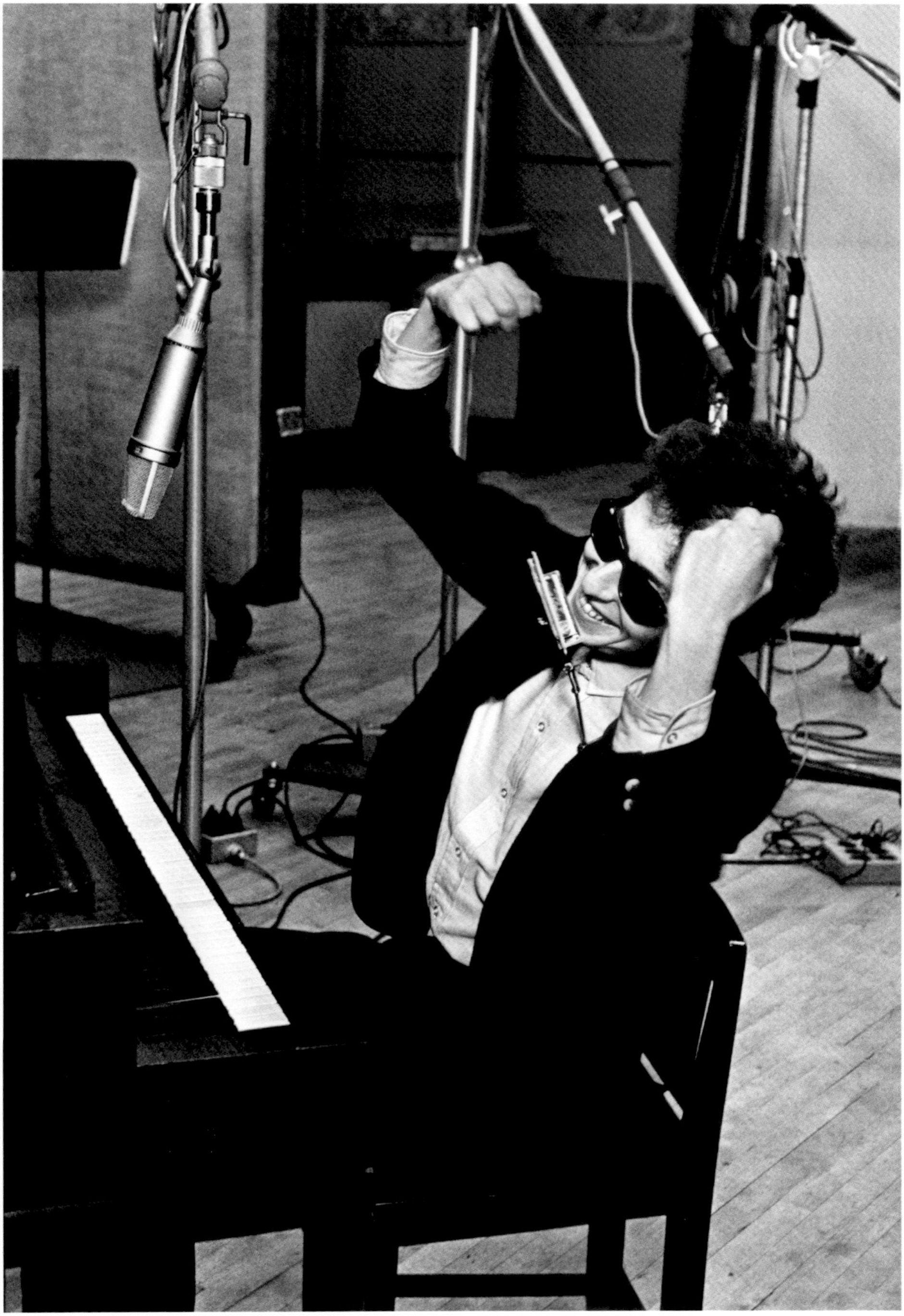

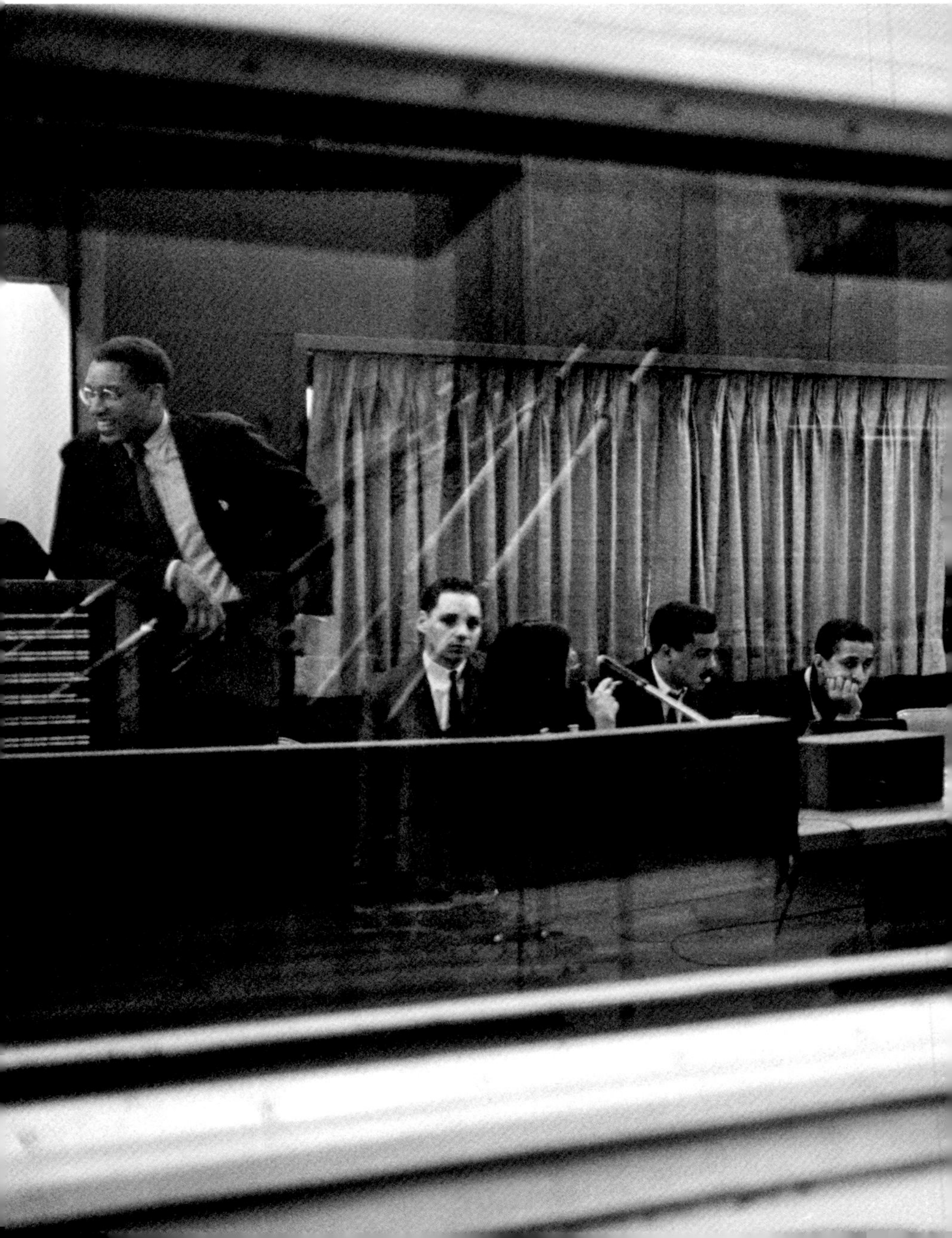

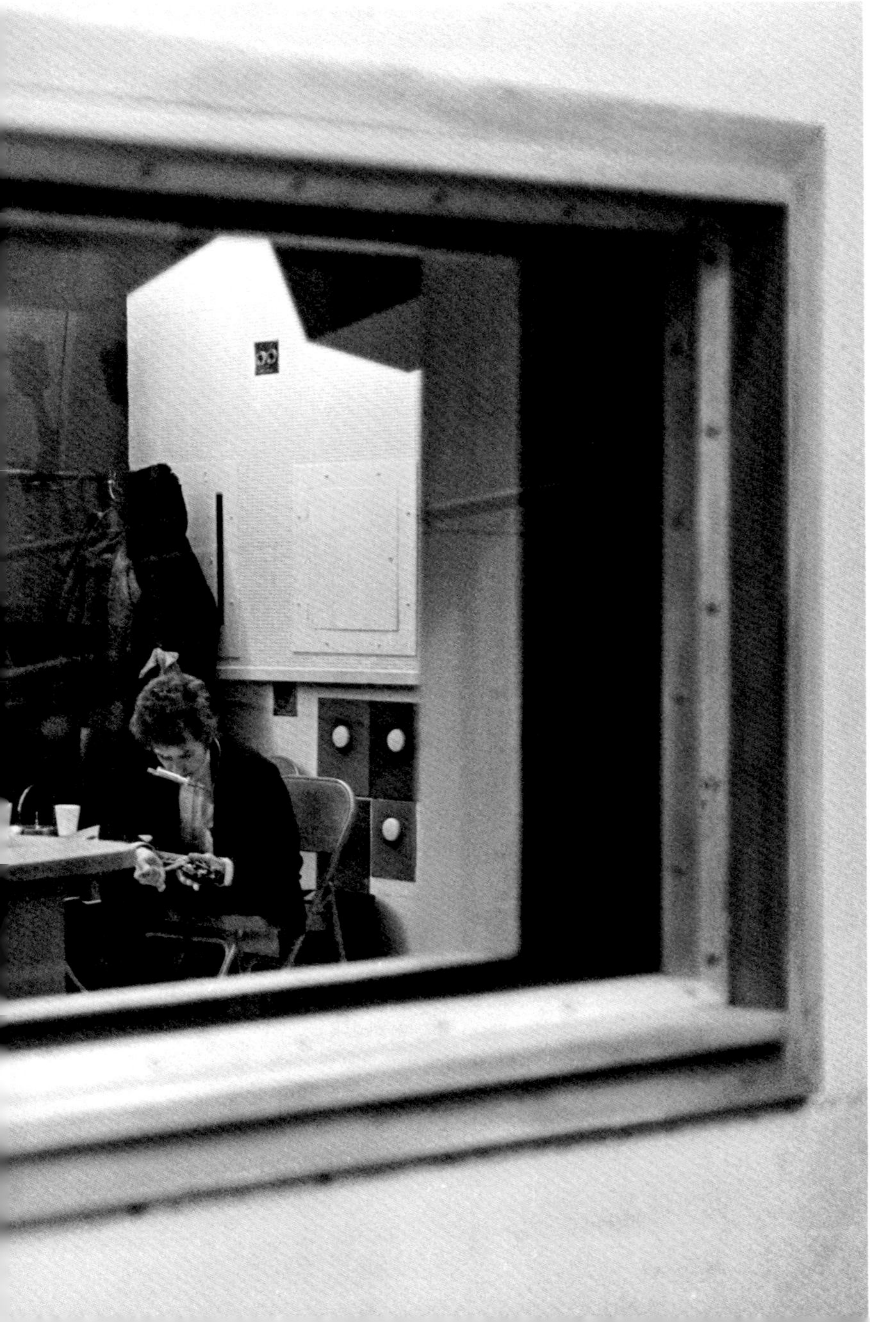

You never turned around to see the frowns
on the jugglers and the clowns

When they all come down
and did tricks for you

You never understood that it ain't no good

You shouldn't let other people
get your kicks for you . . .

How does it feel
How does it feel
To be on your own
With no direction home
Like a complete unknown
Like a rolling stone?

LIKE A ROLLING STONE

Inter-
mission

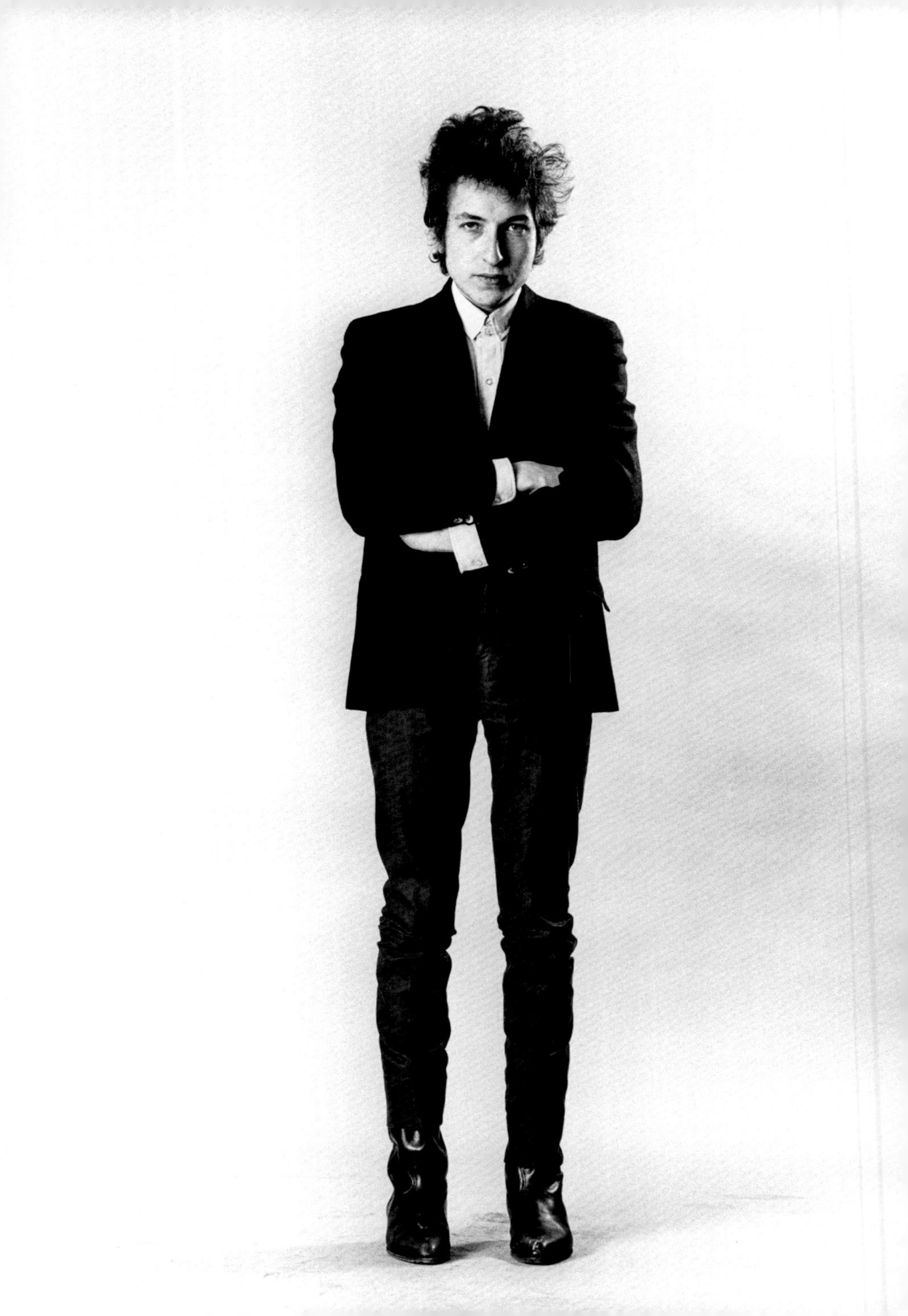

The Bringing It All Back Home album-cover picture probably elicits more questions than any photograph I made of Bob Dylan. Although it seems complicated from the outside, it was actually a fairly simple photographic endeavor and not made the way most people think it was done.

During the time that Bob was recording the songs for Bringing It All Back Home, he asked me to do the cover photo. That was great news for me, especially since up to that time I hadn't photographed an album cover. Although it made me feel good to be asked, it also gave me a bit of concern since covers have a number of special requirements that need to be met. The most bothersome part was that John Berg, the art director responsible for assigning the shoot, said no way. He said I was an unknown without an extensive portfolio of covers, that Bob Dylan was a star and needed a star to make this cover. Needless to say my disappointment ran high, but he did make sense. I could see his need to guarantee the outcome and keep his job.

Later that day in the Columbia Records commissary, while having lunch with Bob and Albert Grossman, I explained that I would not be able to shoot the cover and why. I cannot recall if Albert finished his lunch or just stood up right then and beckoned Bob and me to get up. He took us each by the arm and off we went to the art director's office, where Mr. Grossman proceeded to make a series of predictions of what bad things would happen if I did not get this assignment. It was settled right then and there. I would shoot the cover.

Now, what to do. First and foremost, after hearing the music at the sessions, I realized that this album would certainly be a turning point for the new electrified Bob Dylan. It would not be a continuation as much as it would be a new path in Dylan's music and career. I needed to make a photographic statement that would show this departure while heralding the newly reinvented Bob Dylan.

For quite a while I had been experimenting with a rig I made to fit in front of my 4x5 view camera, enabling me to make multiple exposures on one sheet of film while moving, blurring, or keeping sharp parts of any single exposure -- an effect I had intended for a fashion portfolio. For this album cover I made two exposures on the same sheet of film. After making the first exposure of the full scene with Bob and Sally in the center of the picture, I made a second exposure after placing a black piece of paper on a sheet of glass held in front of my lens so that it would cover the images of Bob and Sally on the couch only, keeping them unaffected by the second exposure for the rest of the final image, which was made while I revolved the film holder on the back of my camera -- one complete revolution during a long exposure. The second exposure blurred the scene around Bob and Sally, giving the visual effect of a spinning record.

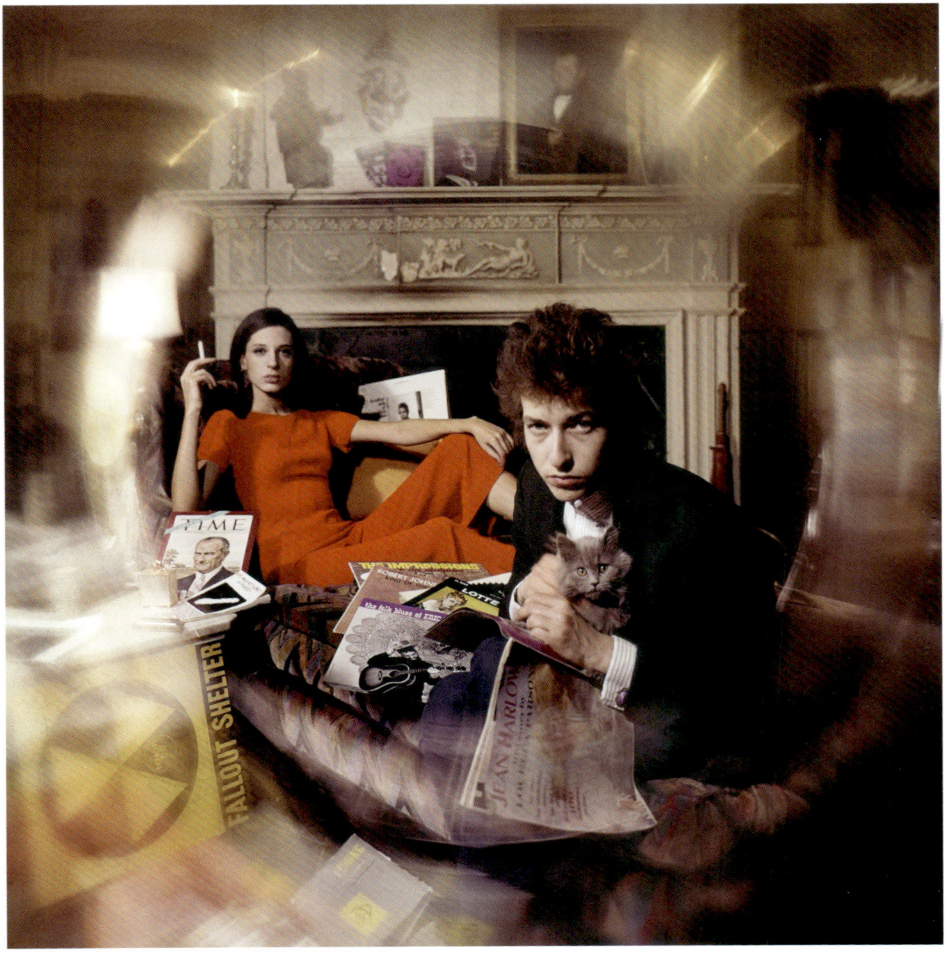
TIME
FALLOUT SHELTER
JEAN HARLOW
LOTTE

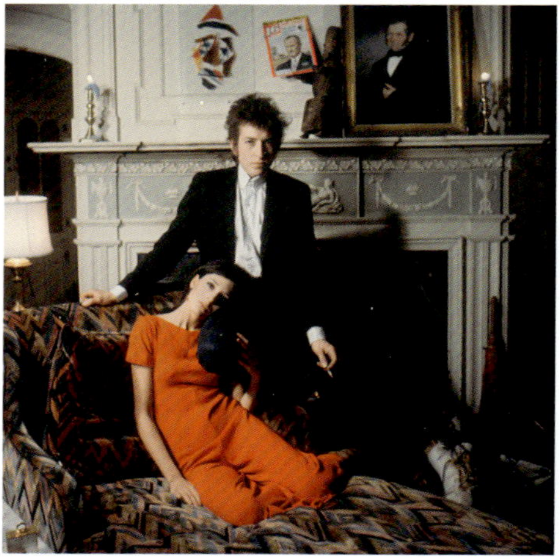
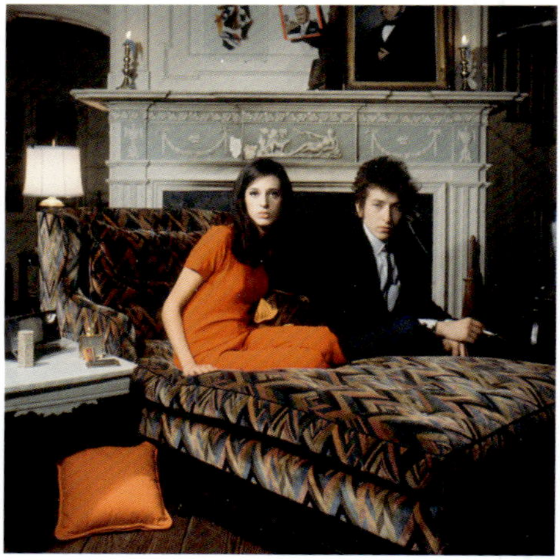
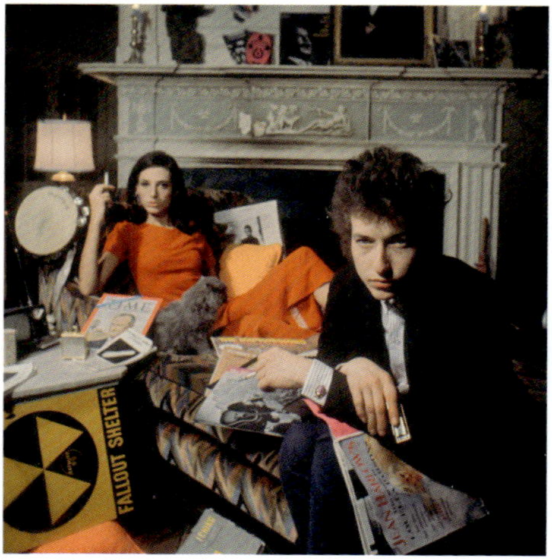

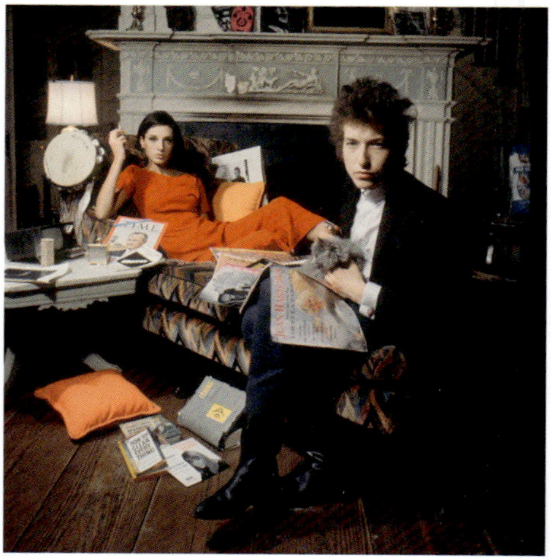

Bringing It All Back Home
Albert Grossman's House
Woodstock, January 1965
with Sally Grossman

On a cold snowy night Bob came by my place with his station wagon, into which we loaded close to a hundred pounds of photo gear and drove to Woodstock. We would shoot the next day in Albert Grossman's house. The next morning I put together a set in front of an old fireplace--when we saw the test Polaroid with Bob and Sally we were all enthused. We scoured the house and basement to find things to put in the picture so there would be things to "move" when the camera back was revolved. We started the shoot with Bob and Sally on a colorful divan, a wedding gift to Sally and Albert from Peter, Paul and Mary. We then dressed the set with all of the stuff we found and finally made the "turning" picture--and we were lucky to get one exposure with the cat looking into my lens. I wanted my statement to say that Bob Dylan was less a folksinger and more a prince of music. So there in the center of the turning record is Bob Dylan without an instrument, in this beautiful room, seated with a beautiful woman in a red dress, wearing his dark blazer and sporting the beautiful cuff links given to him by Joan Baez. And I was very happy for me and for John Berg when this, my first cover, was nominated for a Grammy Award for best album cover photograph.

In March Bob called and asked if I would come up to Woodstock, where he and Sara Lownds, who later became Mrs. Dylan, were renting a house that belonged to Peter Yarrow's mother. Bob told me he was working on a book--later called Tarantula--and wanted to shoot a cover for it.

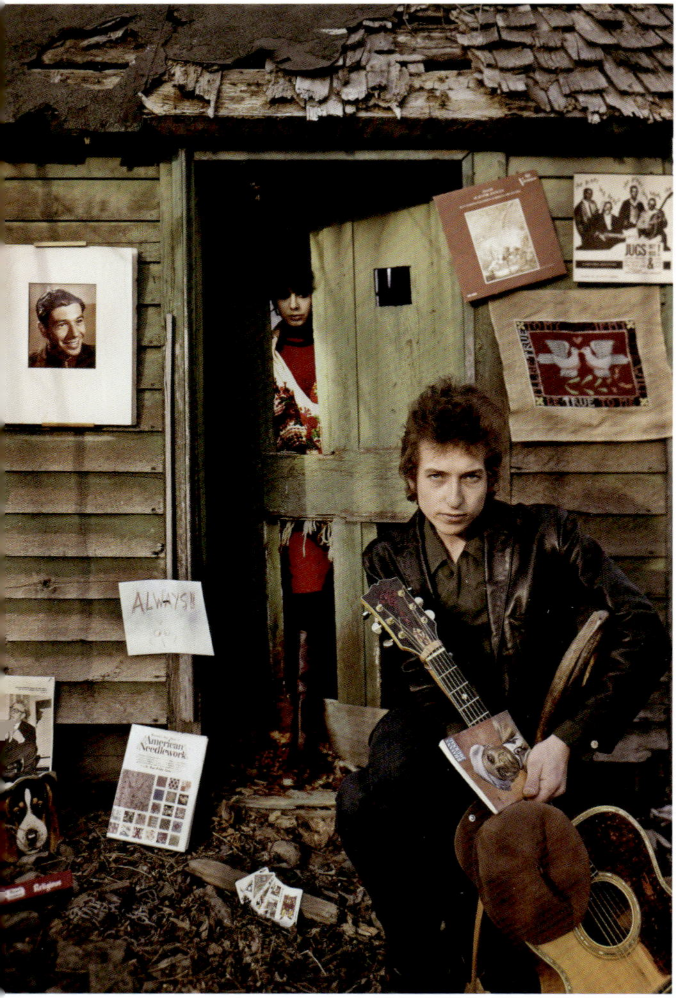

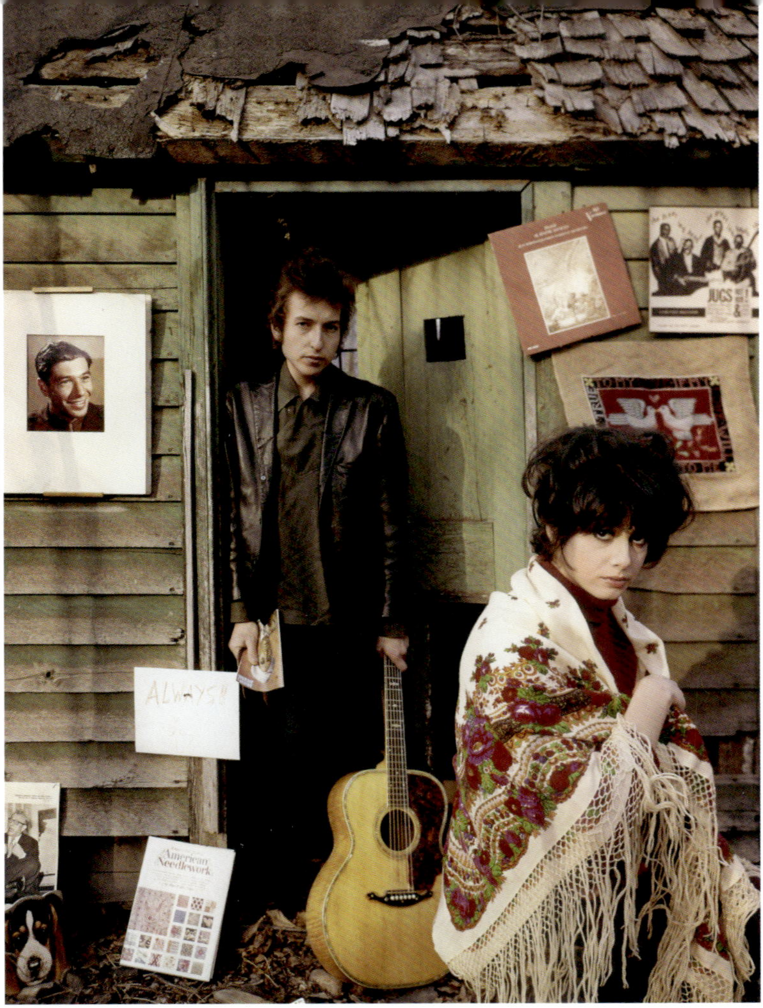

The Shack Behind Peter Yarrow's Mother's House
Woodstock, March 14, 1965
with Sara Lownds

He liked the idea of shooting in front of an old shack behind the house, and in no time at all we couldn't resist dragging out some of the old stuff inside and propping it in front of the little cabin. Although the picture has done well for itself--and was even a cover for a different book--it did not run on Tarantula.

Daniel Kramer's Studio
New York City
January 1965

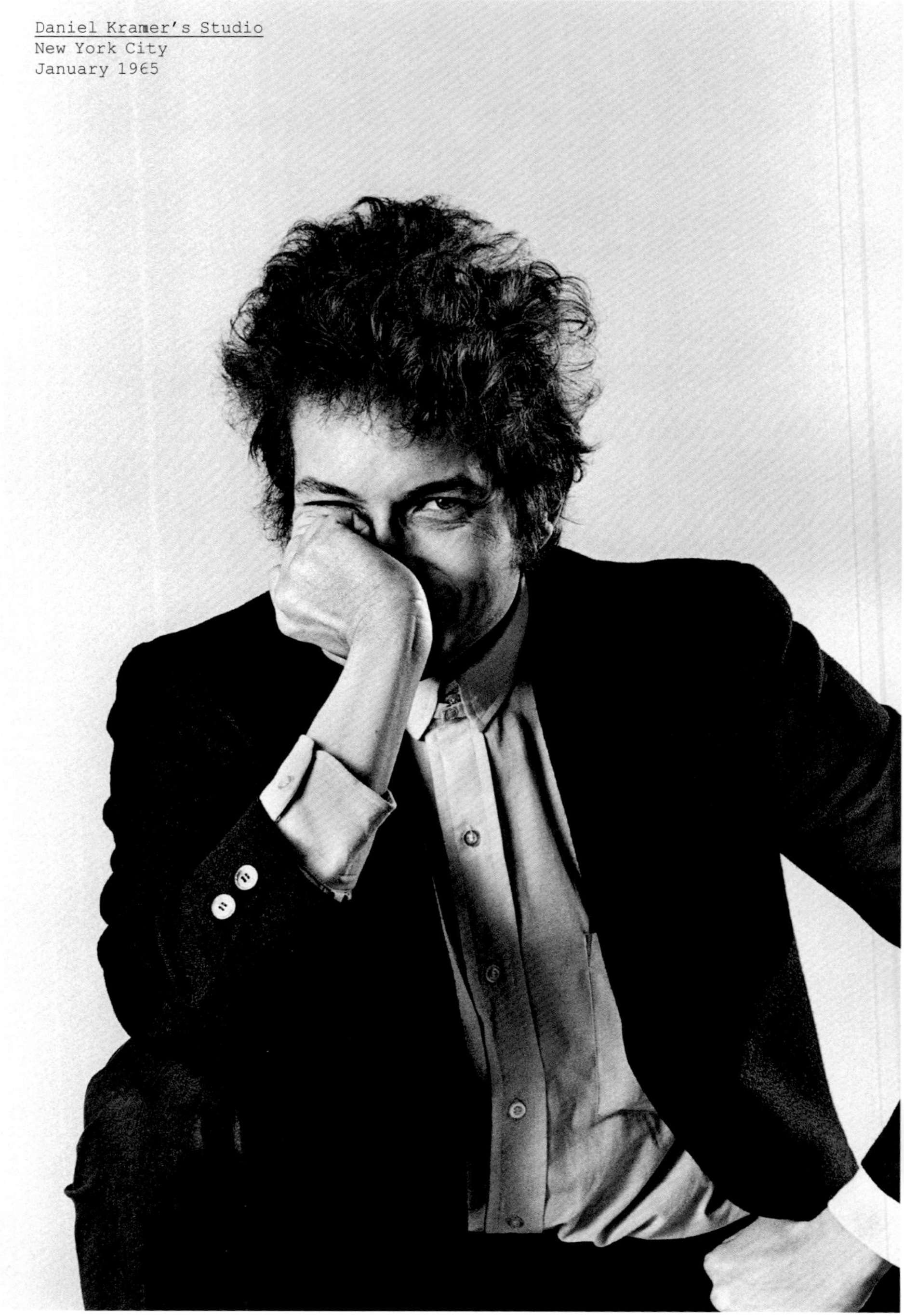

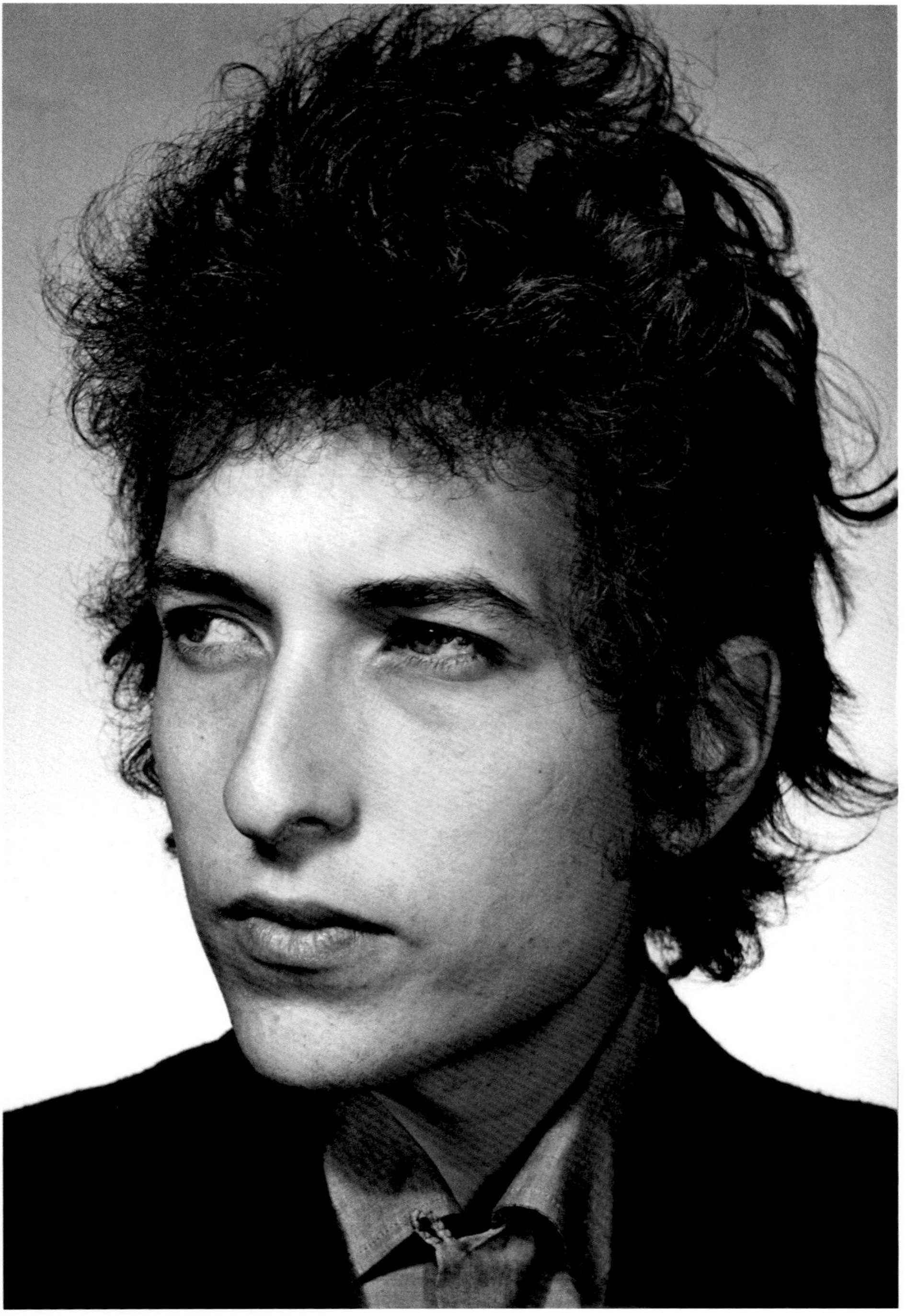

Time and time again, I asked Bob to come to my studio for a different kind of portrait session, one where I would have more control over the lighting. Each time he put me off. Finally, in January of 1965, he agreed to come. I asked him to sit on a stool and do nothing but look into my camera. He did at first, but again he wasn't happy. It was the old rocking-chair story; he didn't like to pose.

He began to avoid the camera, playing with things he found around the studio--holding a dart board or a coffee cup or an ashtray, carrying my camera case, draping himself with my big black focusing cloth--posing with obviously made expressions. I decided to bring out a stool to centralize Bob's activity. Then, instead of sitting on the stool I provided, he put one foot up on it and half-hid his face with his right hand. He was doing what he felt--hiding from the camera but not completely. He was smiling out from behind his hand as if he really knew what was going on. He was playing with the camera the way he played with interviewers and reporters; the way he sometimes plays with the whole world. Catch me if you can, and I believe I did. This picture, for me, depicts the many Dylans.

In April Bob asked if I would do his next album cover. I had photographed Bringing It All Back Home knowing something about the music I heard, and it had helped me conceptualize the image. Now it was just, let's shoot a cover. We met for some discussion in Bob's hotel room, which included a grand piano, on lower Fifth Avenue. The plan was to spend some time in Greenwich Village making pictures with Bob and Bob Neuwirth, his friend and road manager. Not exactly the best way to make an album cover, but with Bob you just never knew...

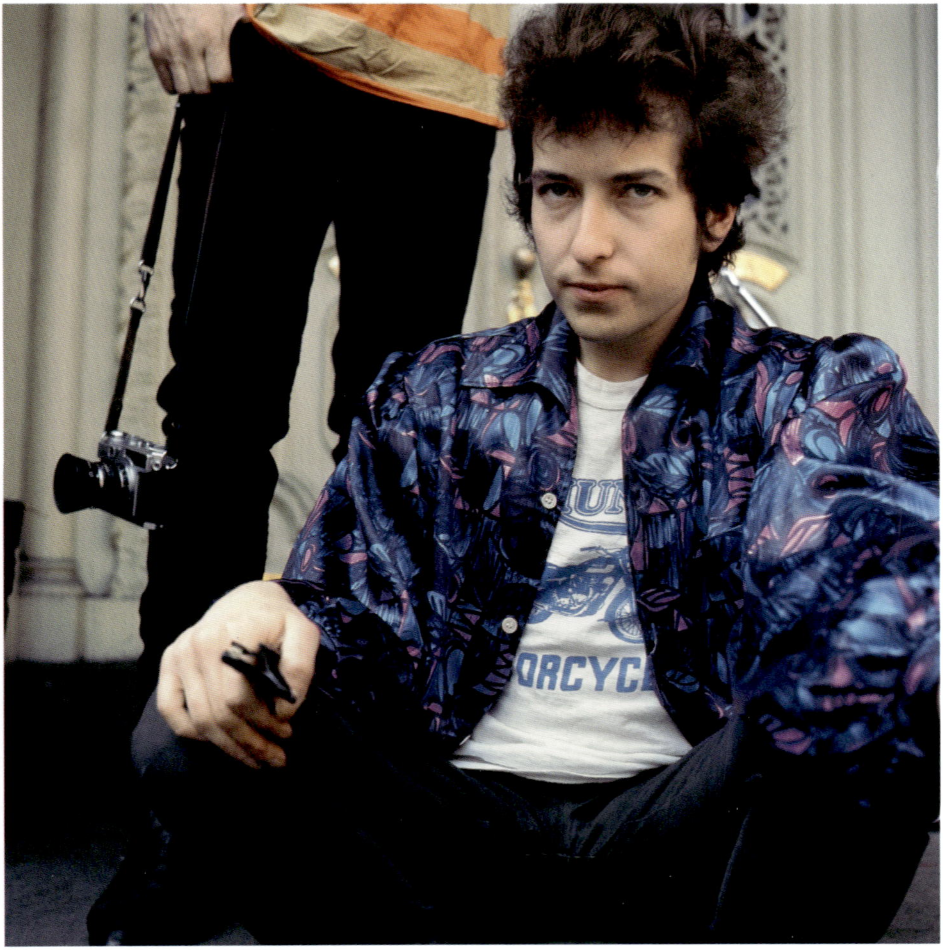

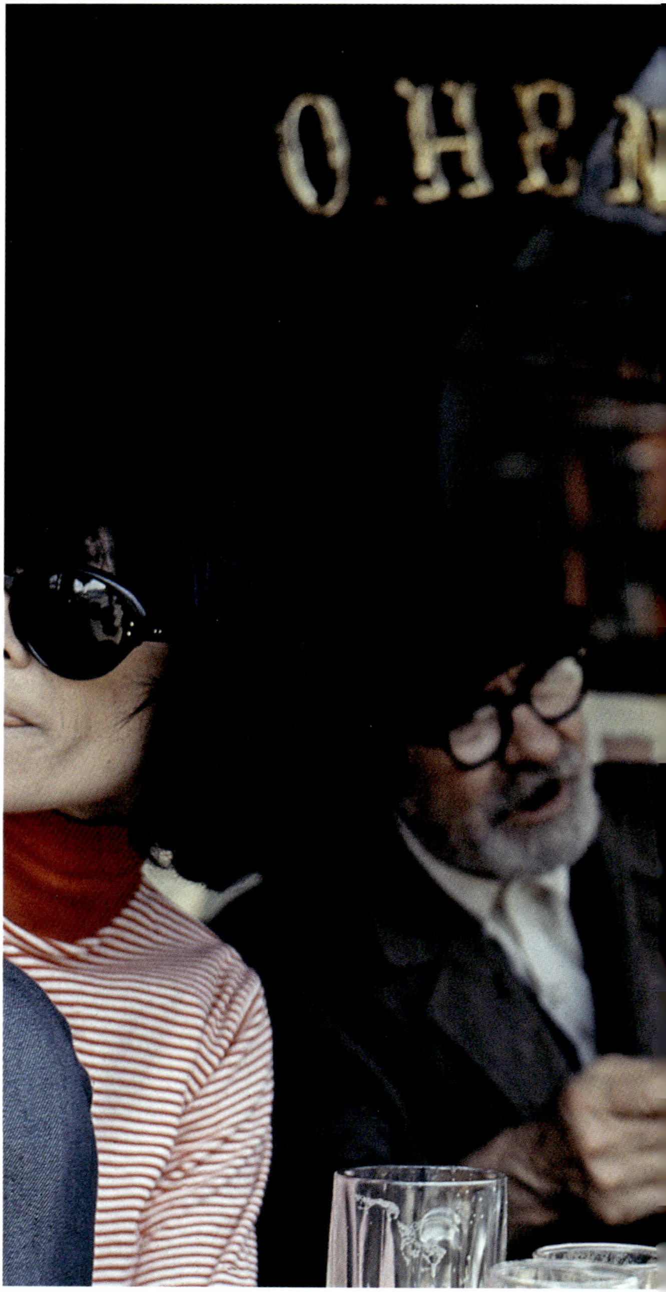
O.HEN

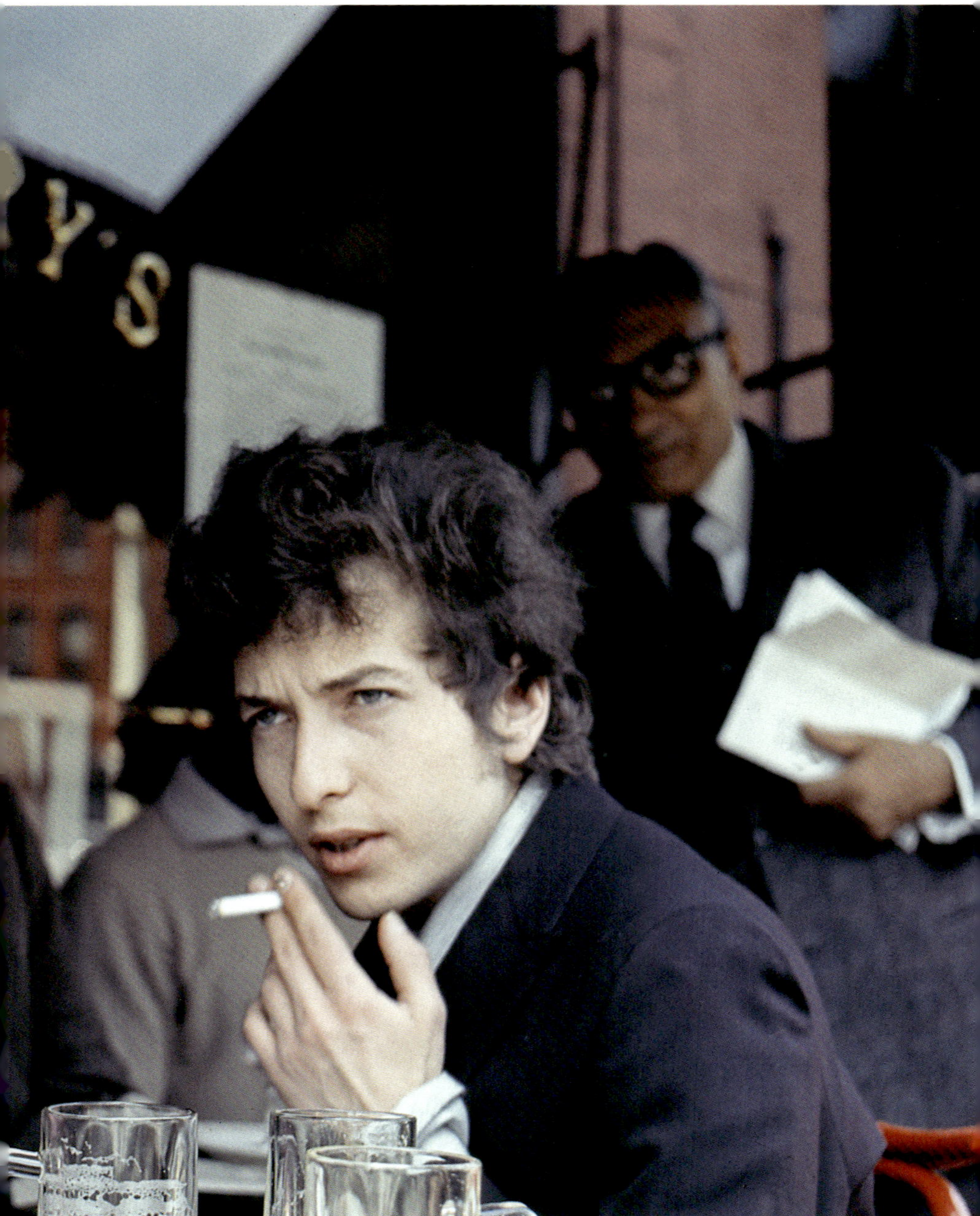
Y'S

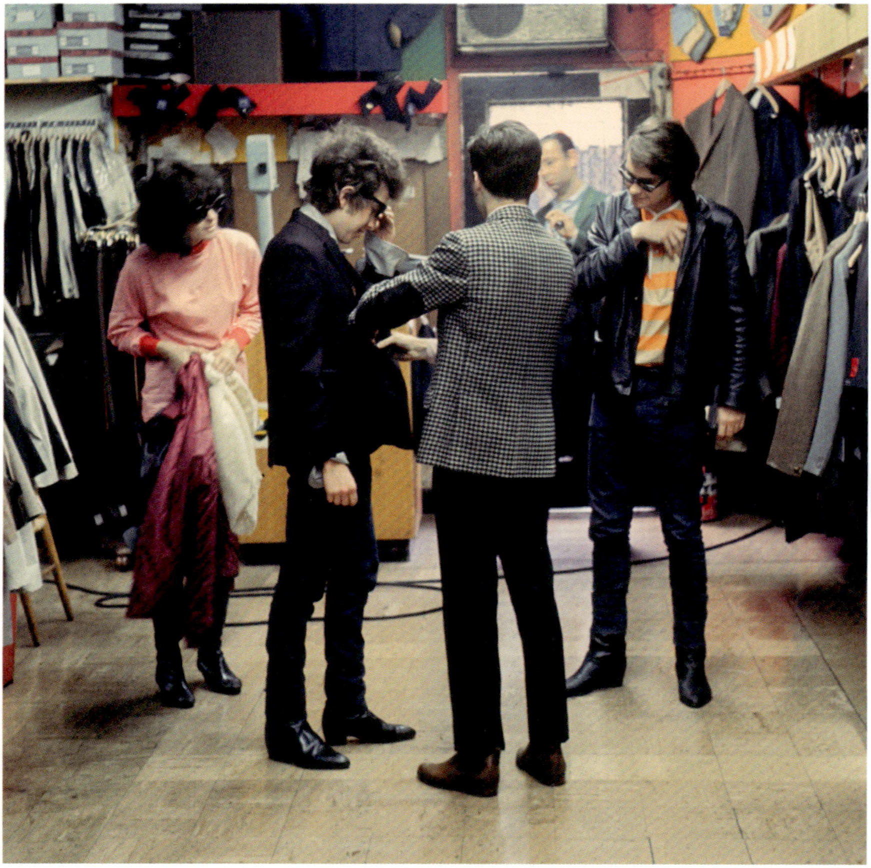

Paul Sargent Men's Store
Greenwich Village
April 1965
with Bob Neuwirth

Our first stop was a great sidewalk café called O'Henry's. The light was good so what more could I ask for? I shot what I could--Bob posing with a lemon, the other people at the outdoor portion of the café as background--and finally pulled a few shots together I really liked. Somewhere along the line I thought we could improve our chances with some different clothing for Bob, so we invaded a nearby terrific men's shop. Although the pictures we made in the store were interesting, they just didn't feel like covers. So back to O'Henry's armed with the new clothing, tags still on the suit jacket Bob was now wearing, for more pictures--some good ones.

The light was changing to not-so-interesting, so we made our way to Gramercy Park, where Bob shared a townhouse with the Grossmans. We were all a bit worn out and milling about on the stoop of the house when Bob said he would like to be photographed wearing his new T-shirt. He disappeared into the house and reappeared wearing the now famous Triumph shirt. The light was good and the colors on Bob's overshirt were working well, so I started to work fast with 35mm film. It was okay but not yet really happening, so I switched to a 2-1/4 film camera to make a square cover picture. The light was still good but disappearing fast. The back of the shot was empty and needed something, so I asked Neuwirth to stand behind Bob to fill some open space and to add some mystery.

It was still not right, so I handed Neuwirth my Nikon 35mm camera. Dangling by the strap into my frame, somehow it looked like it belonged there. I saw a chance for a cover in the viewfinder. I made two exposures and the good light disappeared. At this point we all agreed that we had had quite a day--made a lot of pictures--and now it was over.

When we edited, Bob, who has a very good eye for choosing pictures, liked the Triumph T-shirt pictures for his cover, and so did I. In the final frame--the one used on the cover of <u>Highway 61 Revisited</u>--Dylan's head is cocked slightly to one side, and the almost hostile look on his face could be depicting the lyrics to "Like a Rolling Stone."

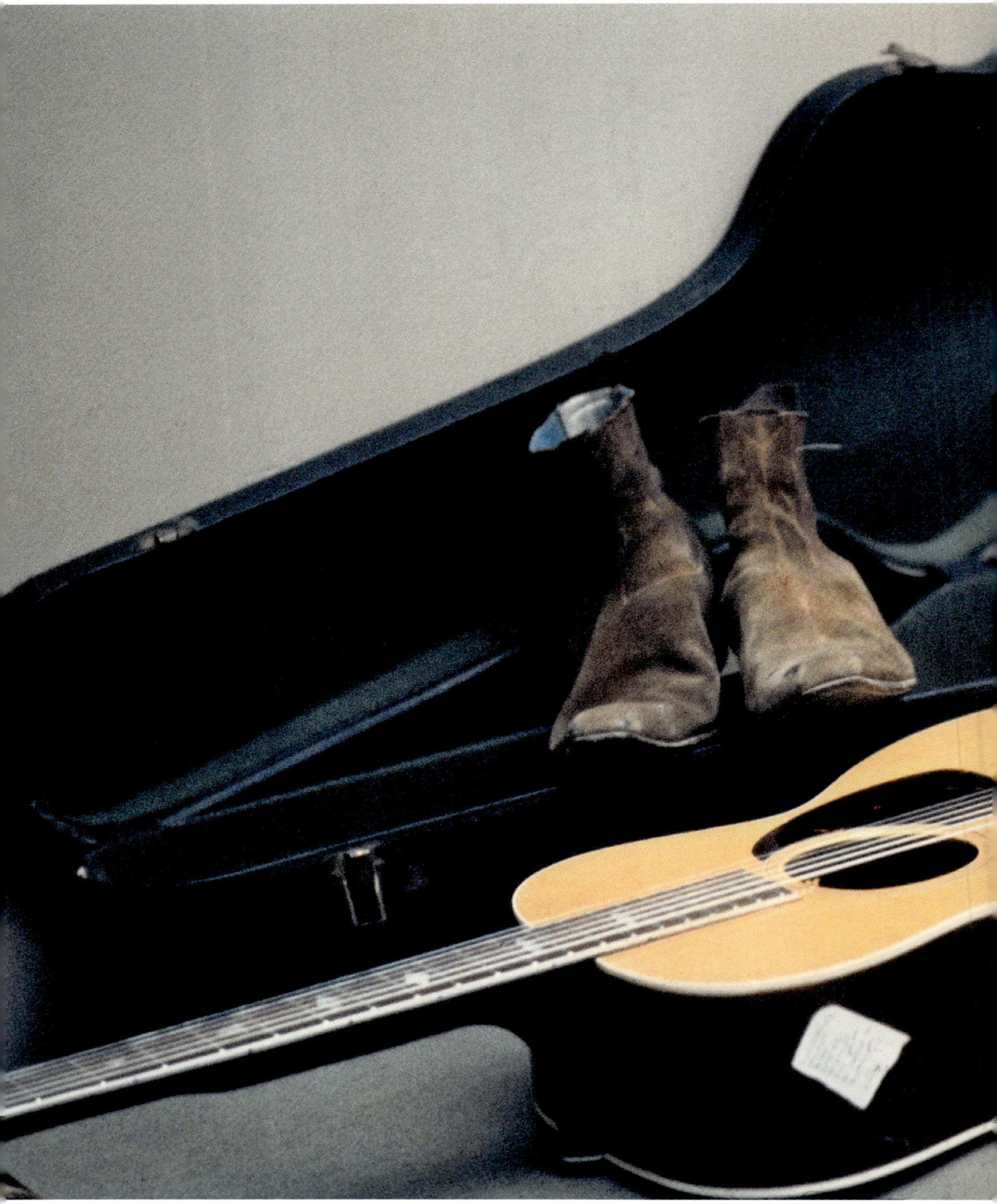

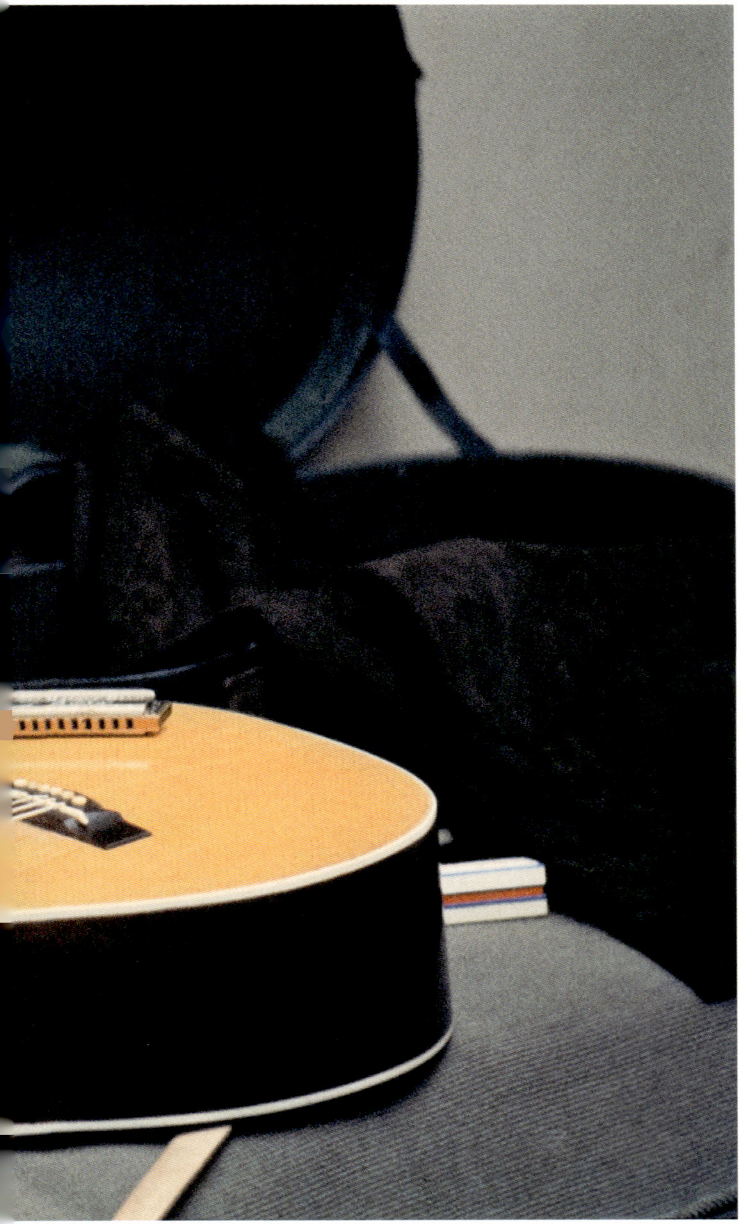

Close your eyes, close the door
You don't have to worry anymore
I'll be your baby tonight.

I'LL BE YOUR BABY TONIGHT

Chapter Four

Bob & Joan

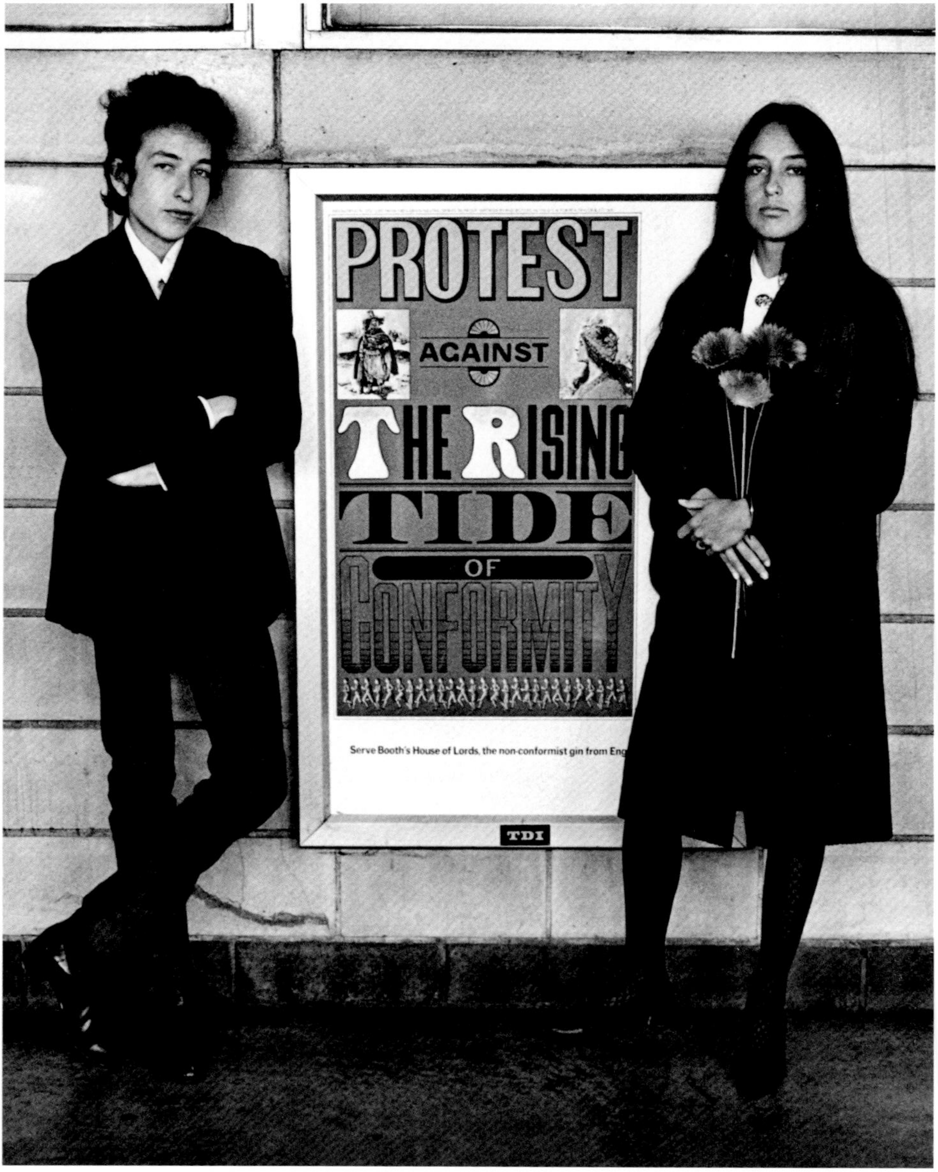
PROTEST
AGAINST
THE RISING
TIDE
OF
CONFORMITY
Serve Booth's House of Lords, the non-conformist gin from Eng
TDI

It seemed inevitable that the particular talents of Bob Dylan and Joan Baez would find their way onto one stage during the winter of 1964-65. They had performed together at the Newport Folk Festival. Then, on several occasions they performed together at each other's concerts, sometimes unannounced. Eventually several joint Dylan-Baez concerts were produced in major cities. Joan gave Bob the credibility, because she was the queen.

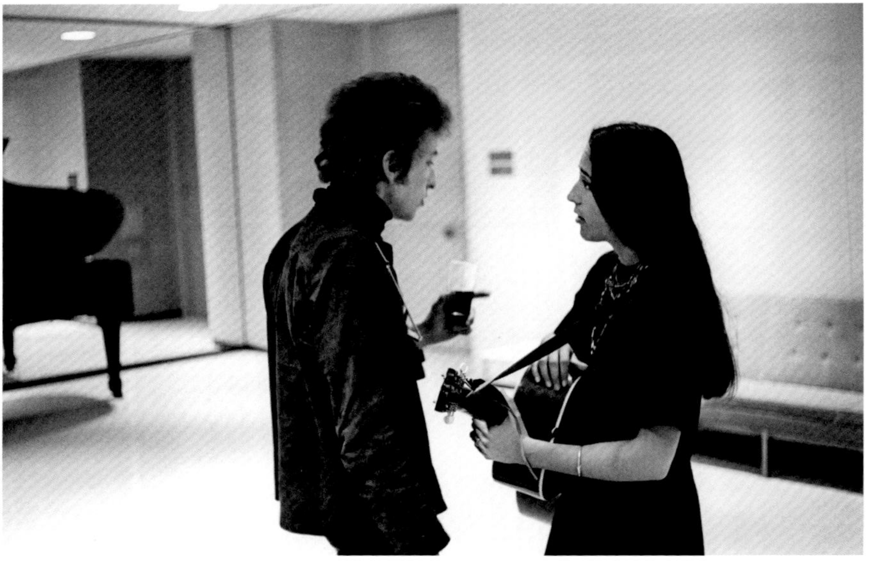

I didn't expect to shoot another concert after Philadelphia, but when I learned Bob and Joan would appear together at a concert in Philharmonic Hall at Lincoln Center for Halloween, and the next day at a concert in Buffalo, how could I not shoot those shows?

The rapport Bob and Joan generated with their audiences was tremendous. These shared performances were often more than just a combination of the two performers. A third entity emerged, producing a wonderful effect.

Philharmonic Hall Lincoln Center
New York City
October 31, 1964

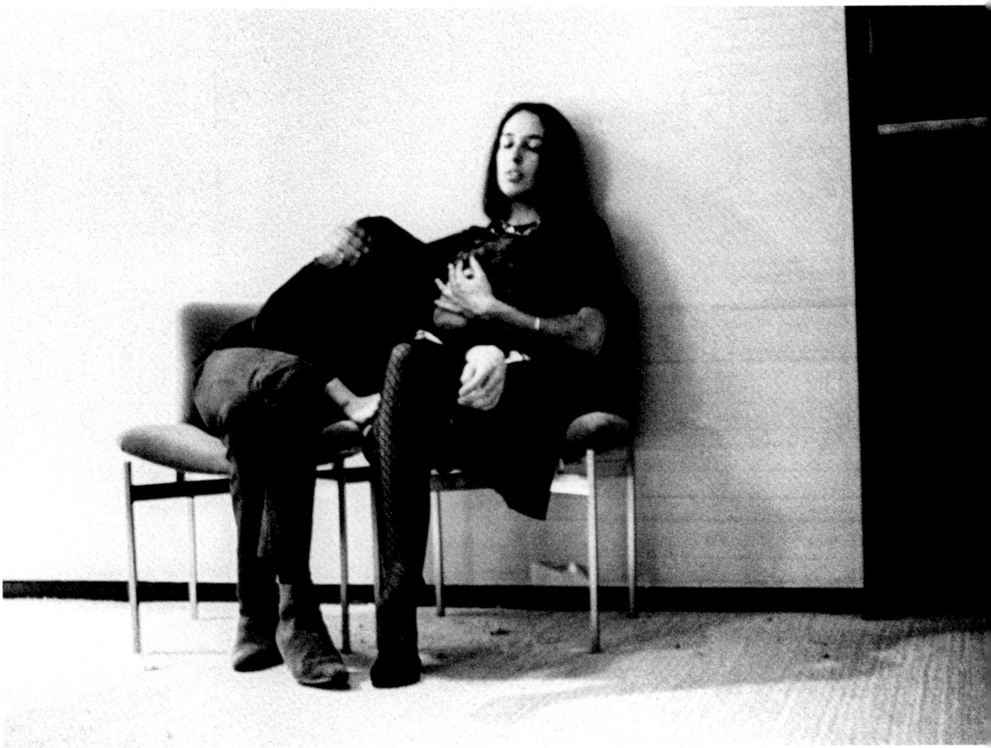

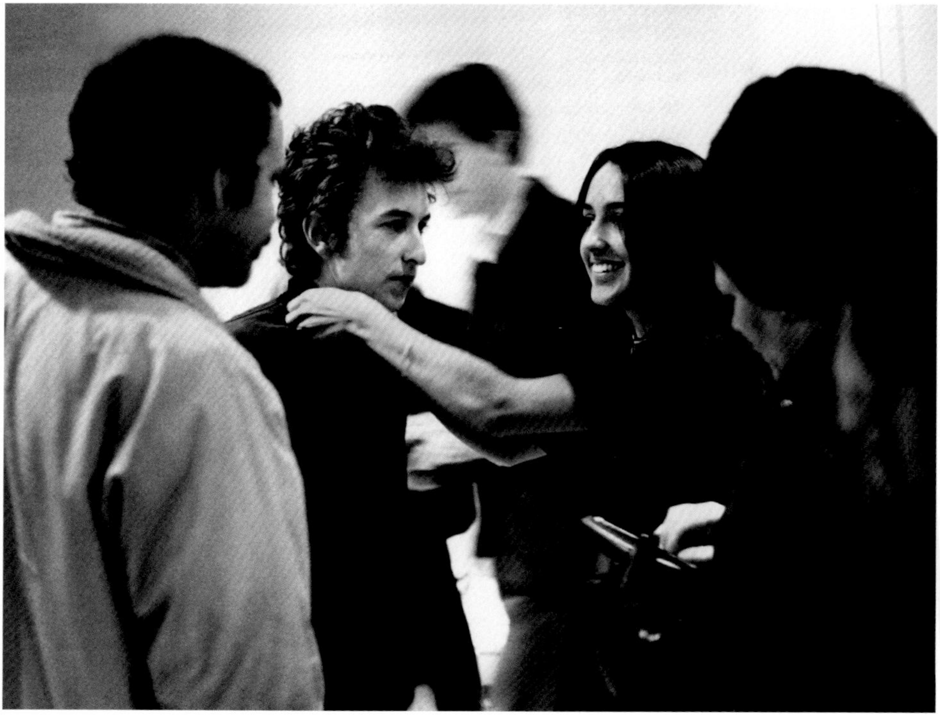

The beautiful concert hall at Lincoln Center was a full house. Just before showtime, while I was wandering around looking for vantage points, I was told by house management that photographers were relegated to the glass-enclosed press booth somewhere in the balcony area. In the last minutes before the curtain opened, I went backstage to check on the lighting and ran into Bob and Albert Grossman. Bob asked if everything was all right.

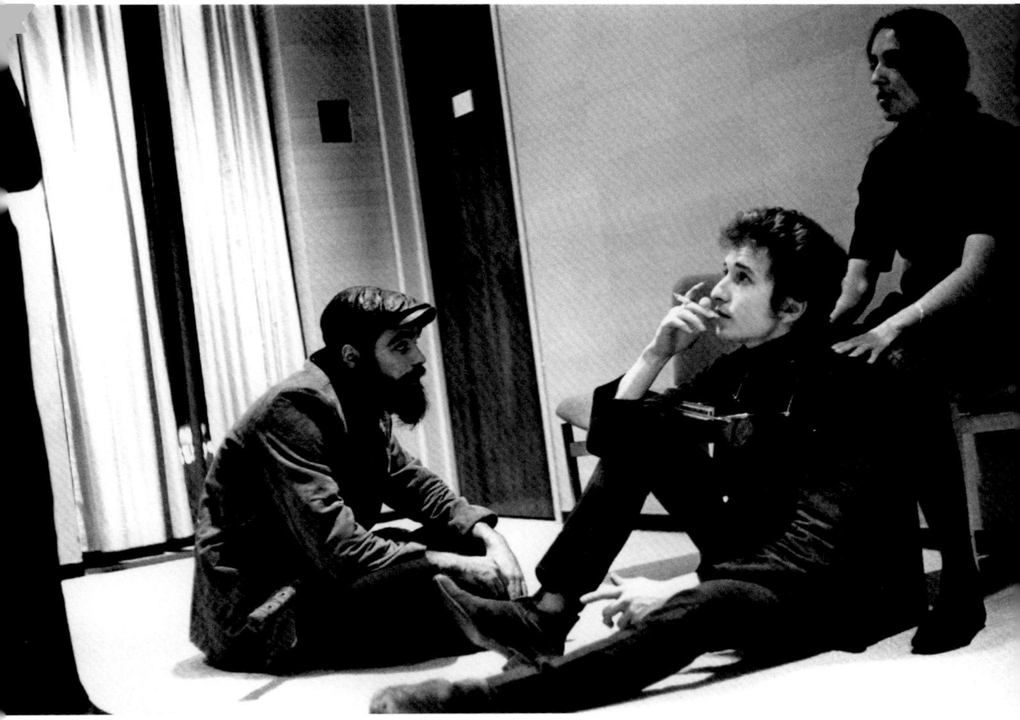

I told him it was, but that I had to stay in the press booth on the second balcony and wouldn't be able to shoot as I usually did. Bob asked Albert if he would fix that for me. Just then the house manager approached us to ask if Bob was ready to start. "Yes, he is," said Albert, and then, to my complete jaw-dropping surprise, he added, "just as soon as Dan gets permission to shoot anywhere he wants to." And I did.

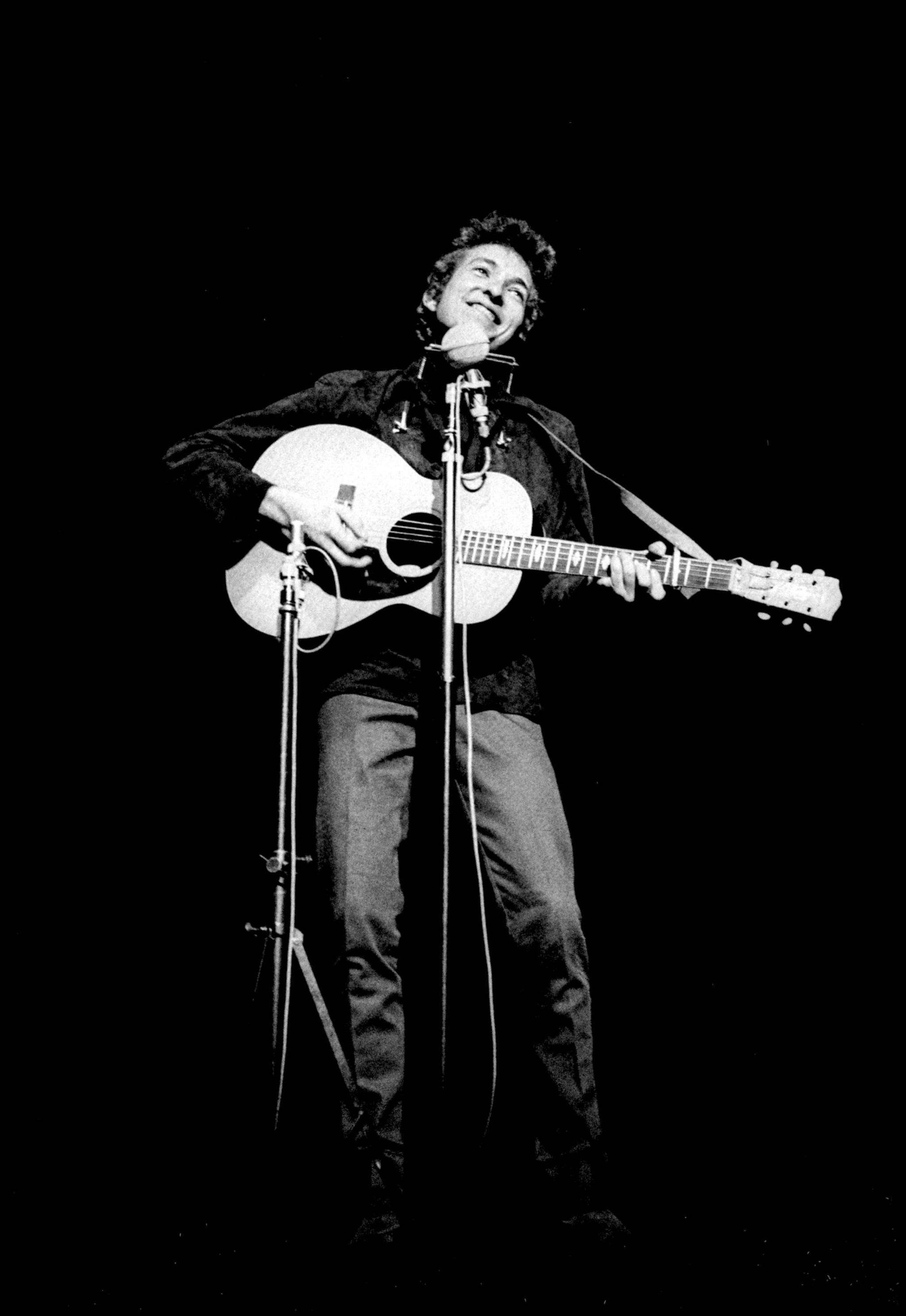

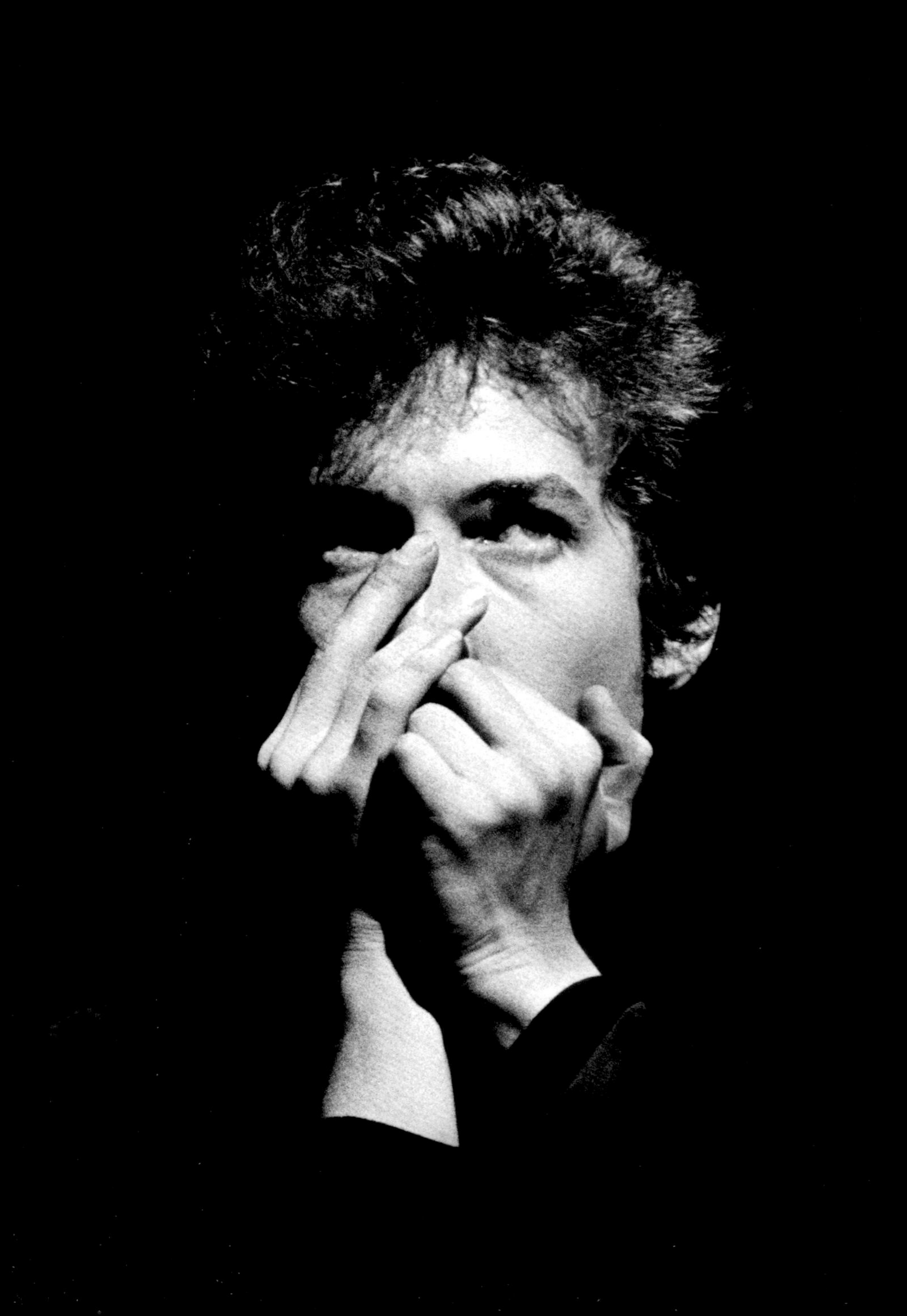

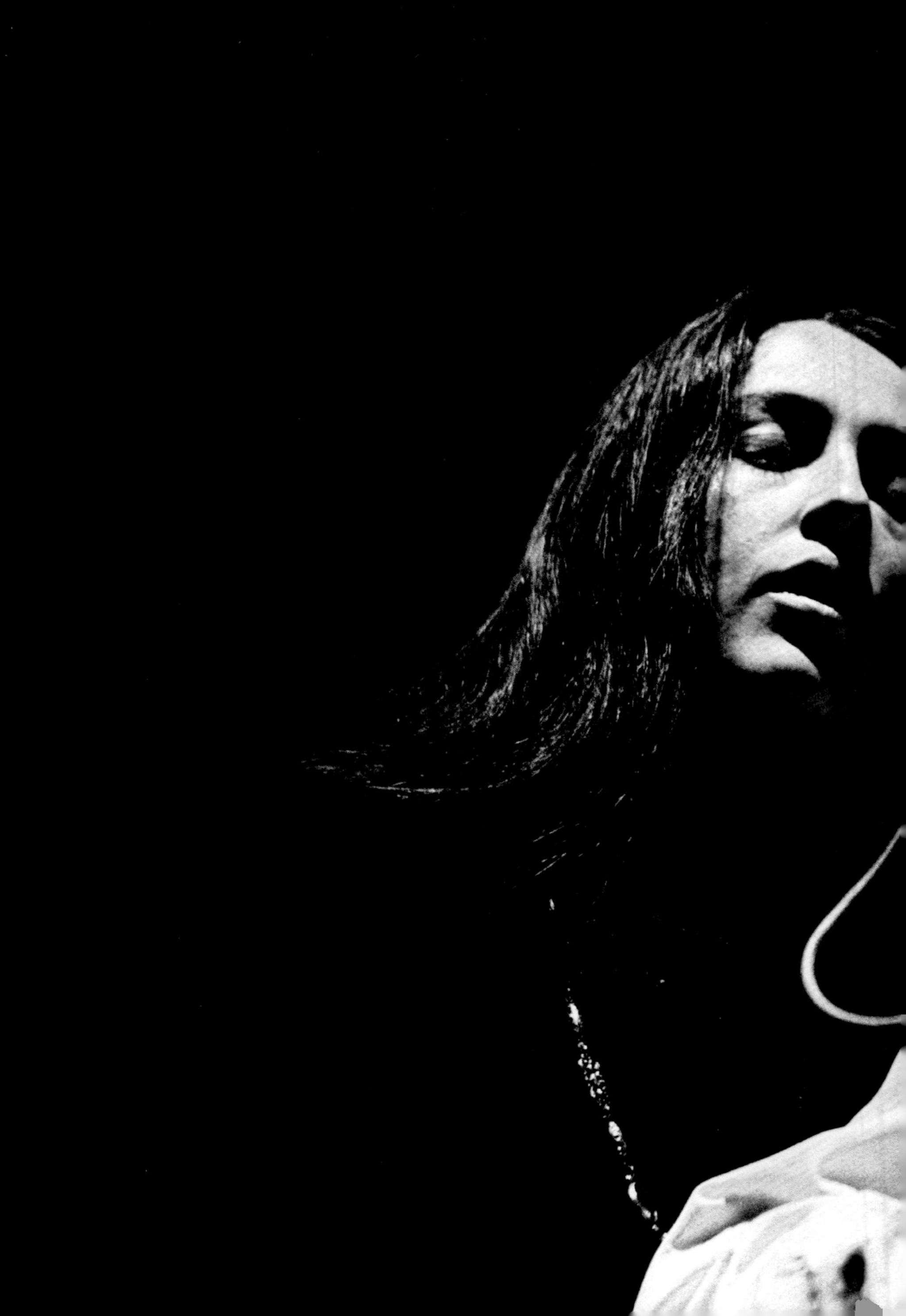

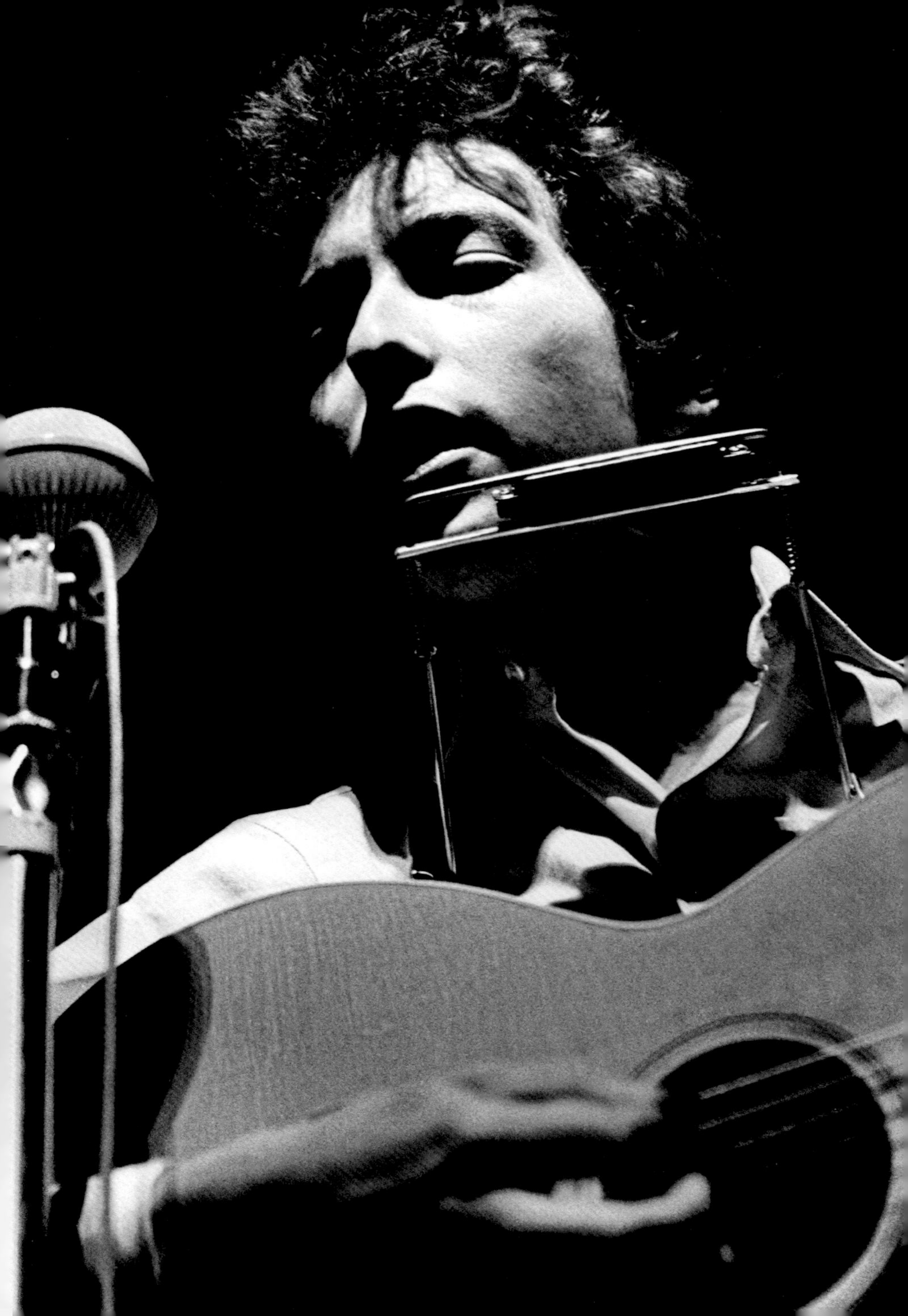

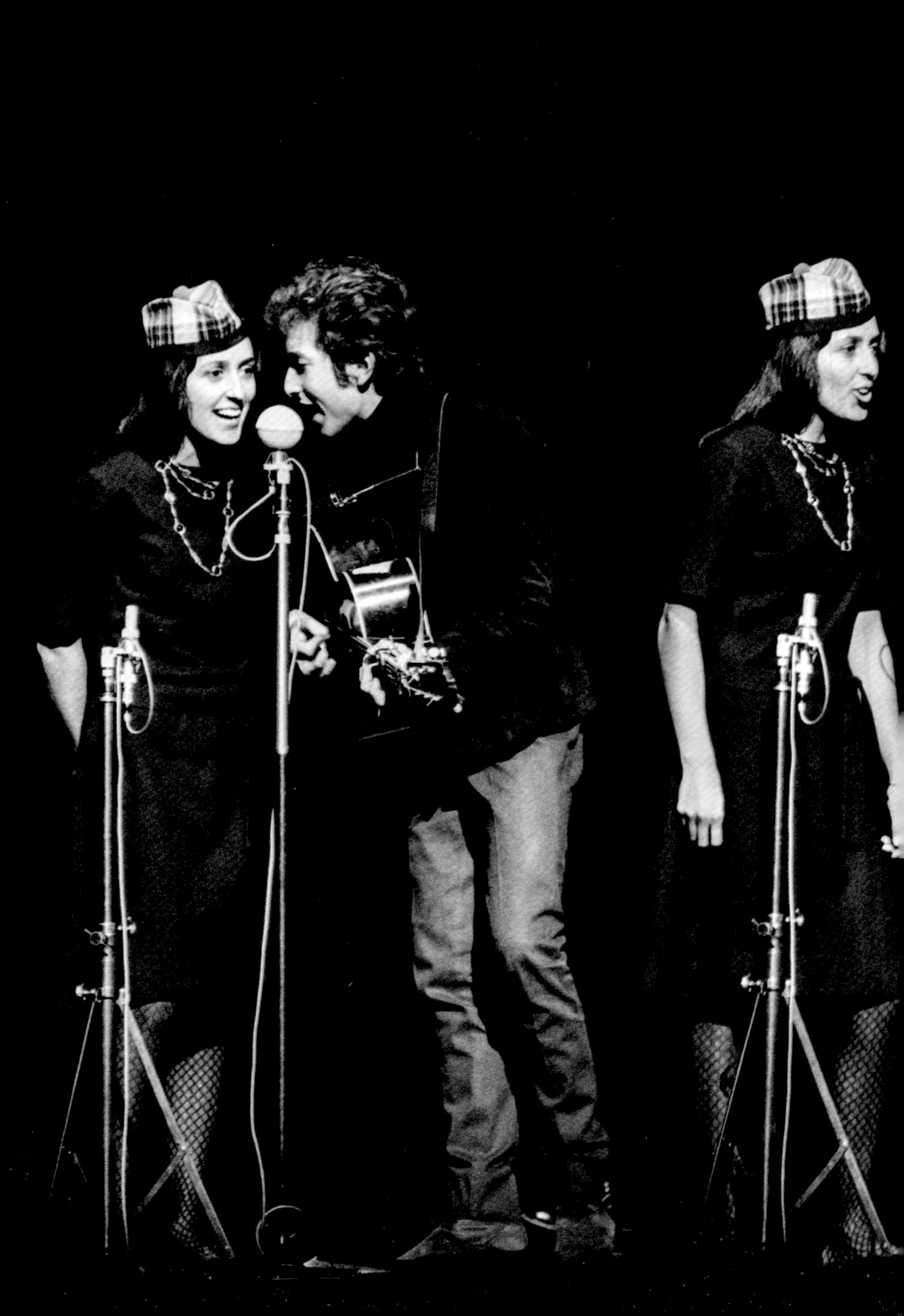

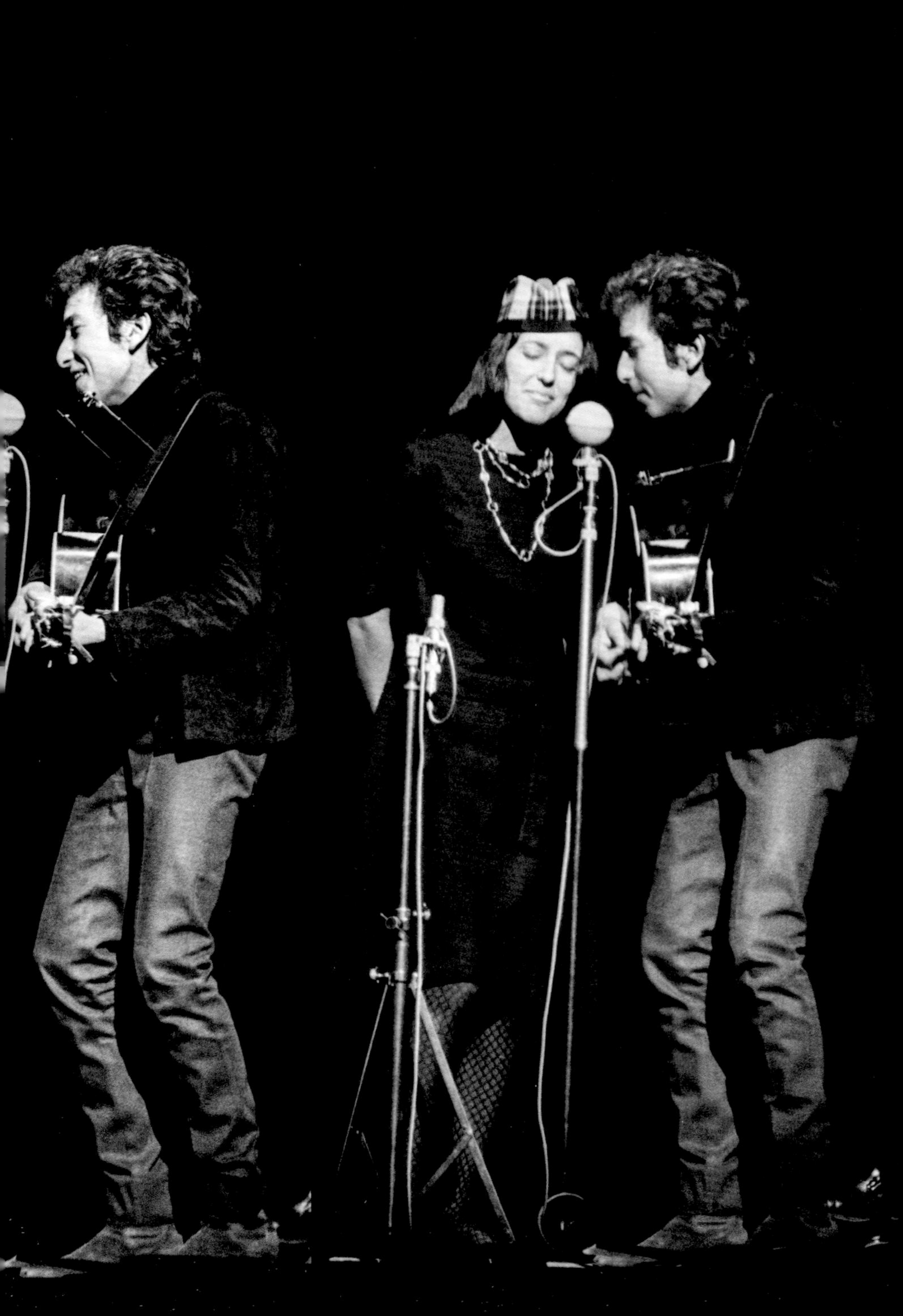

A story was now starting to emerge on my contact sheets--this was really an incredible year for Bob. Bob and Joan made for some very special moments, and I was glad to be photographing when they were happening. Every photographer talks about the decisive moment in one way or another. For me, the decisive moment is the one that occurs for the photographer just before the special moment you see in the picture. Photographers need to develop a sense of expecting what will happen, so when it does they are already there. This was the case when I caught Bob and Joan in a joyous embrace at the after-concert party in New York. I felt a vibe of some sort and started to shoot. In one frame there is the hug; Joan embraces Bob, then, by surprise, she lifts Bob well off the floor and into the air in the next frame.

With just his guitar and harmonica--without physical gyrations, without beguiling little speeches, without any of the obvious show-business attitudes--Bob was able to captivate and control an audience. I watched him do this during concert after concert. Outlined by one spotlight, the pounding of his guitar or rhythmical strumming, the lilting runs on the harmonica or its staccato punctuation, consistently, time after time, Dylan is a superlative performer. It is not a question of whether he is a great guitar player, or a harmonica virtuoso, or whether we agree that his voice is this or that. He produces a total effect that works, and when working with Joan the effect was heightened.

It is not just a matter of performing on a stage; there is very much more to it. I'm certain that most of the people who came to experience two hours of a Dylan concert were unaware of what effort, energy, and preparation were necessary to support and produce his performances. It meant a great deal of time spent traveling to and from concert locations, often a day or two just going and coming. For someone like Dylan, whose energy and creative abilities are constantly driving him, it is difficult to spend many hours sitting in a car, waiting at an airport, killing time in a hotel room.

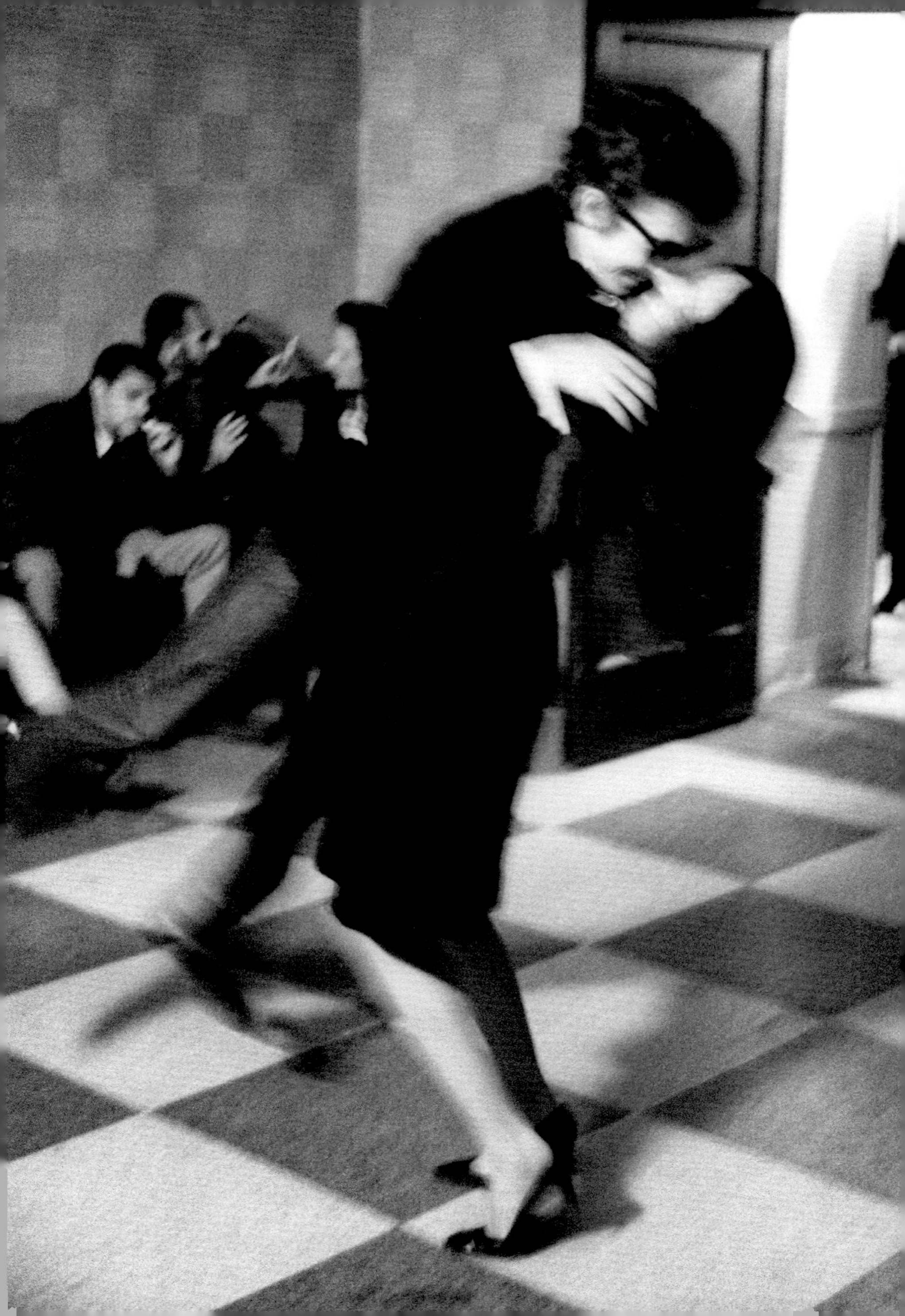

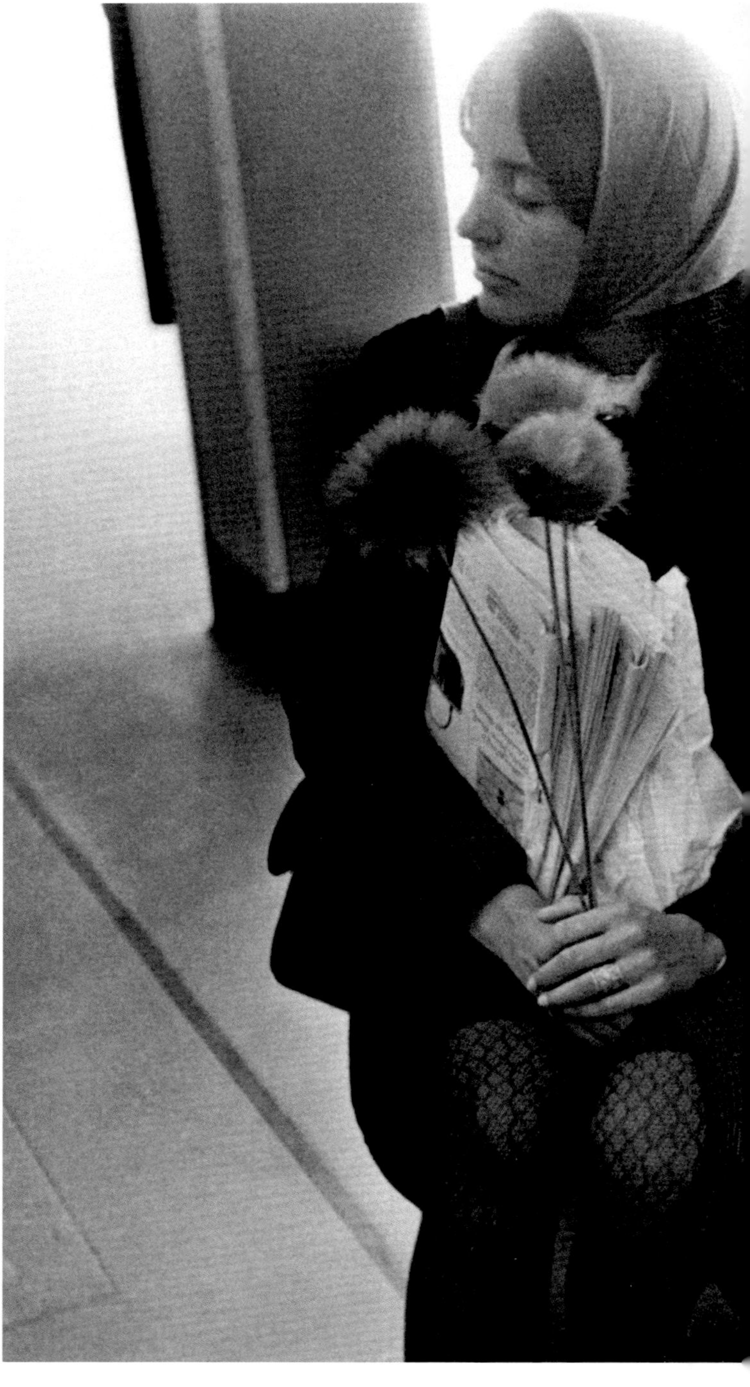

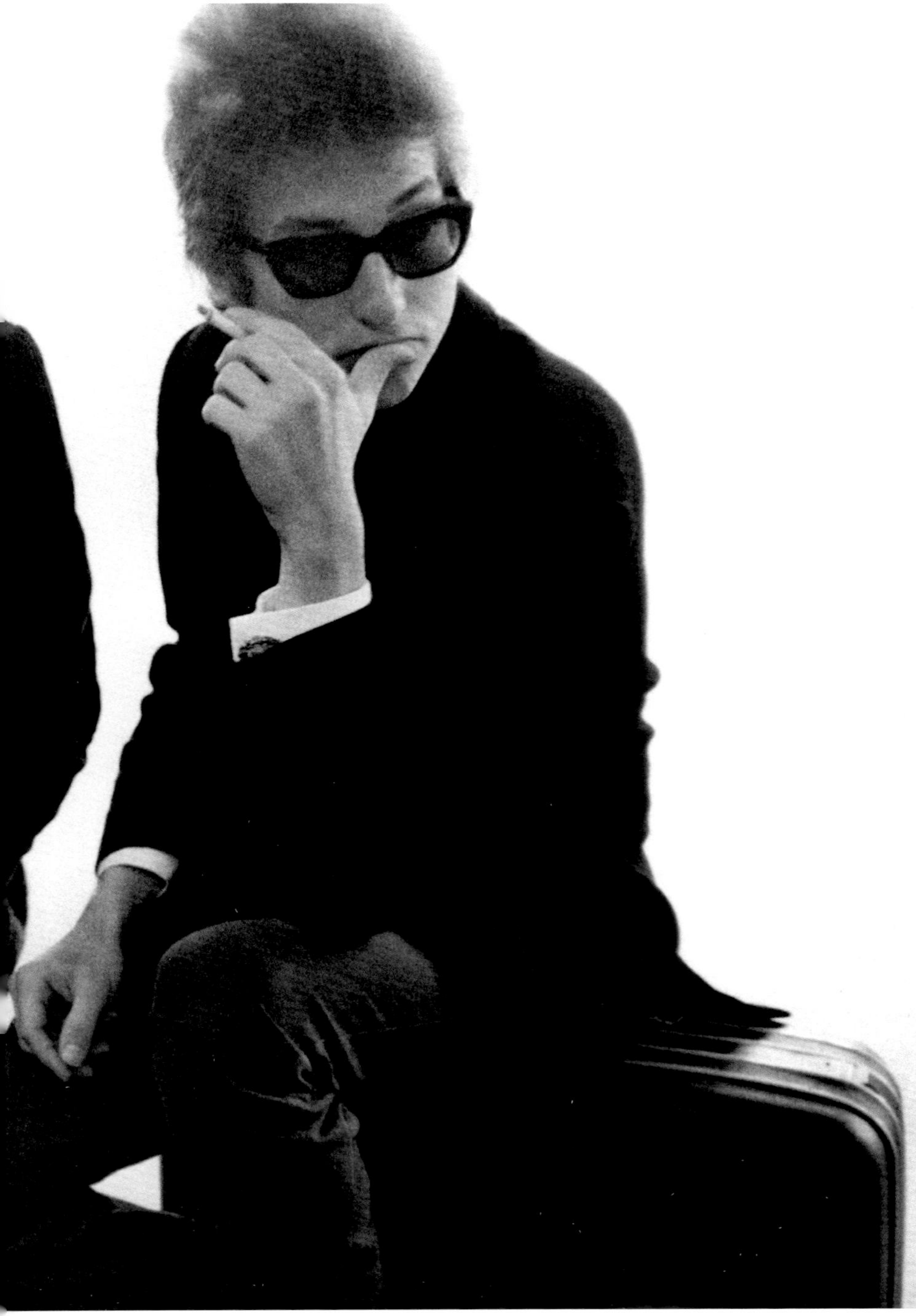

Bob responded to touring like a workman whose job was to go to a theater somewhere. He would take his tools with him--his guitar in an old battered case, several harmonicas, a small suitcase with his own microphones and connecting wires, and the clothes he would perform in. Victor Maymudes always accompanied him. Together, the two men would go off to their day's work, driving in Dylan's late-model Ford station wagon, a little worse for wear. It meant a plane flight, if the distance was greater than a hundred or so miles. It meant arriving at the location several hours before a performance to prepare the microphones and test the stage lights, both time-consuming procedures. This is a necessary part of his work, and during the time I spent with Dylan he met the demands with an incredible degree of professionalism.

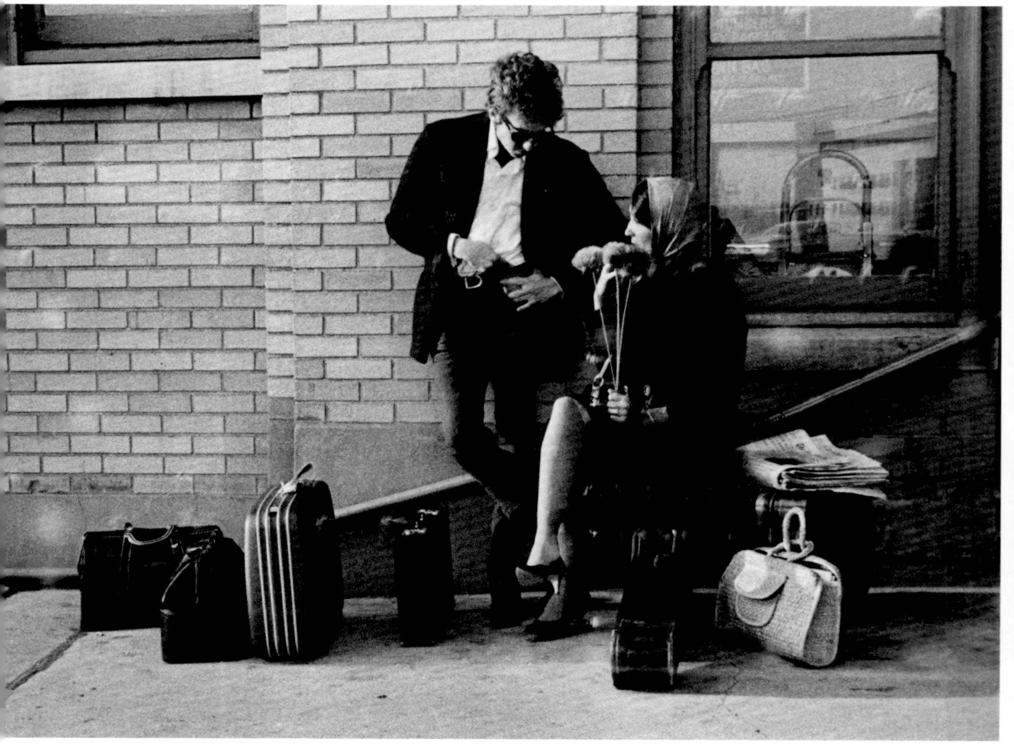

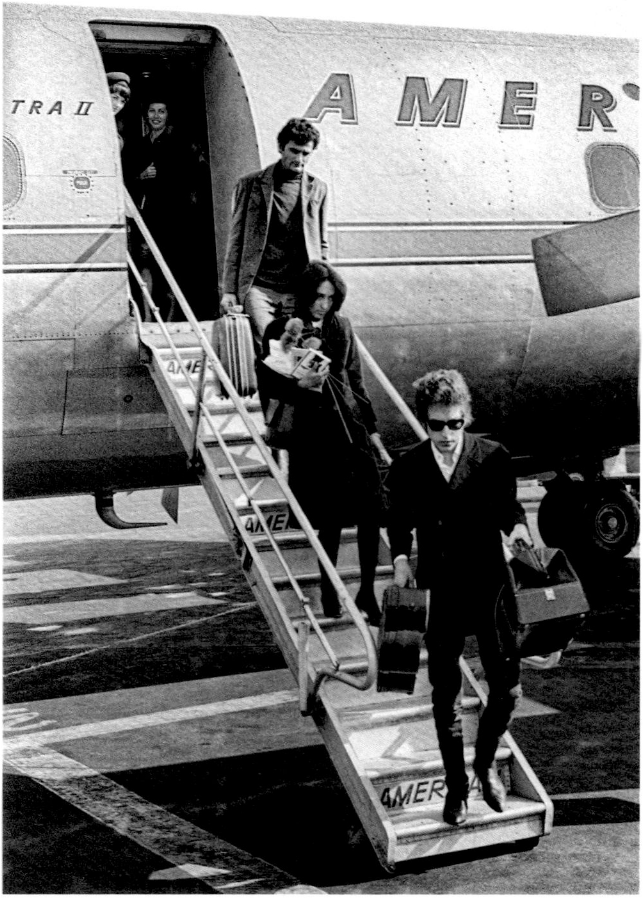
TRA II
AMER
AMER
AMER
AMER

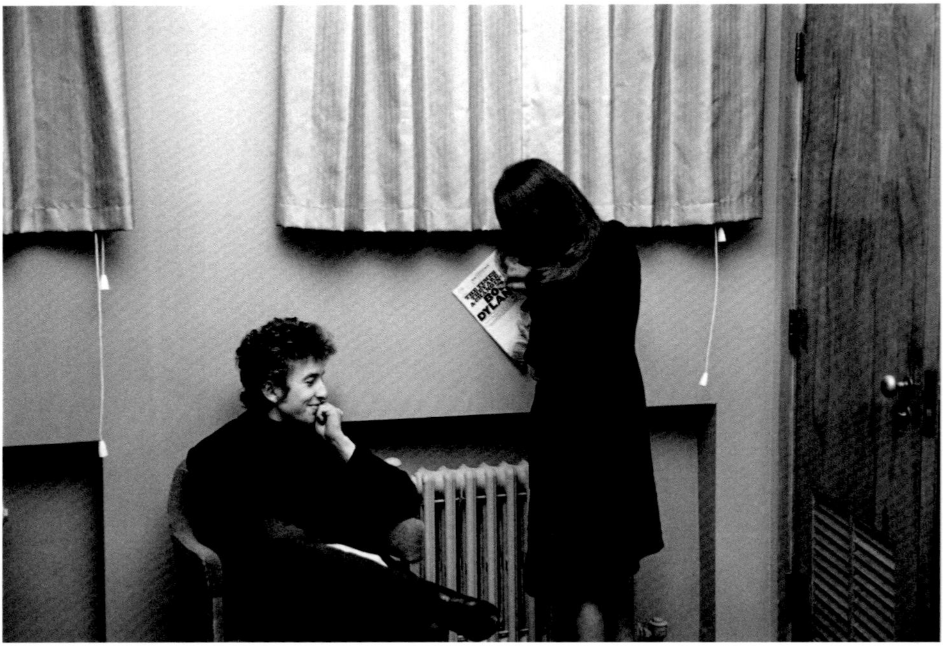

The day after Philharmonic Hall we made it to Kleinhans Music Hall in Buffalo for a show, and the fans were watching Bob's every move. While Bob and Joan were working out their song list, a knock came from the green-room window. A resourceful young girl had found a way to reach Bob in order to get her album signed. She pushed her album through the open window and pleaded for an autograph. Joan accepted the album, signed it, and passed it back. Bob hid behind anything he could find.

After the concert we left the theater by making a great effort not to run down the fans that had collected about the car. We drove past the young blonde girl standing on the curb holding her Dylan album in her hand--the one that had been autographed for her earlier. Tears streamed down her face as we pulled away. We were heading for the motel when Joan suggested we go back and find her and invite her to join us.

We did just that but never found her. Years later when I published this story in a piece I did about Bob Dylan, I got a wonderful letter from the girl, who said getting that album signed was one of the great moments in her life. Maybe I'll hear from her again.

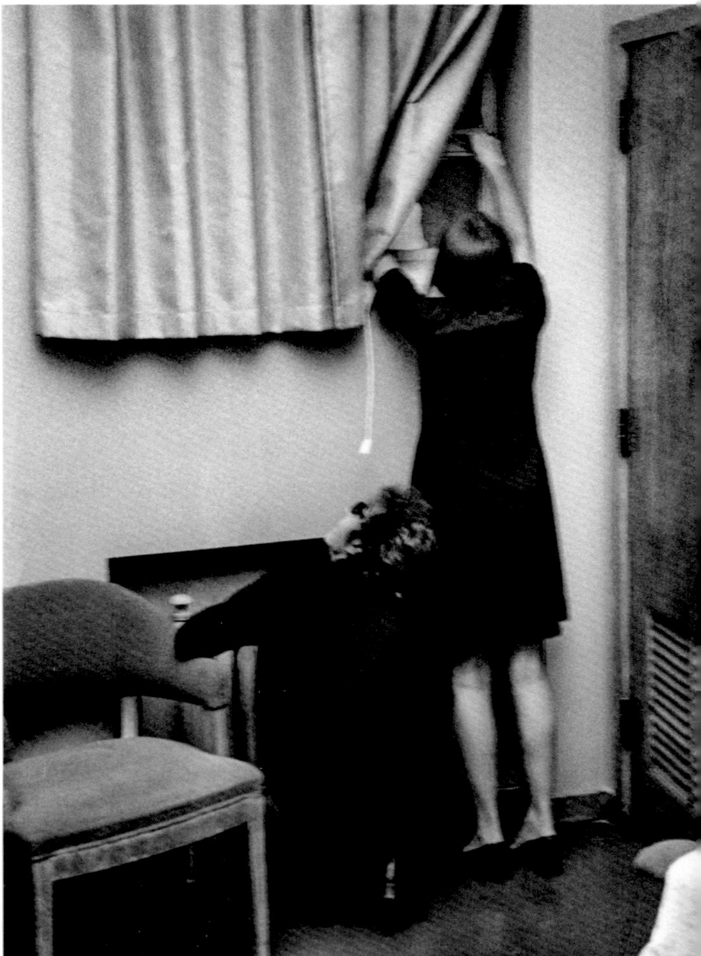

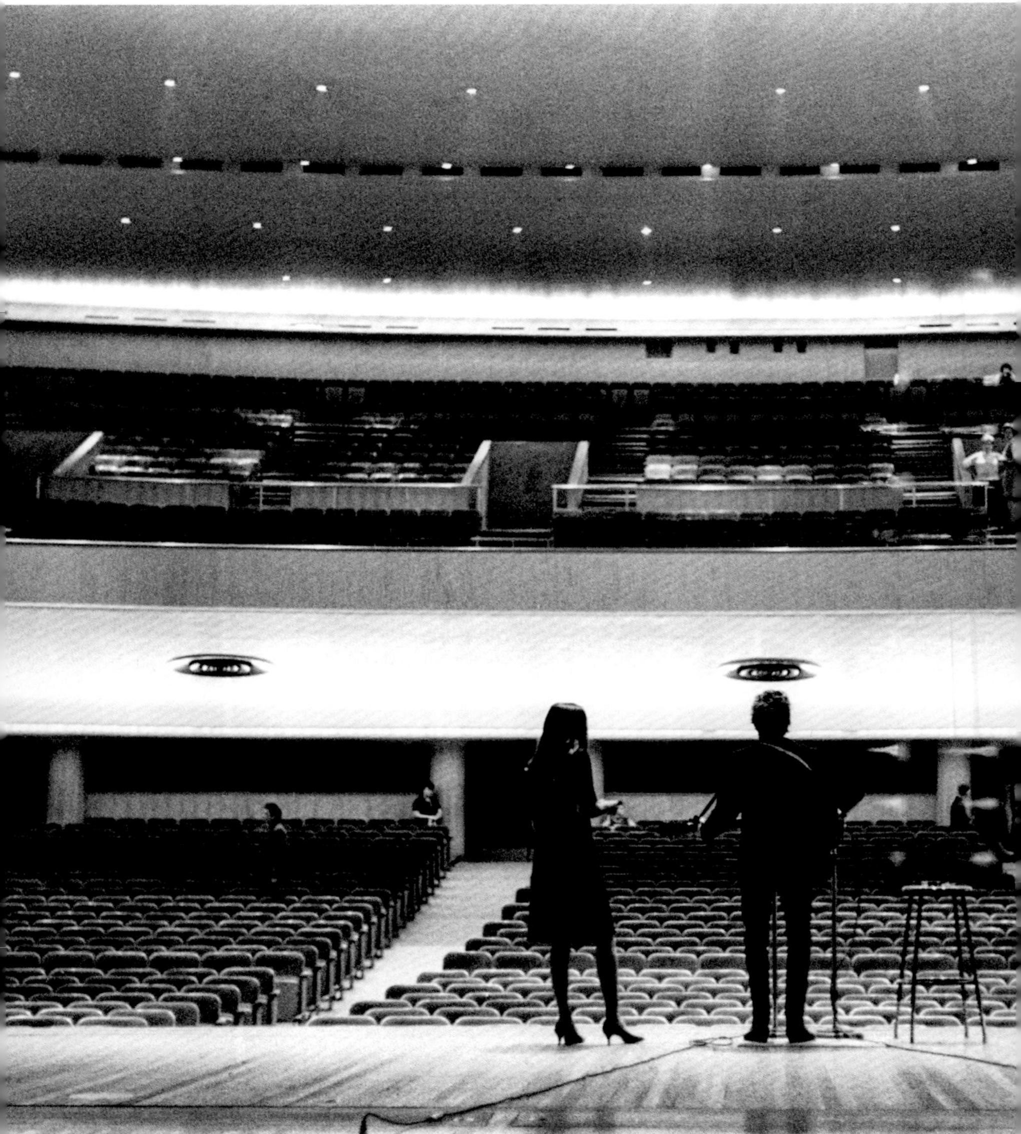

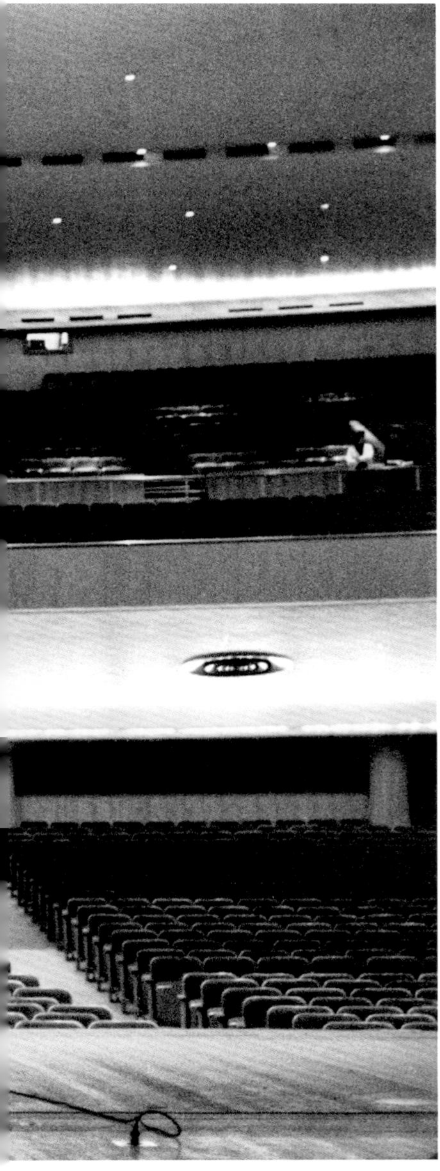

Once at a Dylan concert I stood in the back of the theater, talking with a police officer who was there to control the crowds. He leaned over in the darkness and said, "He sings about some kind of philosophy, doesn't he? He's not like the others we've had here. His audience listens to him -- they're very quiet. I don't have any problems tonight. Last week, we had a guy in here with a guitar that just went crazy."

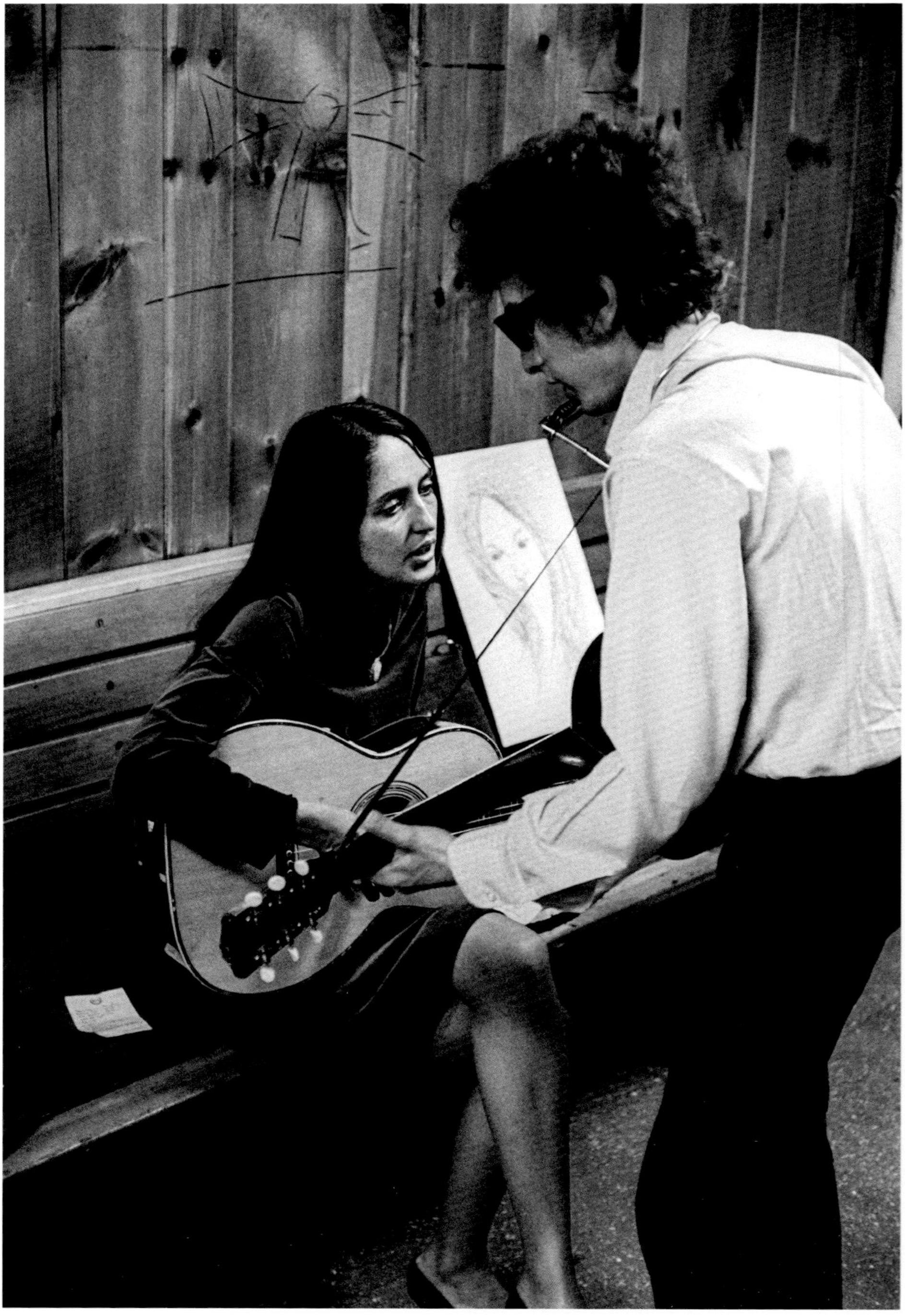

In early March Bob Dylan and Joan Baez gave a joint concert at the New Haven Arena as part of a 10-city tour from Philadelphia to Berkeley. That was the last time I photographed them performing together. Their performances were special moments, but Bob's new music would call for a band and a whole new way for him to present himself. The spring was about to uncoil. Less than two months after that tour, Bob was in England for his first of many international appearances. It would be a number of years before Joan and Bob would share a stage again.

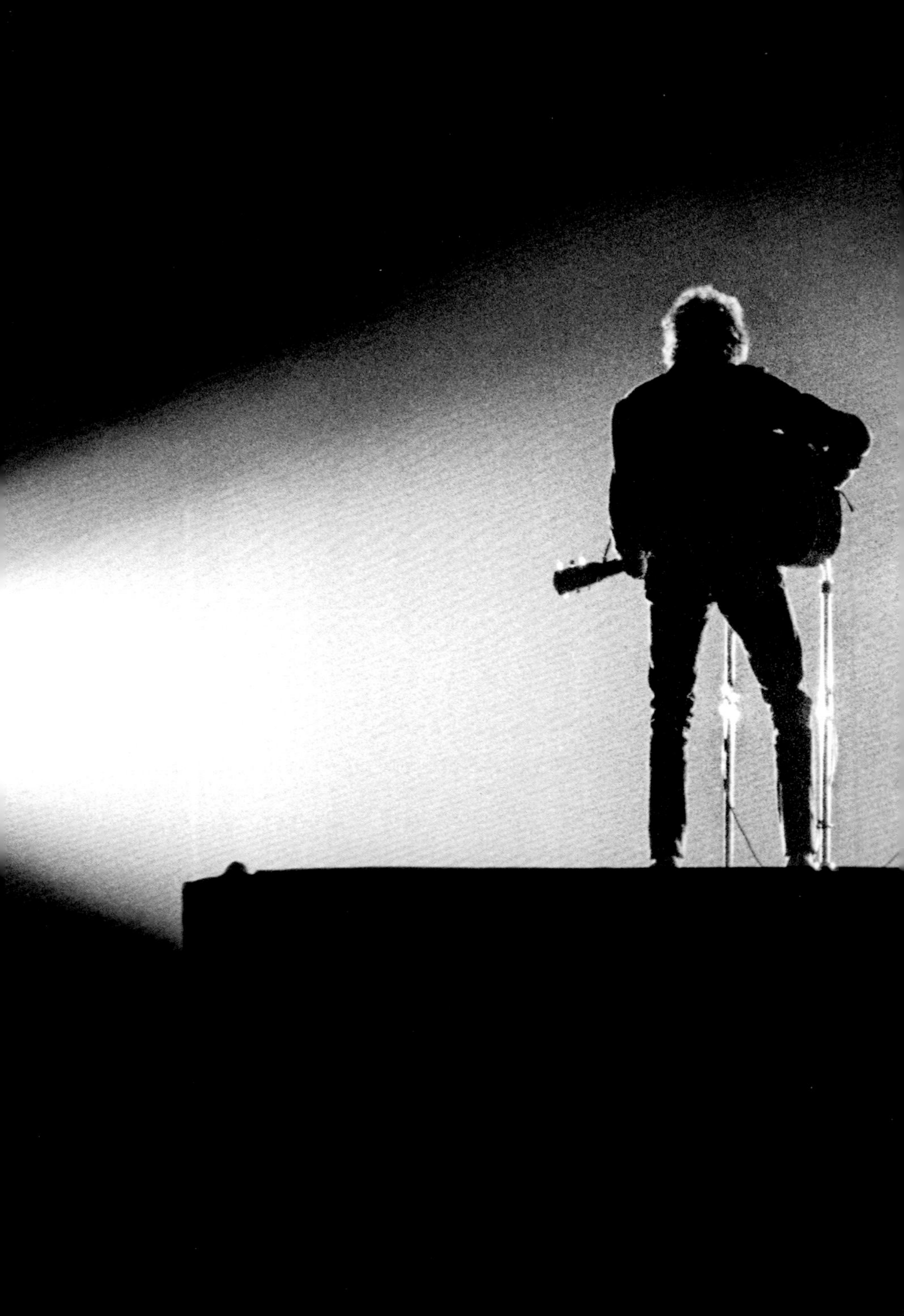

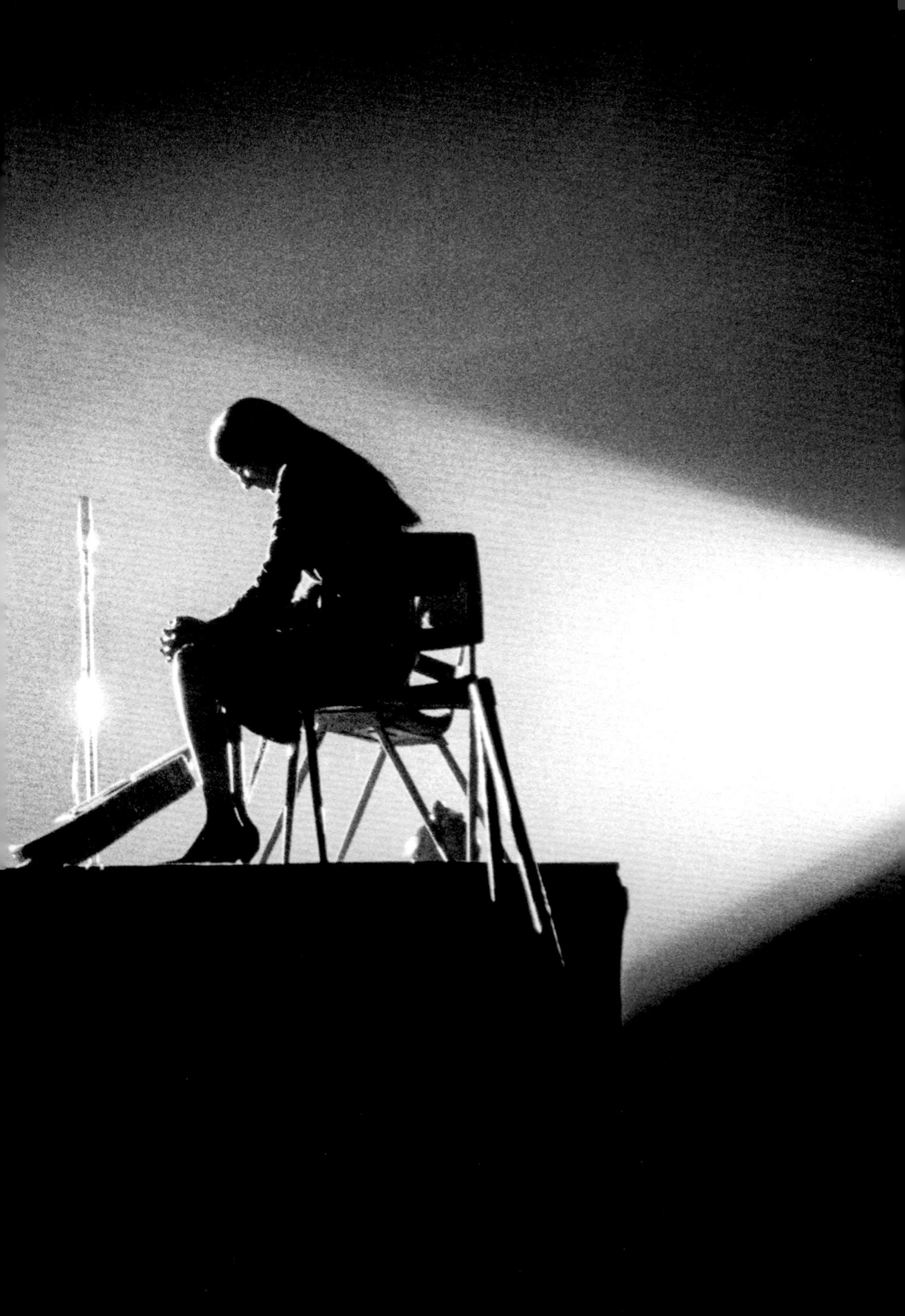

All except for Cain and Abel
And the hunchback of Notre Dame
Everybody is making love
Or else expecting rain
And the Good Samaritan, he's dressing
He's getting ready for the show
He's going to the carnival tonight
On Desolation Row

DESOLATION ROW

Chapter Five

Early '65

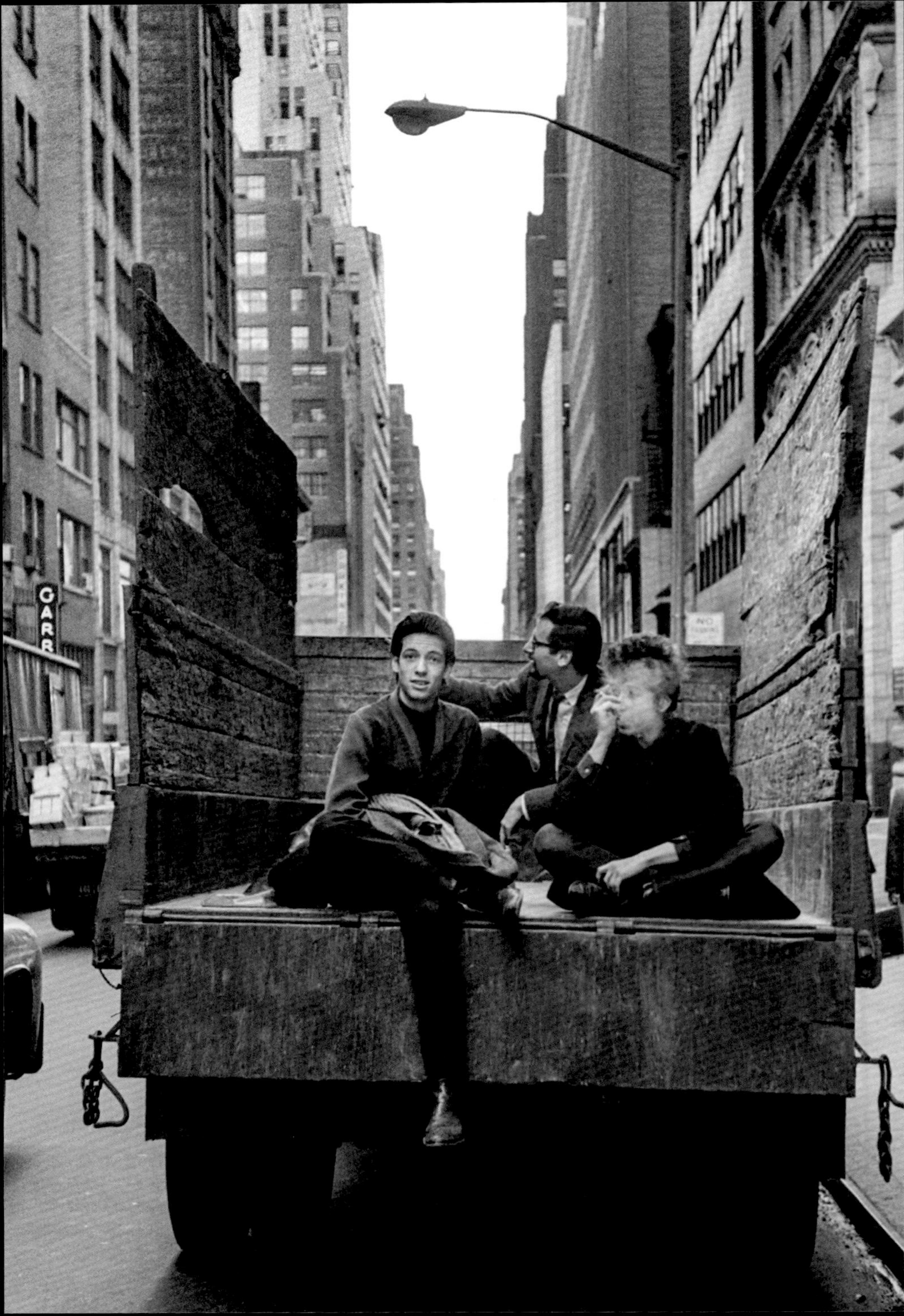
GARR
NO

Back from his British tour in the spring of 1965, Bob was getting ready to launch the new music he had produced for Bringing It All Back Home and for Highway 61. At the Newport Folk Festival he would bring his new sound to a live audience, and after that the Forest Hills Stadium concert would make the transformation complete. The ensuing publicity made it inevitable that invitations to appear on television would follow. He was soon asked to perform and be interviewed on The Les Crane Show, one of the more popular nighttime talk shows of the time. Bob Dylan was fast becoming a household name. At the same time he was double-timing his efforts in preparation for what was ahead--more touring, new albums, more songs, and a larger audience.

Fifth Avenue
New York City, January 1965
with Peter Yarrow and John Hammond, Jr.

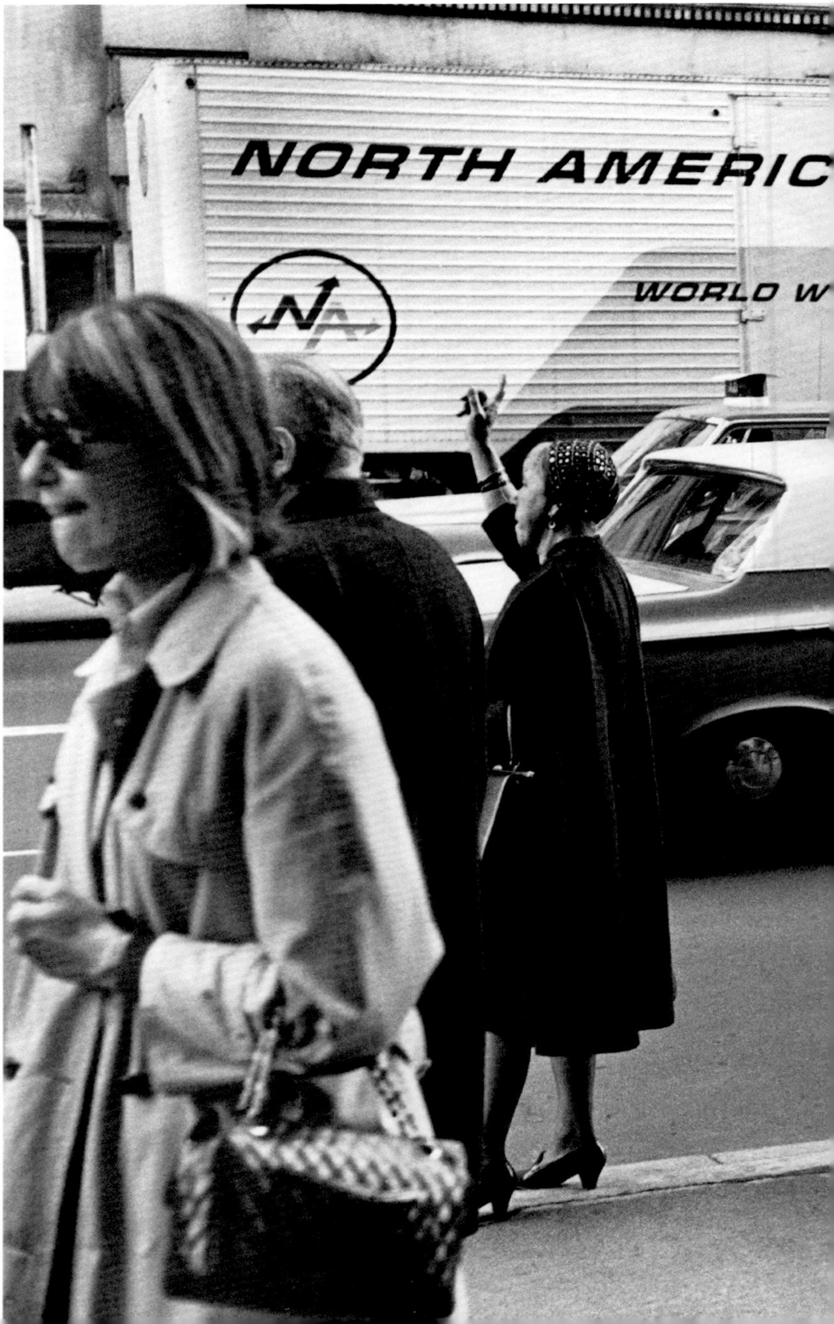

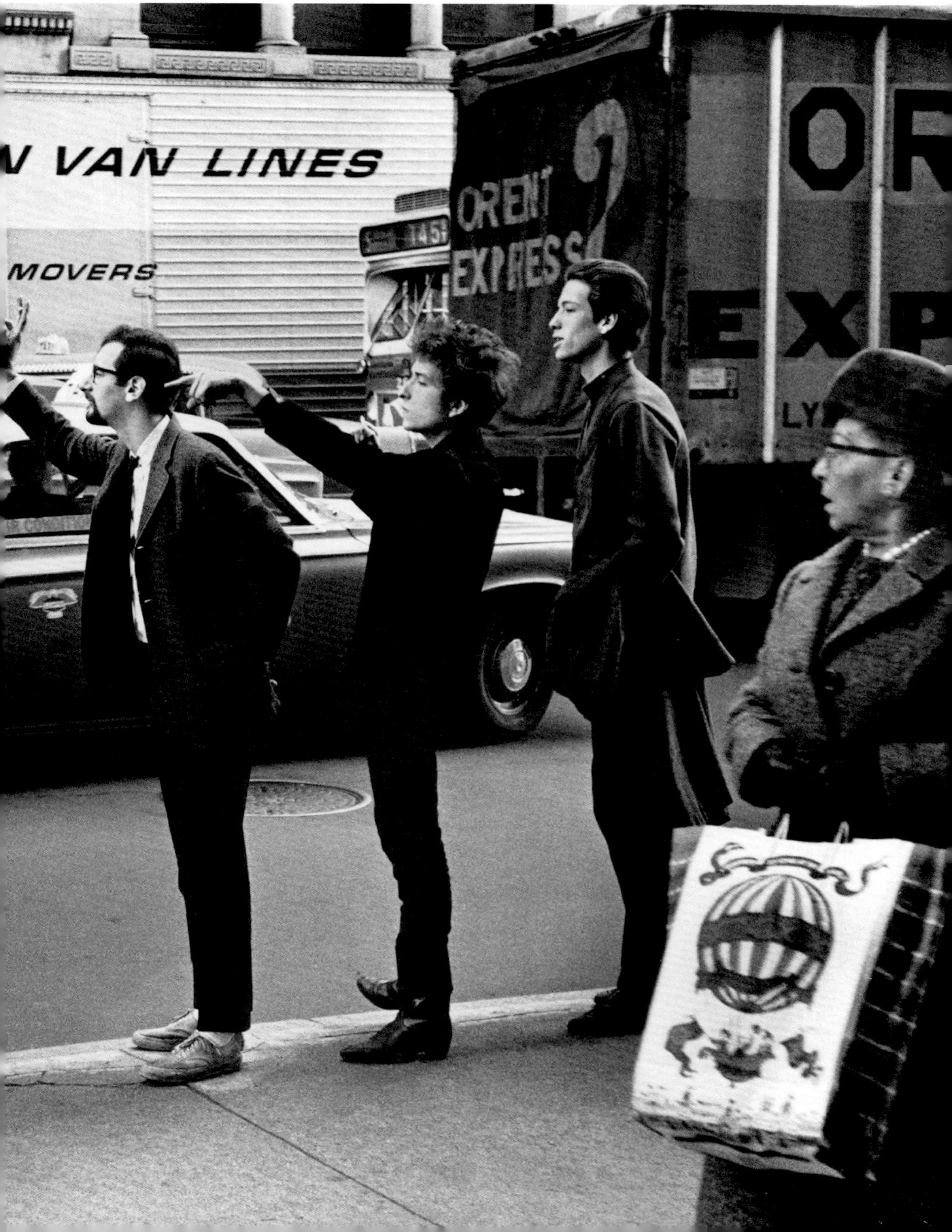
VAN LINES
MOVERS
EXPRESS

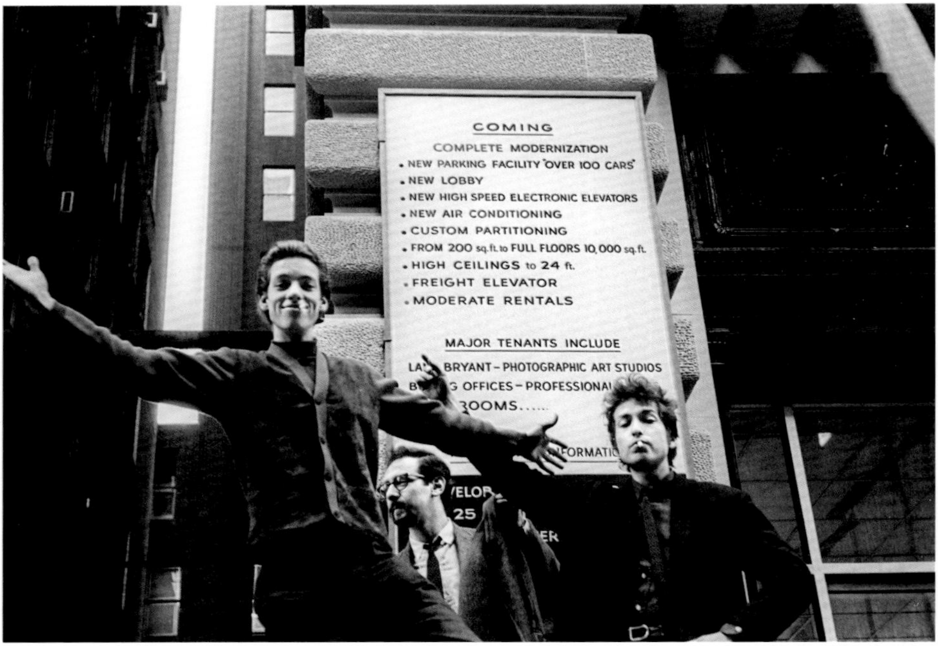

Eventually, photography became something that Bob enjoyed. One day he called and asked if I'd like to make some pictures. He soon arrived at my studio with his friends--Peter Yarrow of Peter, Paul and Mary and John Hammond, Jr., the folksinger--and suggested we go out to the street and have some fun. We got a few pictures I really like very much, and I do believe that my subjects worked hard to make it happen.

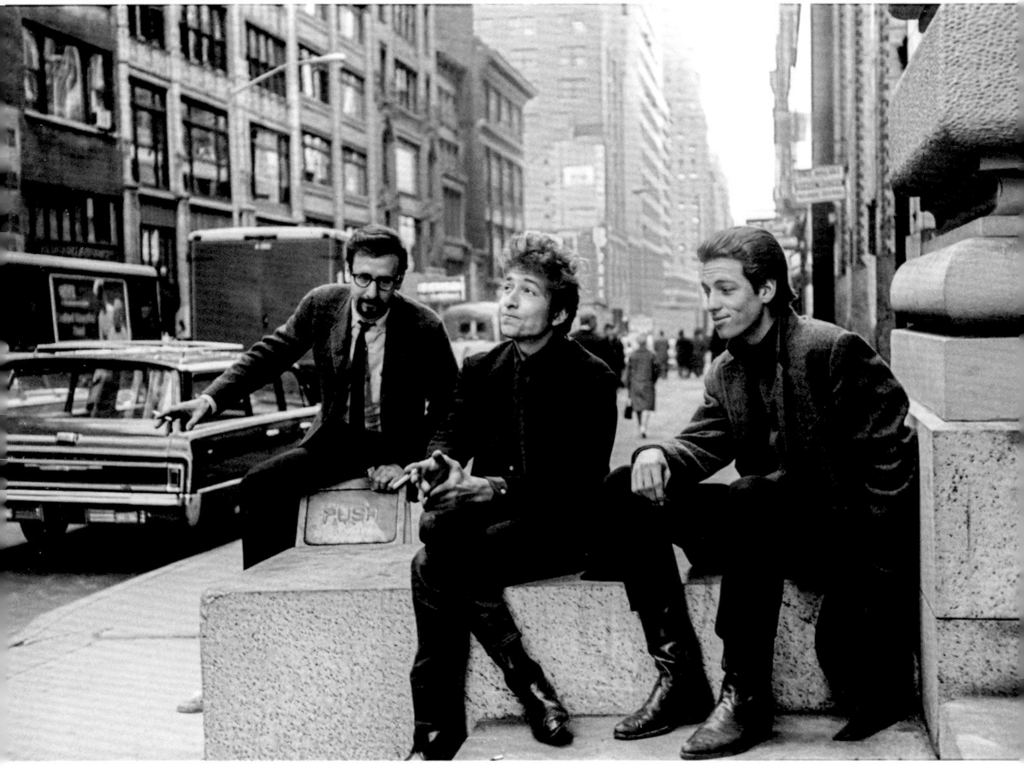
PUSH

Backstage With Johnny Cash
Rutgers University Gym
New Brunswick, New Jersey
February 10, 1965

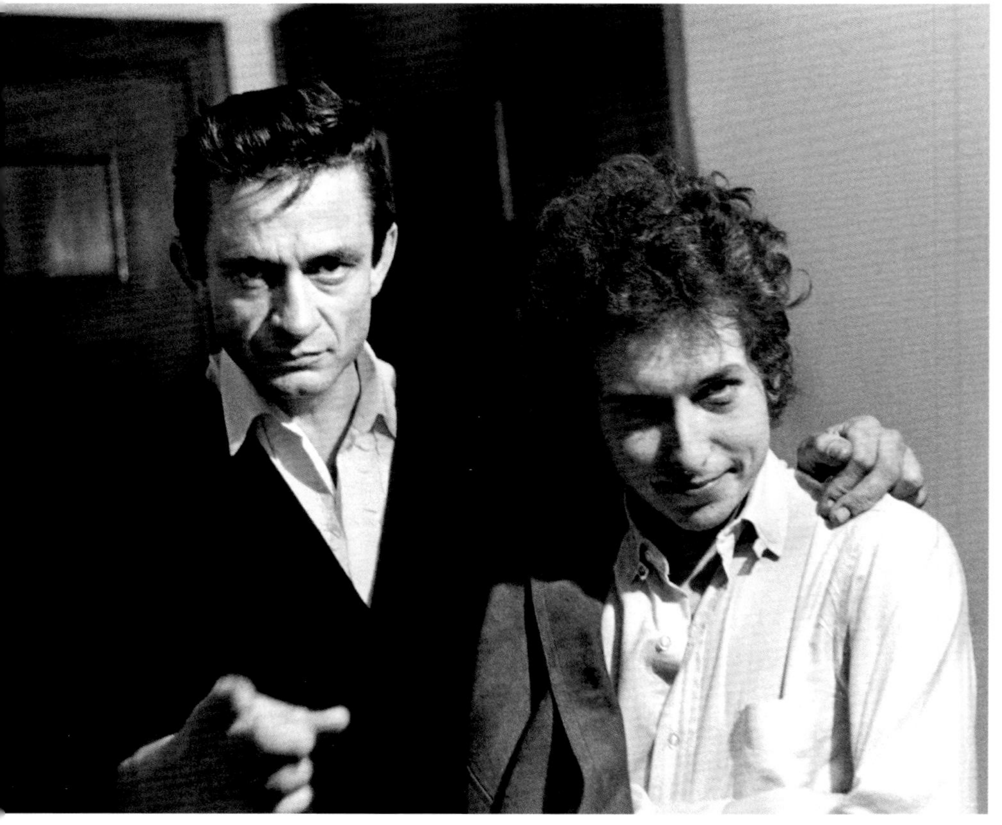

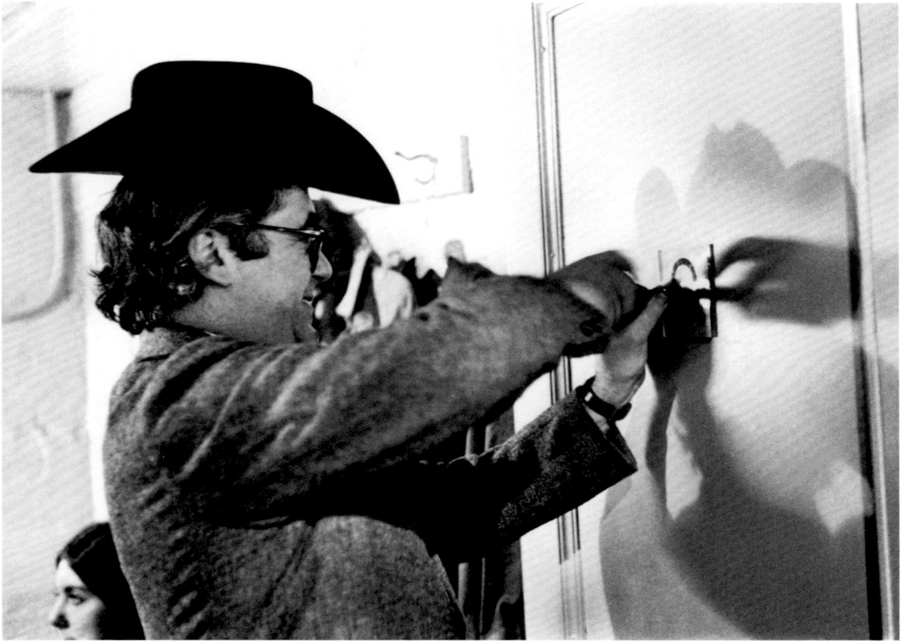

The Les Crane Show
New York City
February 17, 1965

Bob did a concert at Rutgers in February, and I didn't know it but Johnny Cash was coming to the show.It would be one of Bob's last solo acoustic guitar performances. Cash did not arrive in time to see Bob perform, but he did make it to the dressing room just afterward. There was some fooling around in the dressing room, and then it was decided to get dinner. Bob joined Johnny in his limousine, in which he had a portable record player. He wanted Bob to hear his new album. At dinner I managed to photograph some intimate moments between the two men.

It was only a week later that Bob appeared on The Les Crane Show. Everyone seemed to enjoy the experience. Albert Grossman decided to loosen and turn the number six on Bob's dressing-room door to make it a nine.

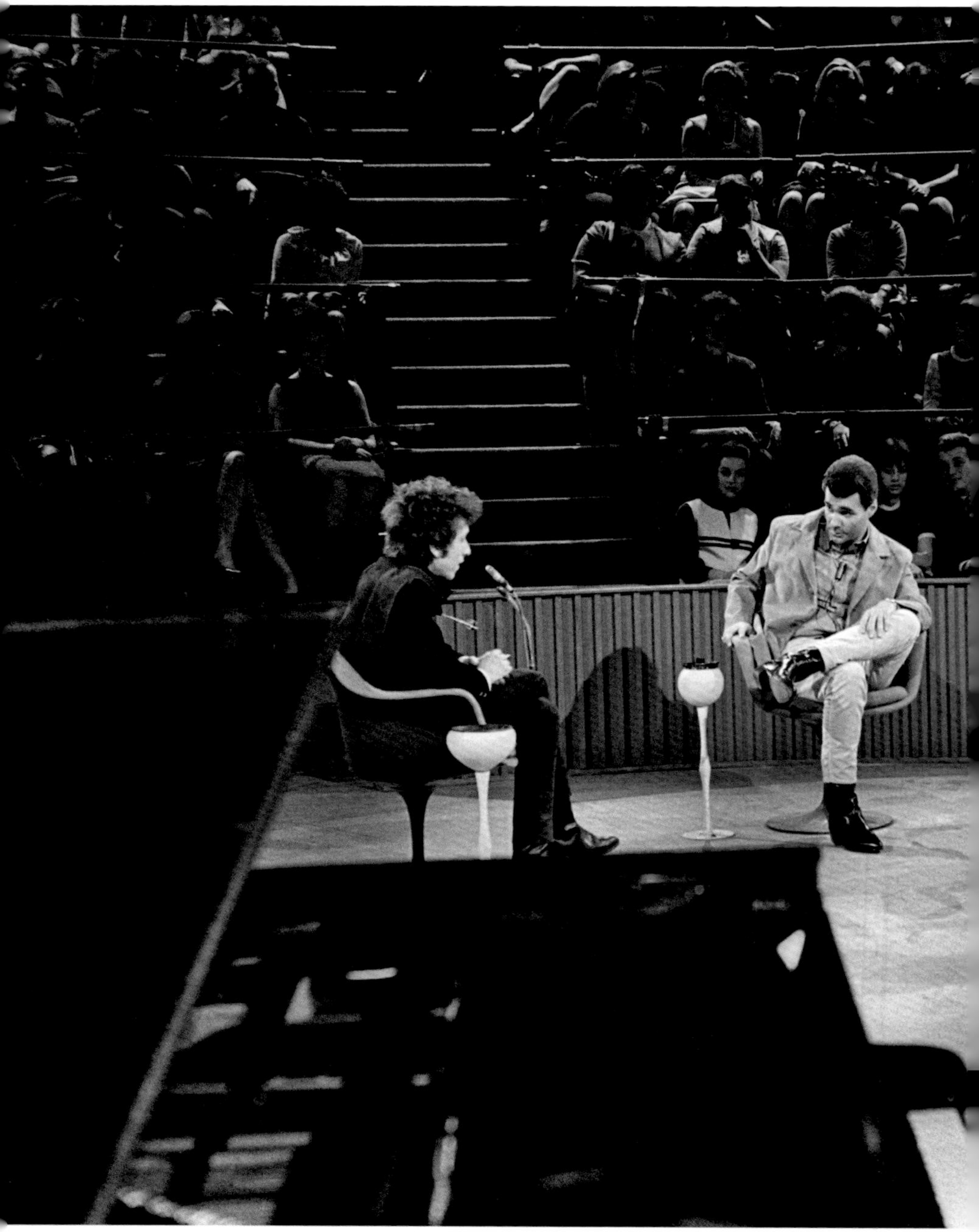

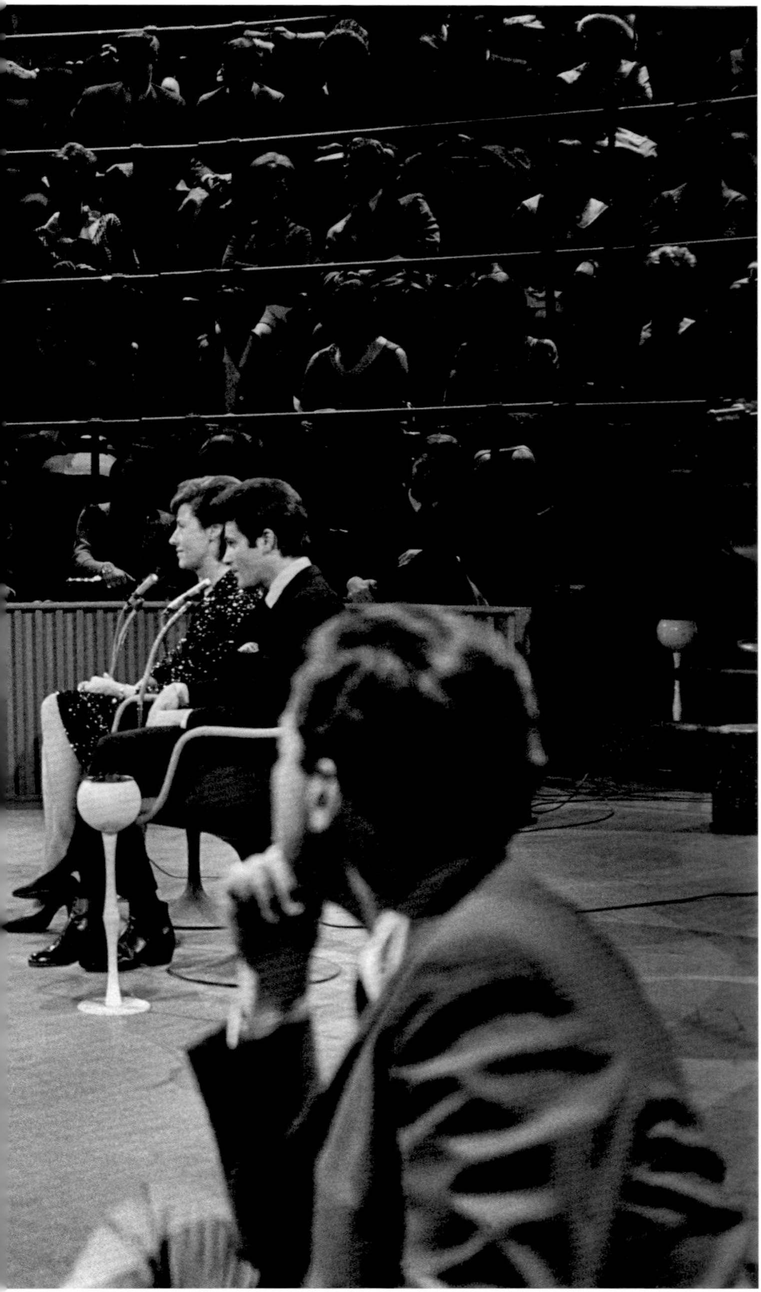

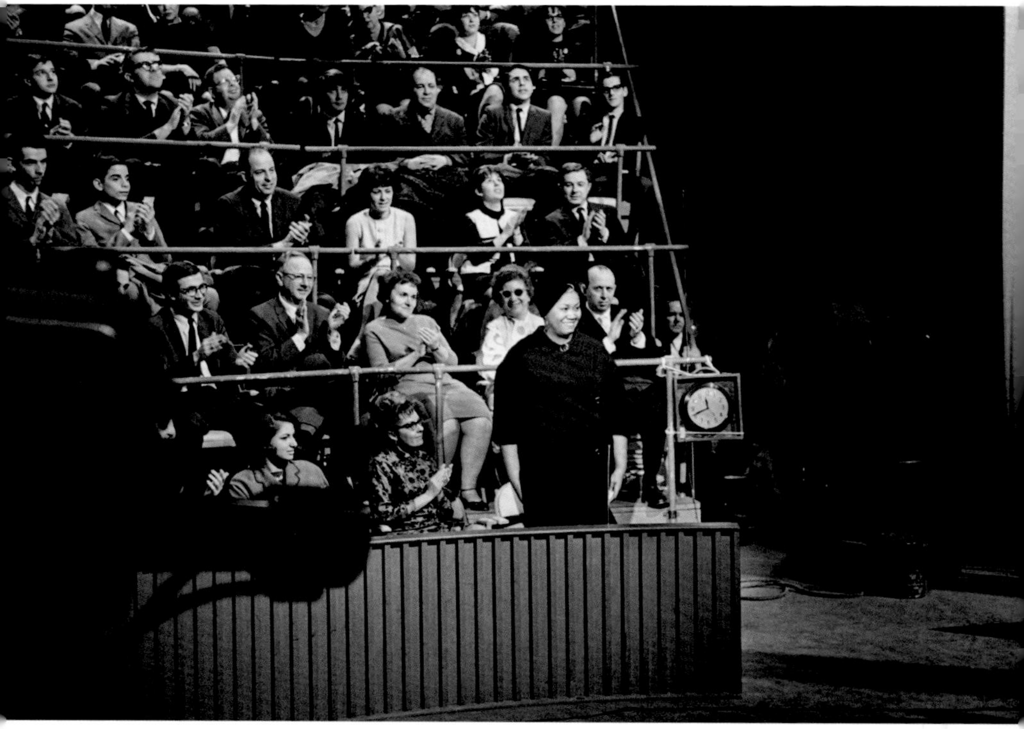

The wonderful folksinger Odetta came as an audience member, but when Bob noticed her and waved she was asked by Les Crane to take a bow. Best of all, Bob decided to answer the host's questions with appropriate nighttime talk-show answers, or at least that's how it seemed. Bob even added that he wanted to get a Maserati and showed a bit of his deadpan humor when Les asked him about what hit songs he'd written. Instead of naming big songs, he listed off his more obscure tracks with a wry smile.

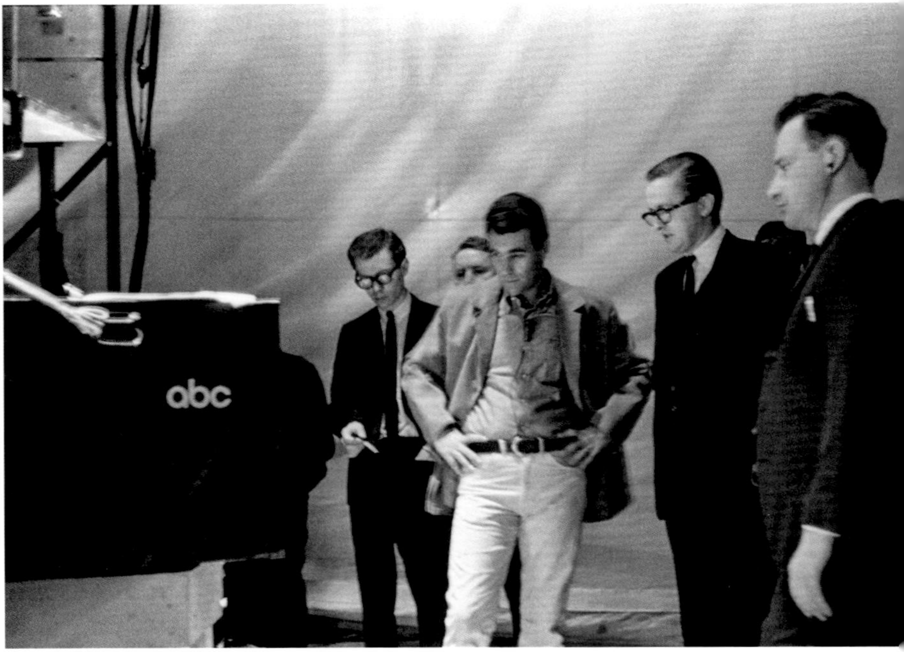
abc

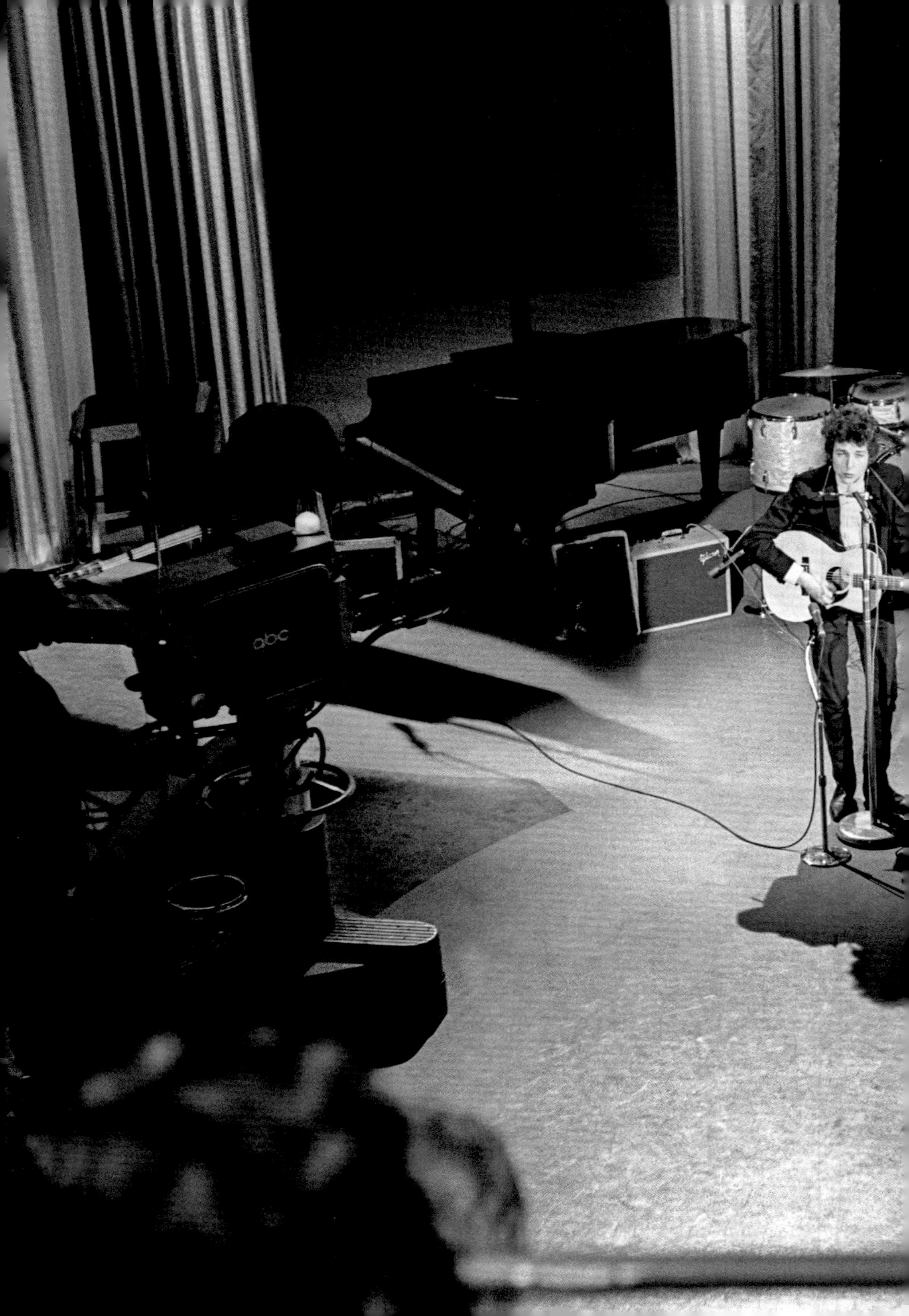
abc

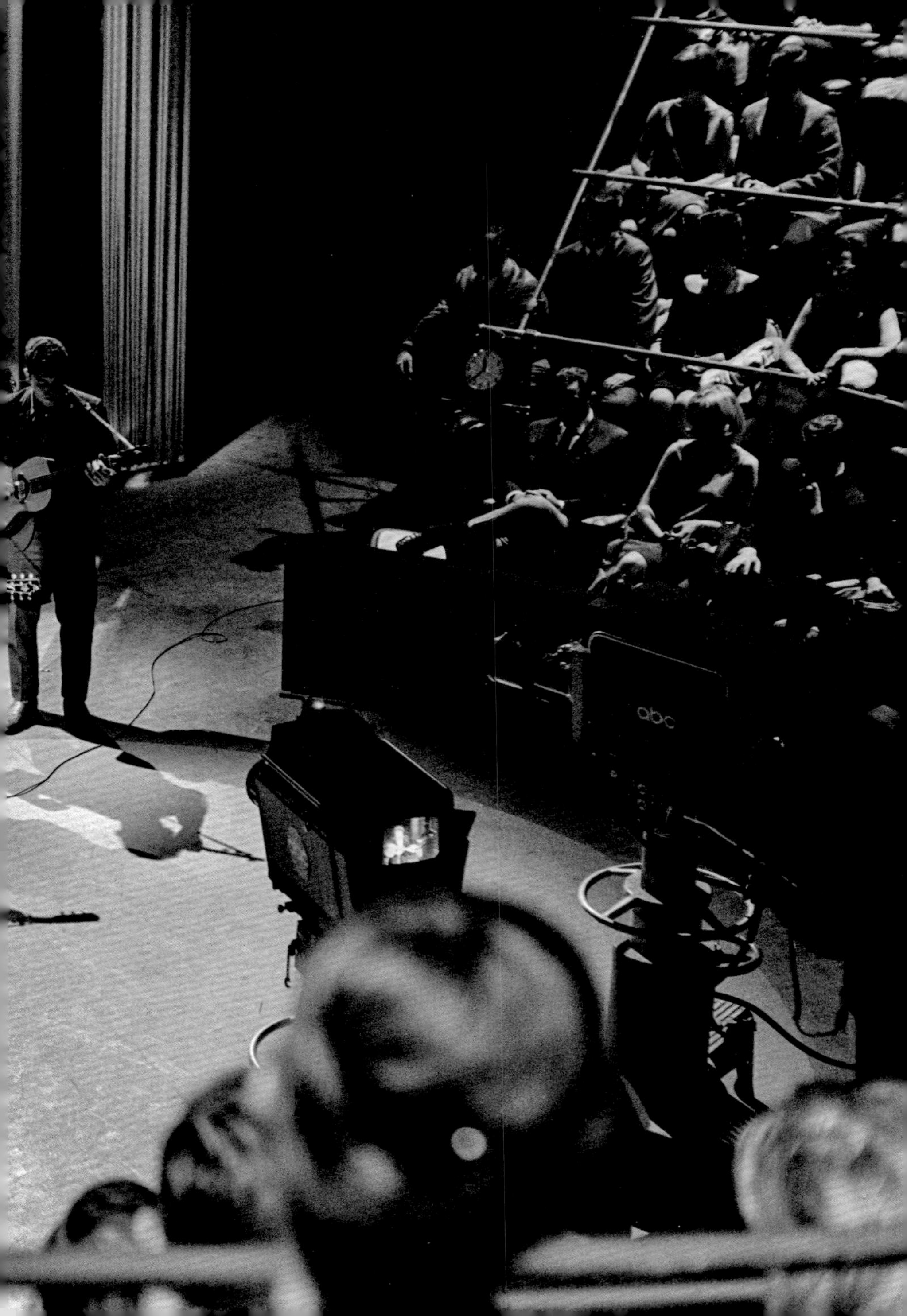
abc

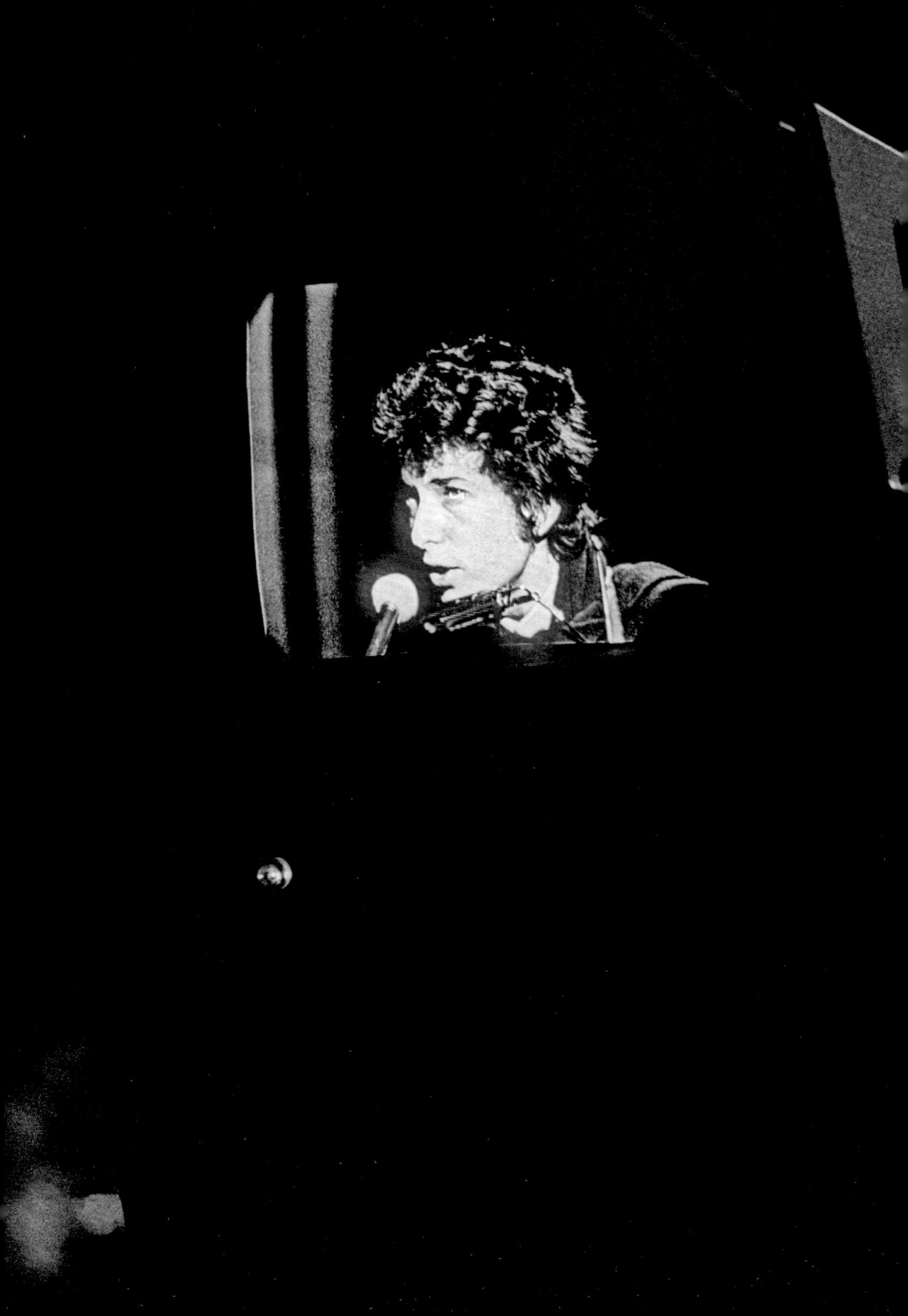

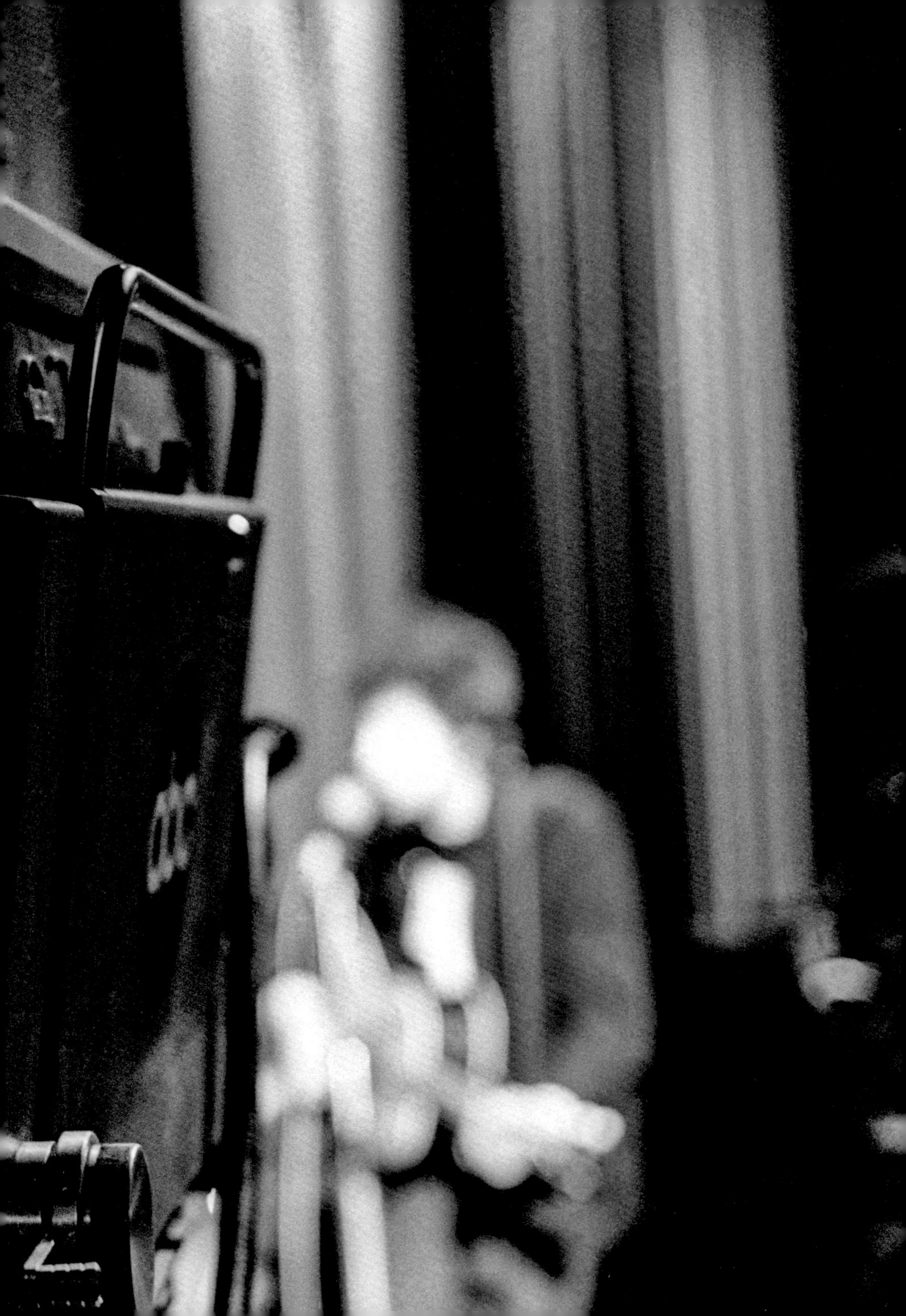

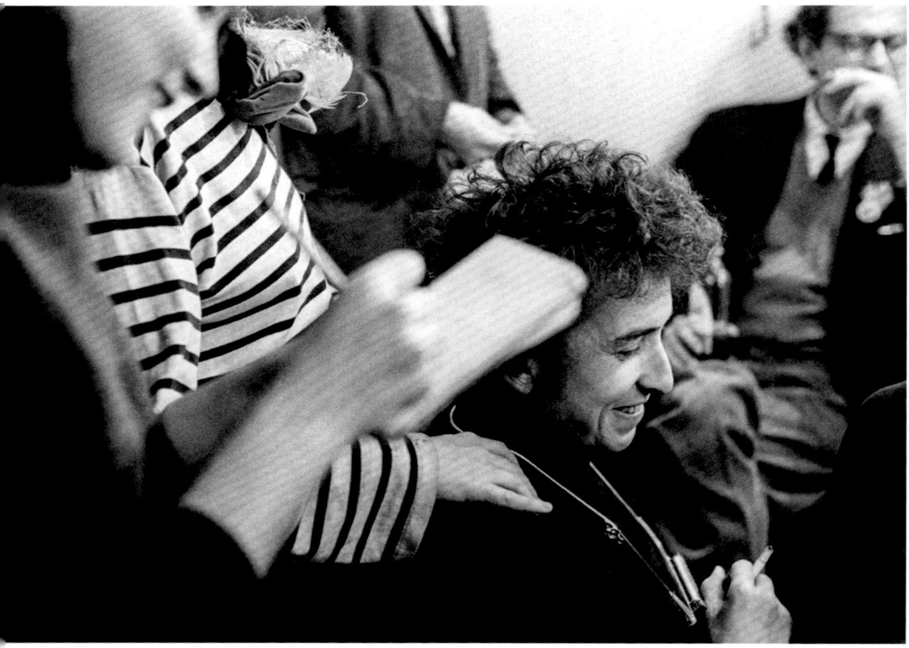

Somewhere along the line Bob told me that no matter how he tried to be reasonable with reporters, the articles about him never really worked out--they became distorted or inaccurate. He would often answer reporters in a way that would make it obvious he felt the questions were silly or naive. He was asked by one reporter, "What do you really want to do?" "Go to college, learn to make money, and be a success," he told her.

It was always the youngest interviewers who had the best chance. Dylan seemed to have the most patience with these people. Once after a concert at Princeton (Allen Ginsberg, a very enthusiastic fan and friend, had come to the show), Dylan granted interviews first to a high-school girl and then to a young man who was reporting for the first time for his college newspaper.

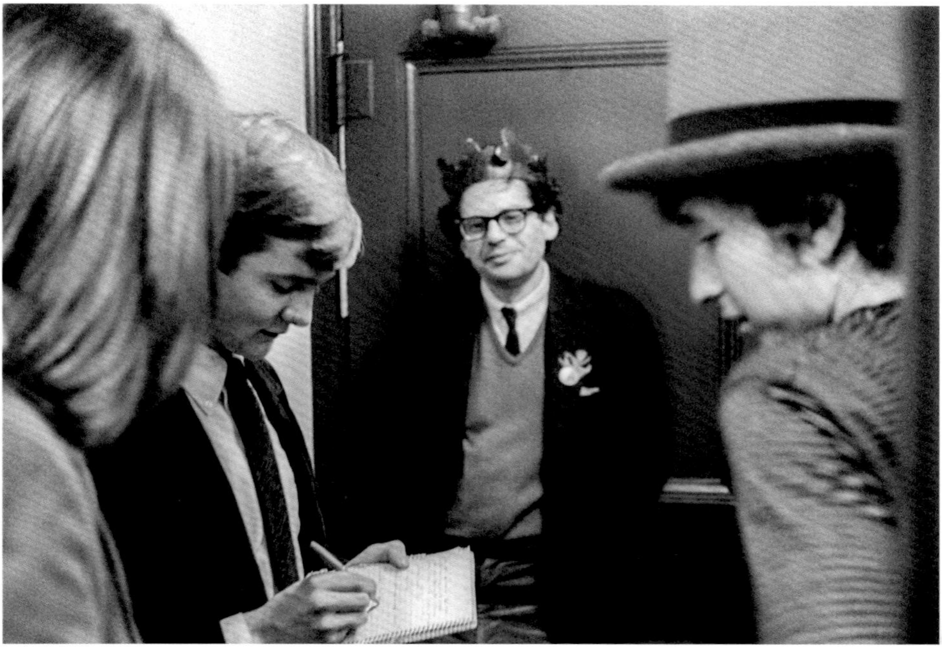

The college student concluded with questions about the song "With God On Our Side." He asked Dylan, "Do you believe in what you say in that song? Do you believe in the words you write?" Dylan replied, "I believe in every breath I take," and with that he embraced the reporter and exclaimed, "and I believe in every breath YOU take!"

Allen Ginsberg, wearing a crown he found in the dressing room, embraced both of them and cried out, "And I believe in every breath we ALL take!" The reporter was a little shaken when the interview resumed, and Ginsberg, noticing this, offered to help by taking the pencil and pad from his hands and continuing the interview.

McCarter Theatre
Princeton, New Jersey
November 7, 1964

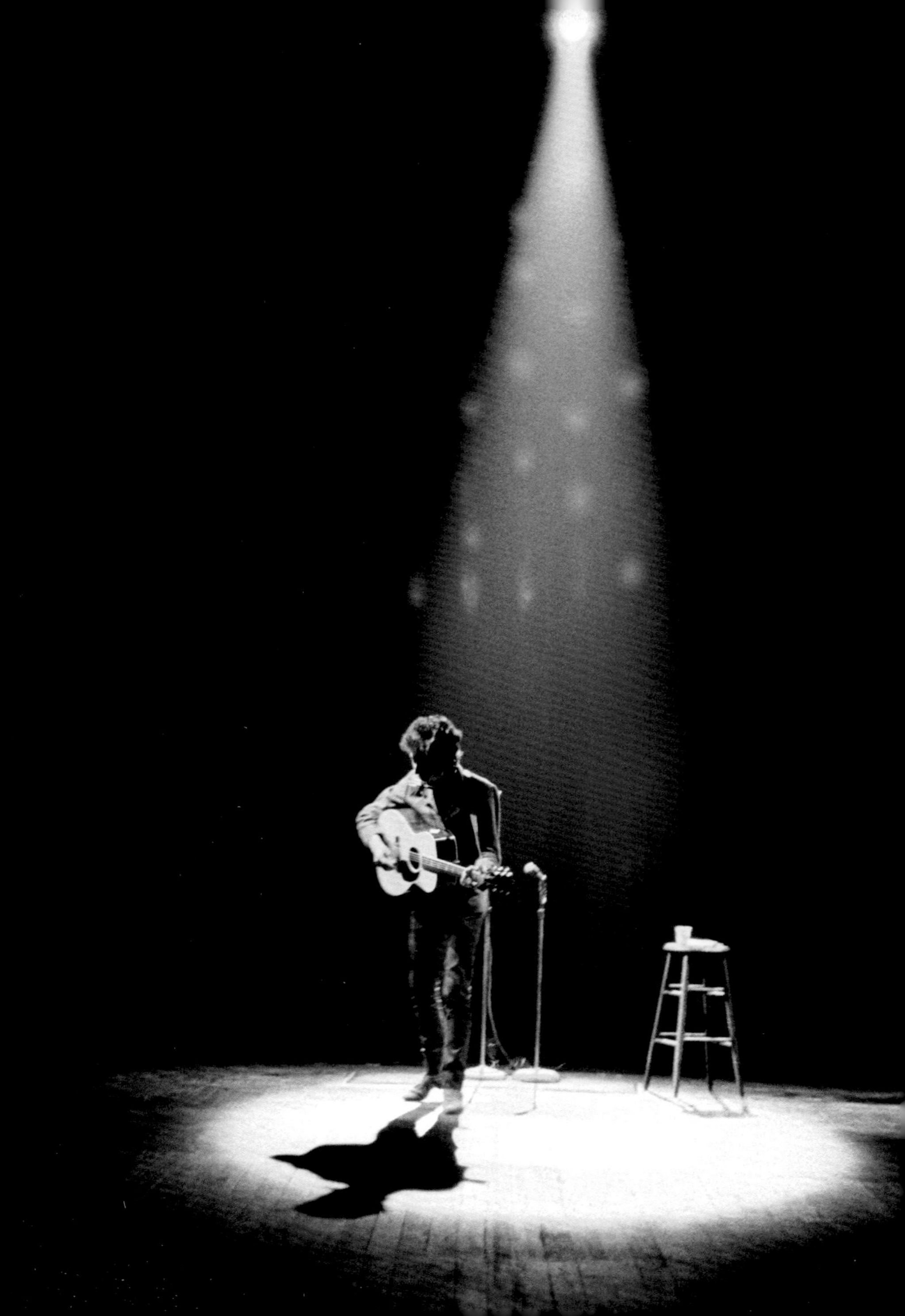

And you say, “Who is that man?”
You try so hard but you don’t understand
Just what you’ll say when you get home
Because something is happening here
But you don’t know what it is
Do you, Mister Jones?

BALLAD OF A THIN MAN

Chapter Six

Forest Hills

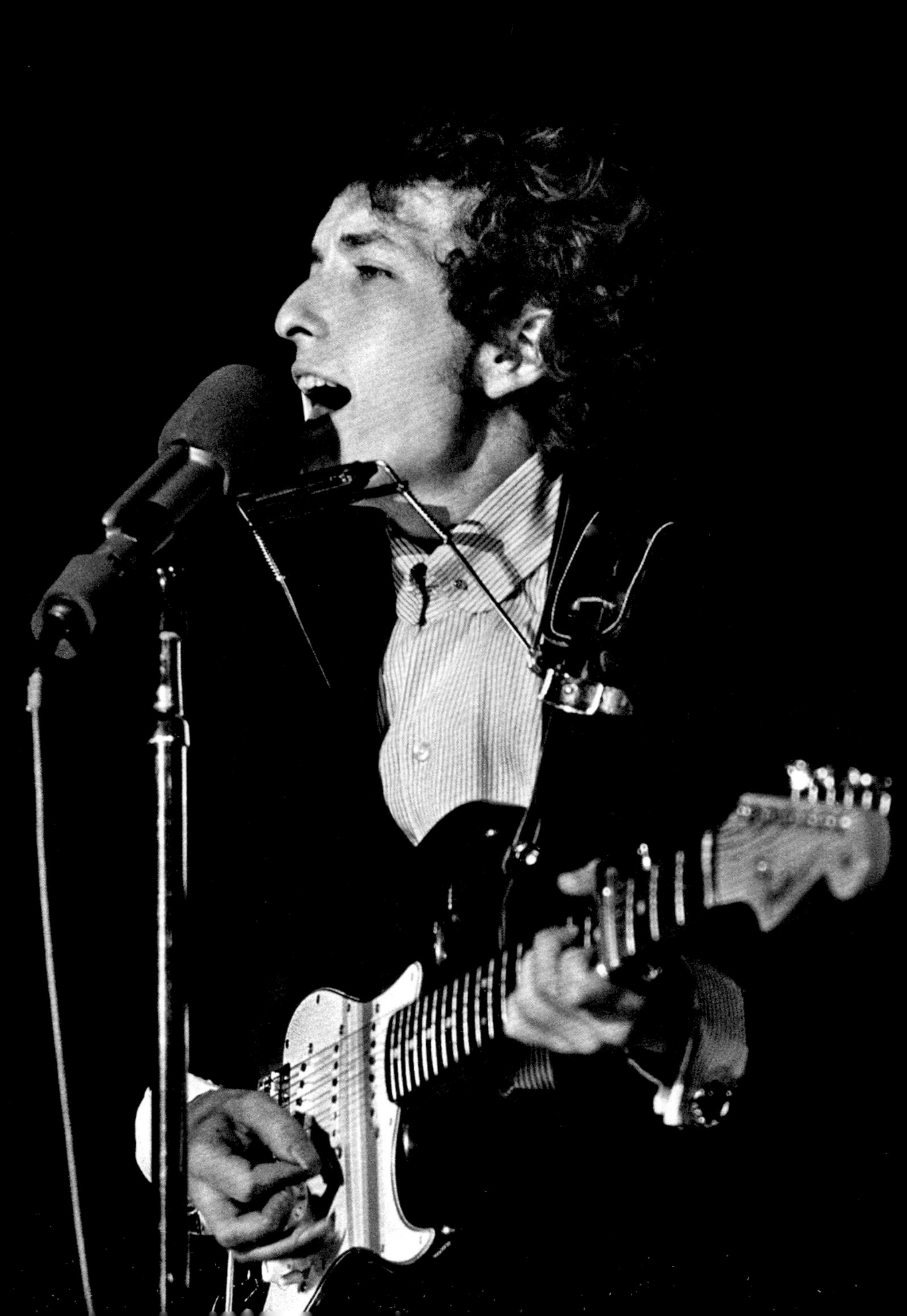

On August 28, 1965, a year and a day from the time I met him in Woodstock, Bob Dylan gave a concert at Forest Hills Stadium in New York City, where 14,000 people filled the stands to capacity. It would culminate in what he had been doing with his music for the past half year--we were about to get the big bang. I arrived at the stadium before Bob so that I could acquaint myself with the photographic problems. The weather forecast called for showers, and this was still a matter for concern since Forest Hills was an open stadium.

A huge horseshoe of seats faced the stage. Large wooden speaker enclosures stood at the edge of the lawn, facing the stands--making it possible for all 14,000 people to hear the same concert as if they were in the front rows. The grounds were deserted except for some musicians and stage and production people standing about in conversation near the stage. A small group of fans had gathered near the gate, hoping to meet Bob and get his autograph. Shadows of clouds were sweeping across the field. At about 2 p.m., Bob arrived with Albert Grossman. Upon his arrival, as though a baton had been lifted, it all began.

Before the show, Bob spent some time with the men who were going to play with him. Programming and problems the music would face in this particular stadium had to be discussed. Later in the night, during intermission, Bob would meet with the musicians who were going to accompany him in the second half of the concert. He told them they should expect anything to happen--that the audience might yell and boo and that they should not be bothered by it. He was aware of the possible reaction from his audience, but he was willing to risk that and stand with his convictions. The artist must be true to himself. He must be satisfied with what he produces--this is the prime factor in the production of his art. I always had great respect for this part of Dylan. He was always true to himself and produced what he believed was his best.

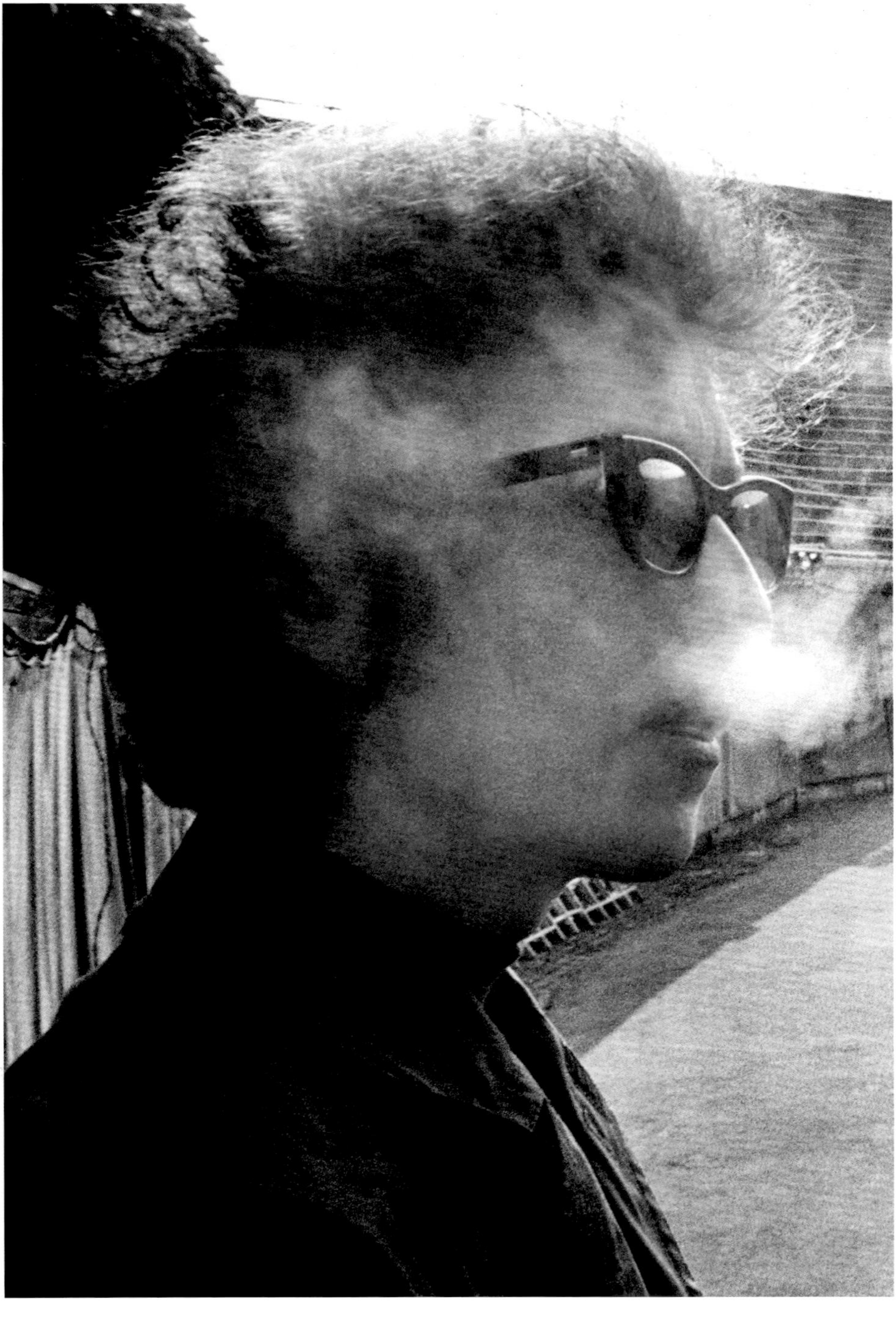

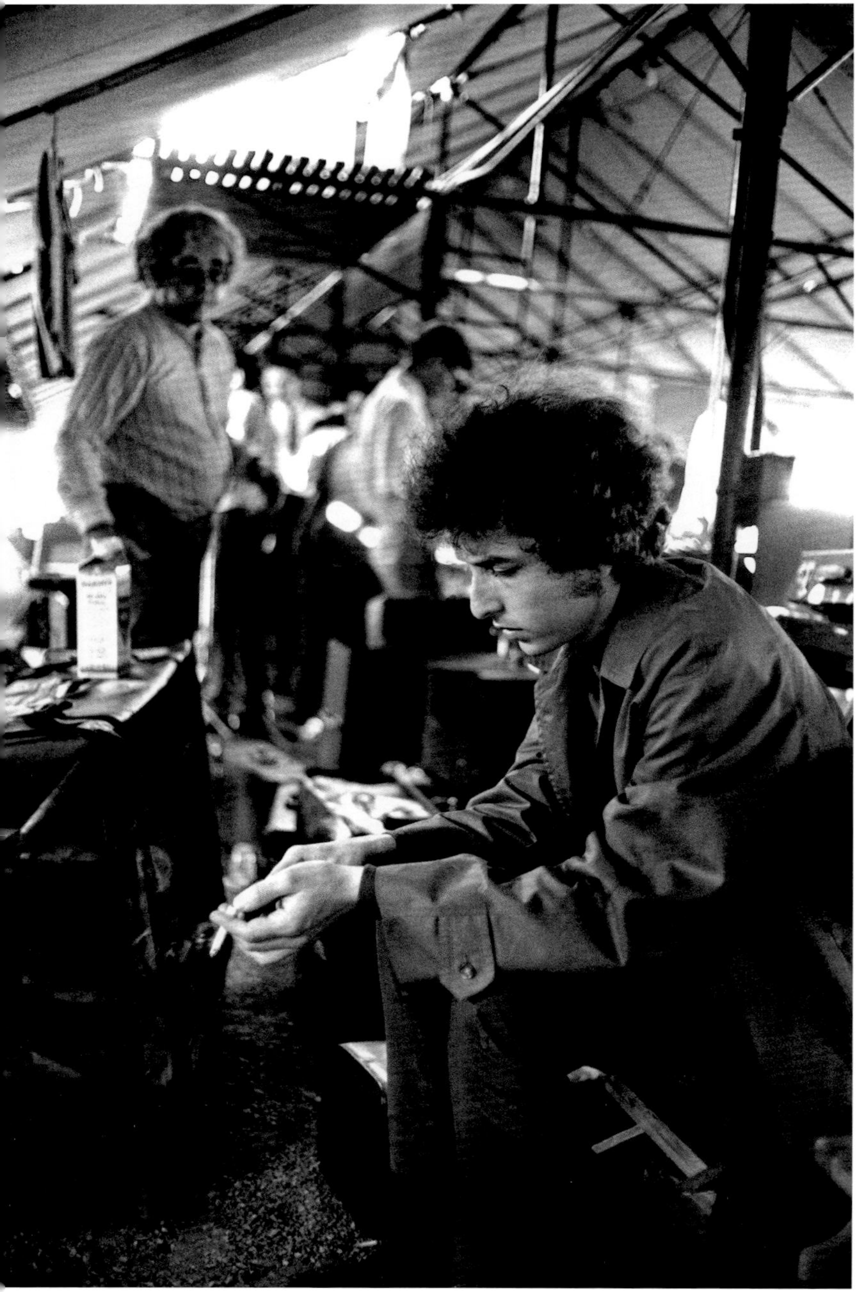

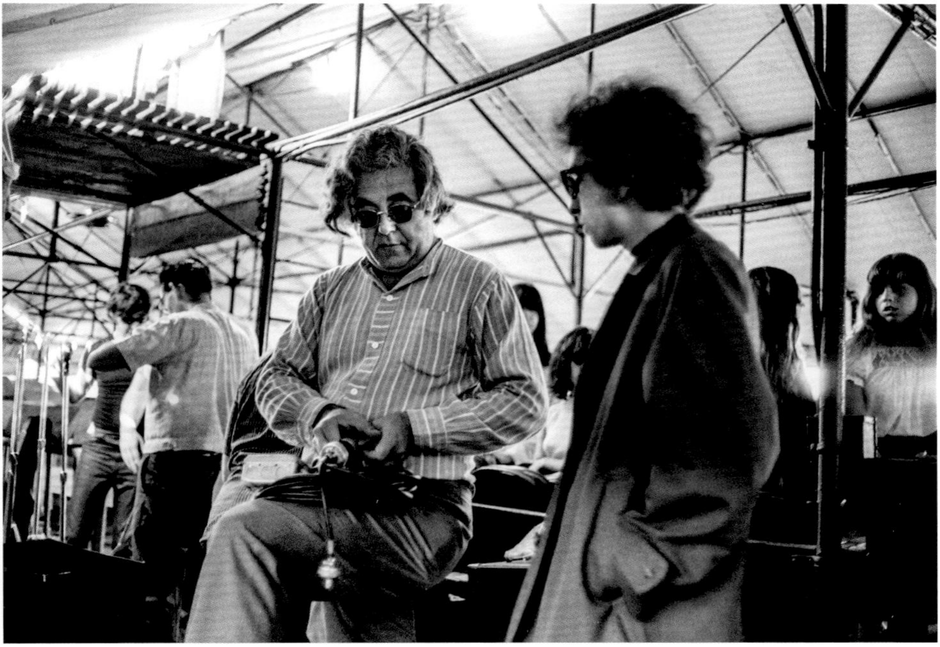

At the Forest Hills concert, as always, Albert Grossman personally supervised every phase of the operation. He seemed to be everywhere at once, always in complete control over the situation. In order to be certain of the sound quality, he sat in the distant stands with a walkie-talkie radio unit and guided the engineers in the sound booth until the microphones were properly set. Although he never tampered with Bob's creativity, he was a great support and guide for the incredible amount of work and planning that went into a production of this magnitude.

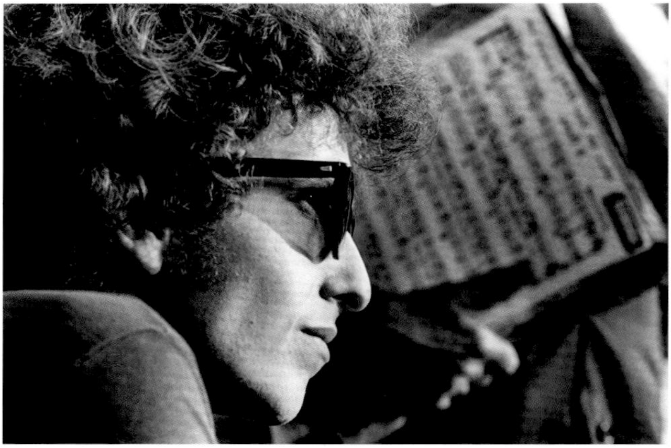

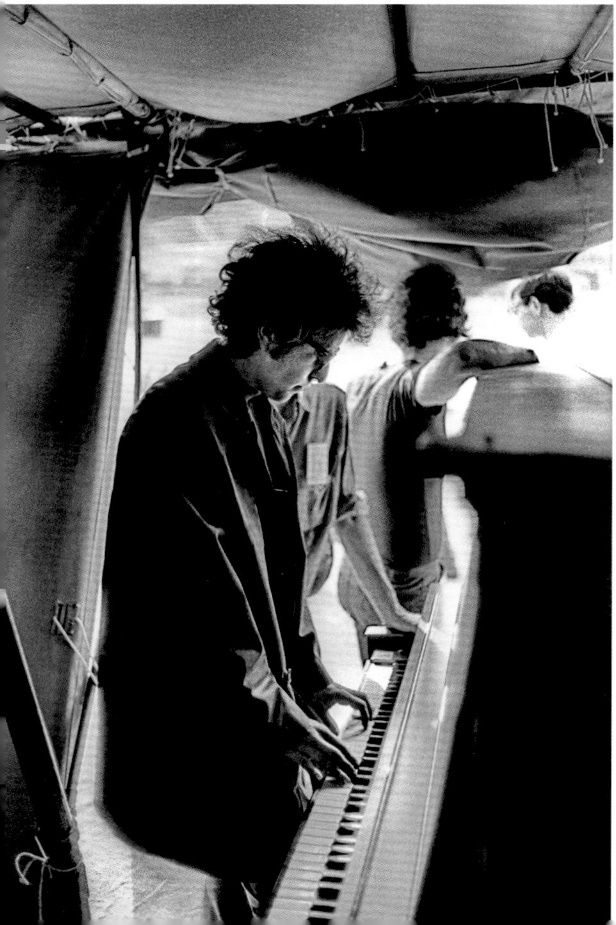

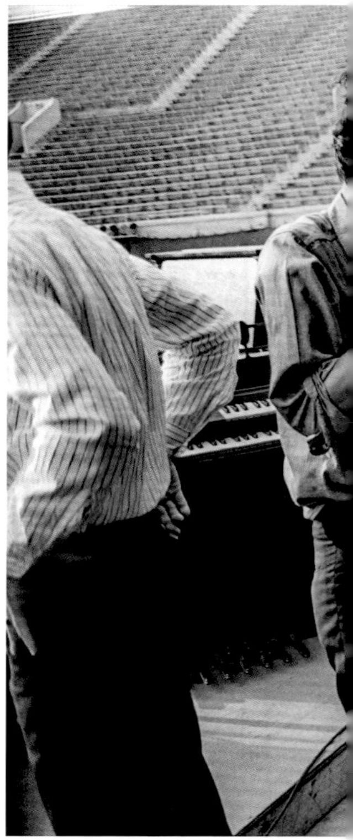

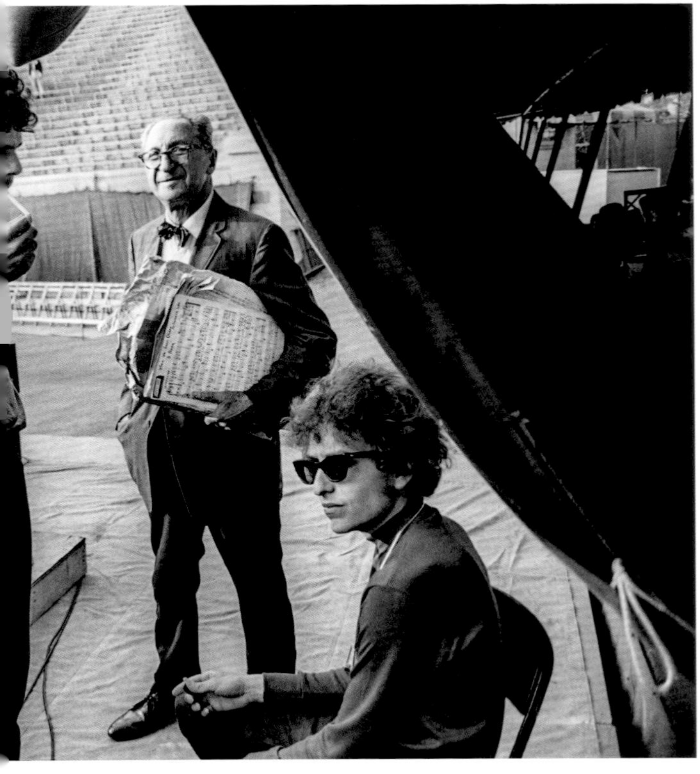

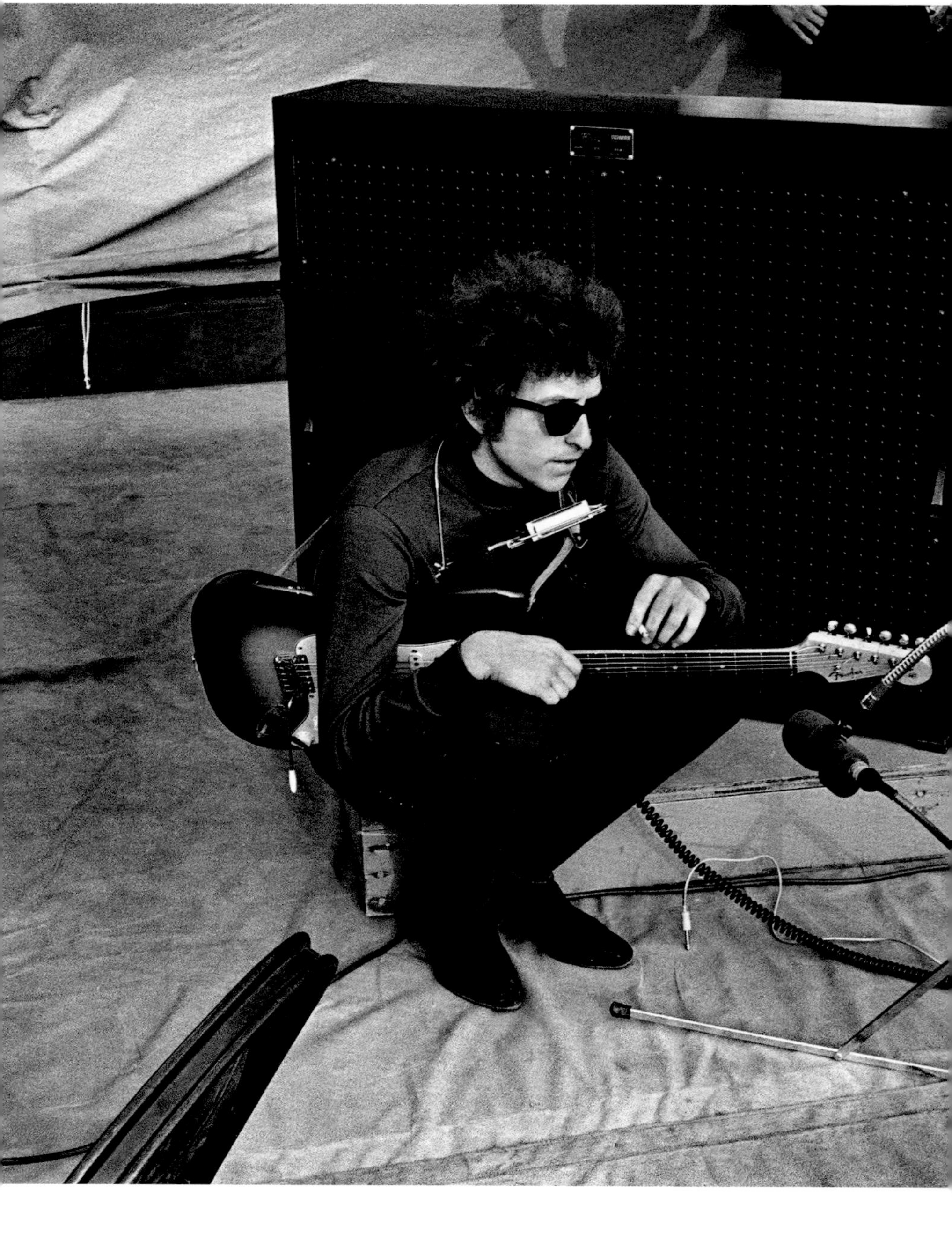

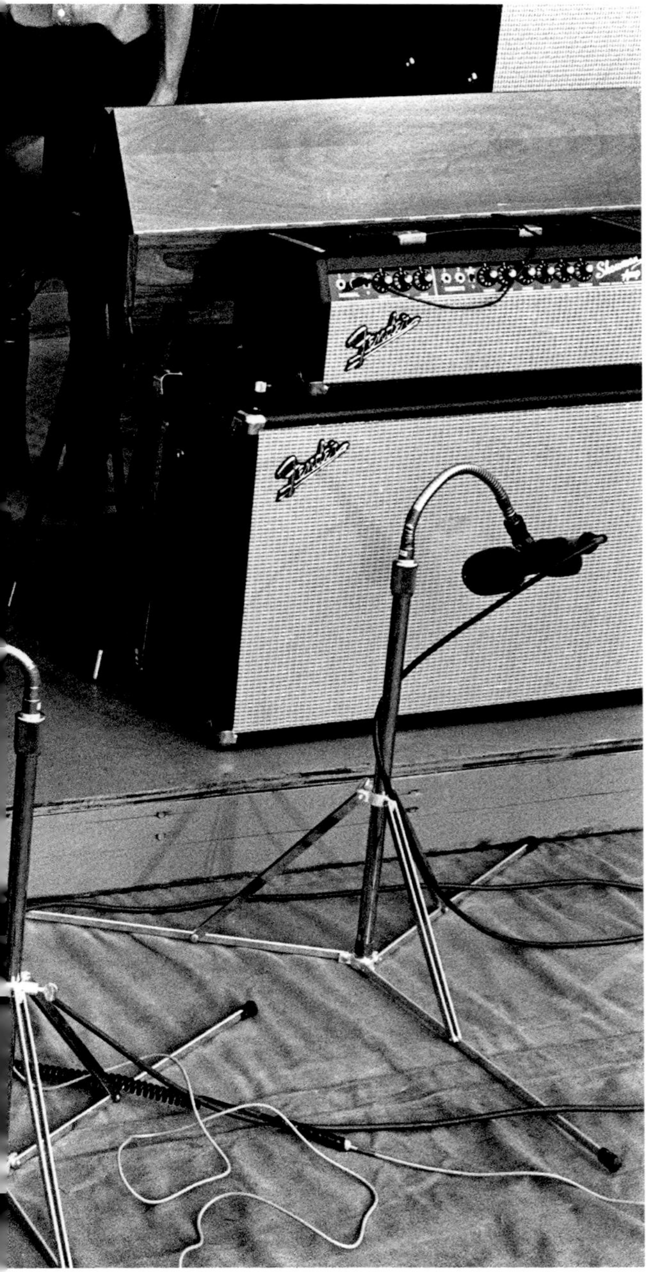
Fender
Fender
Fender

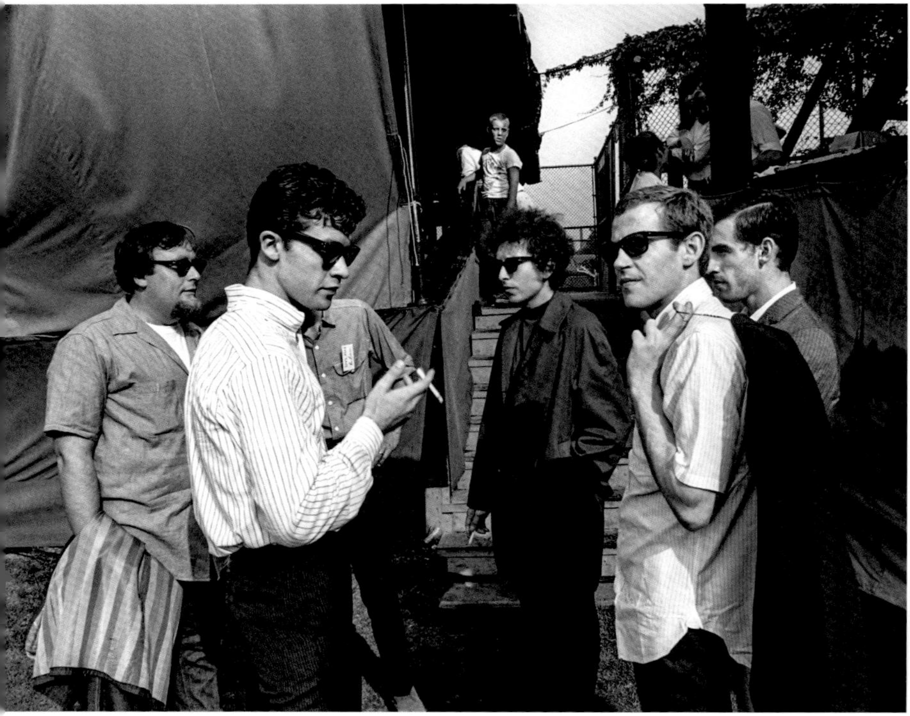

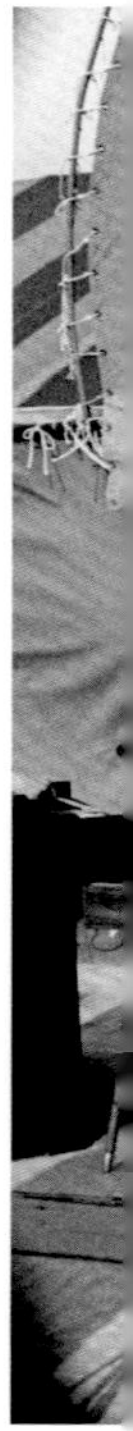

Preparation for the Forest Hills concert was unlike that for past Dylan concerts. Bob would bring his guitar, some harmonicas, and his small case of microphone equipment. On this day, things were approaching the conditions of a recording studio. There were many microphones to unpack, microphone stands to assemble, and dozens of coils of cable to unwind. The instruments had to be set up and arranged on stage. Microphones had to be placed and then balanced for sound.

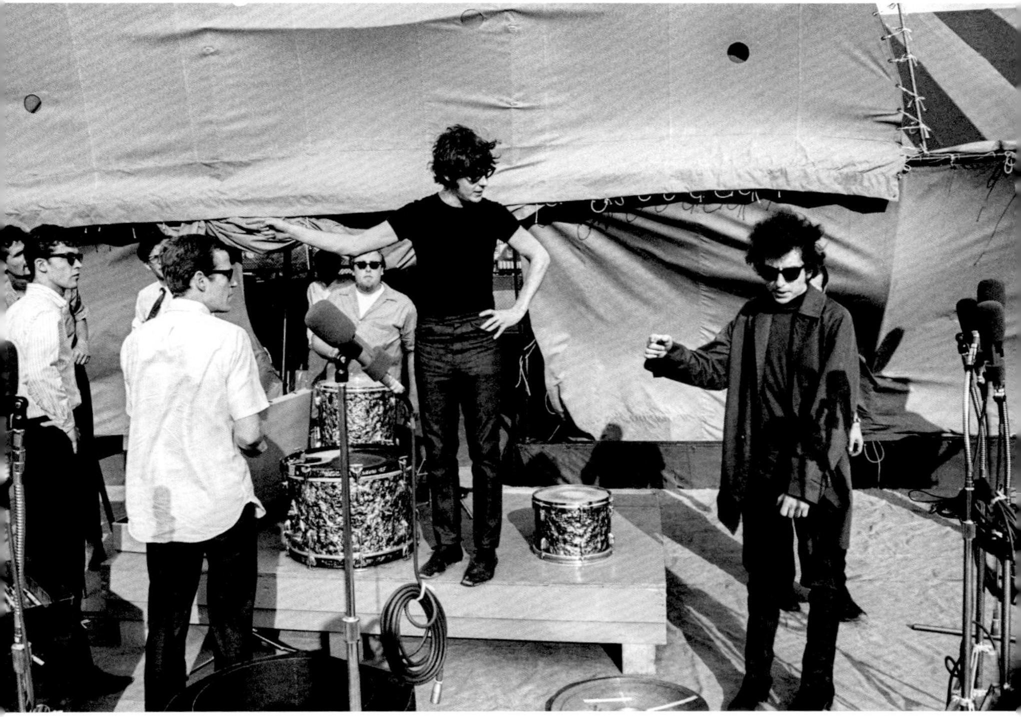

There were problems caused by the rustling sound made by the wind as it rushed by the mike heads. Voice levels had to be balanced so they could be heard over the sound of the instruments. It went on and on. A number of people worked at it, and the musicians and Bob were constantly needed for sound checks. It was an astonishing contrast to the preparation required for the first Dylan concert I attended almost a year earlier.

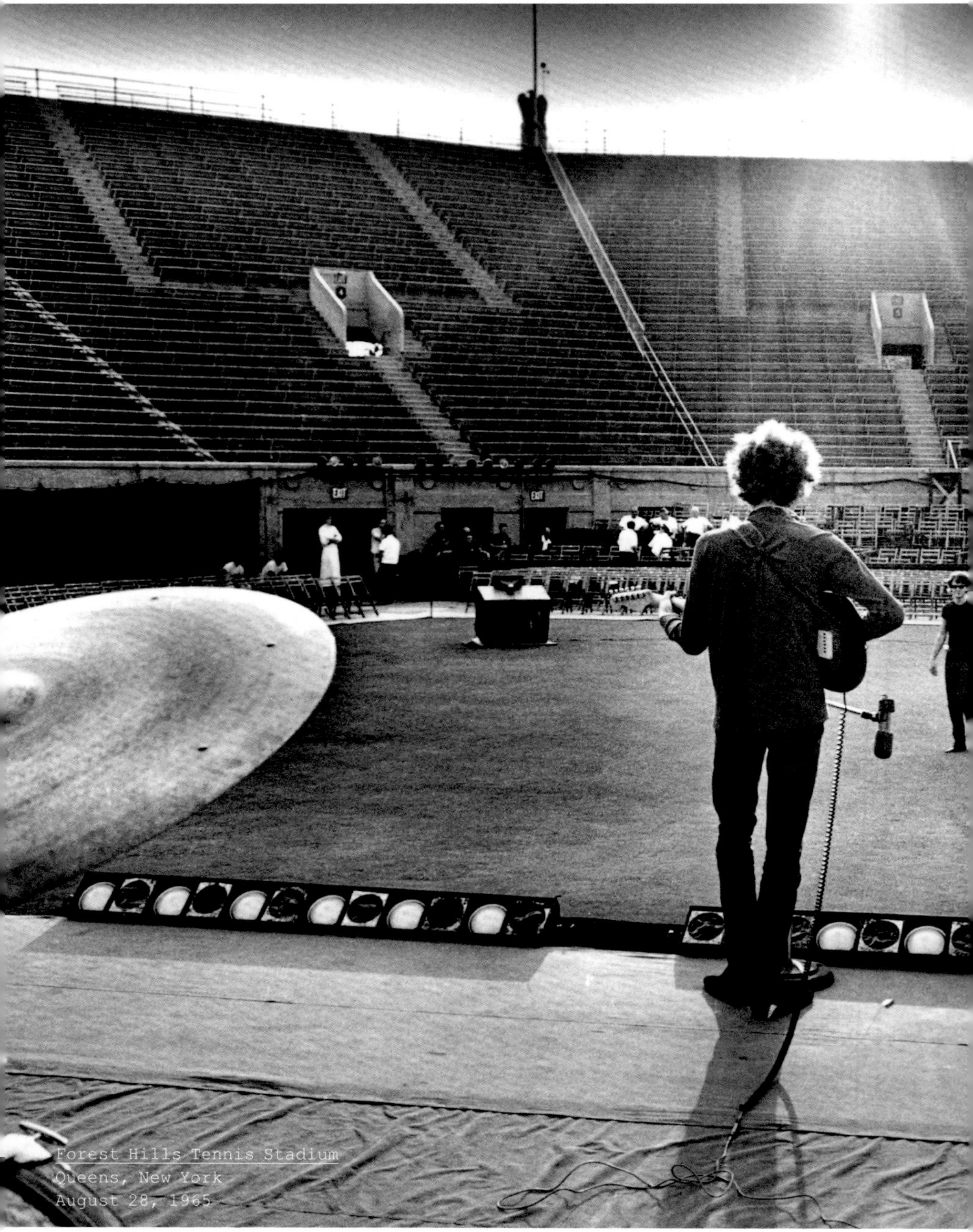

Forest Hills Tennis Stadium
Queens, New York
August 28, 1965

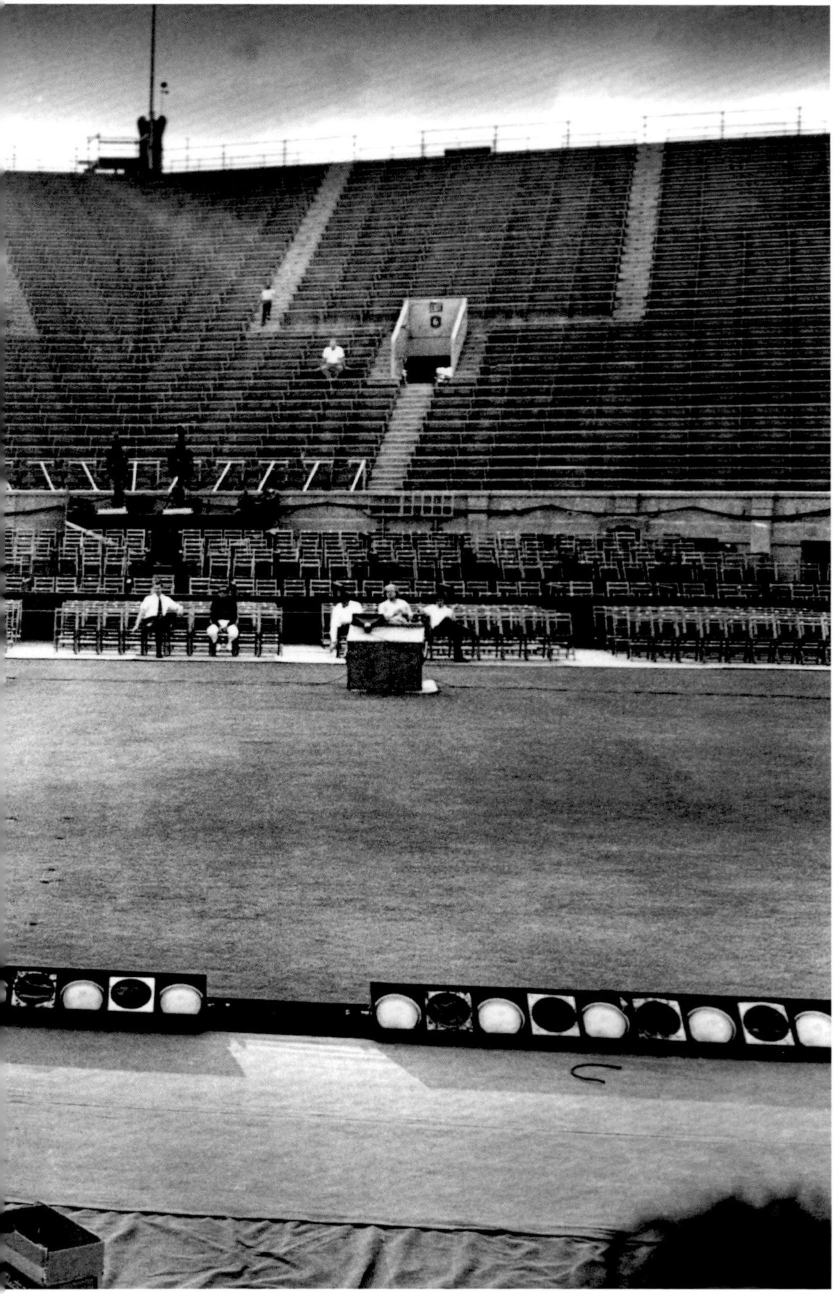

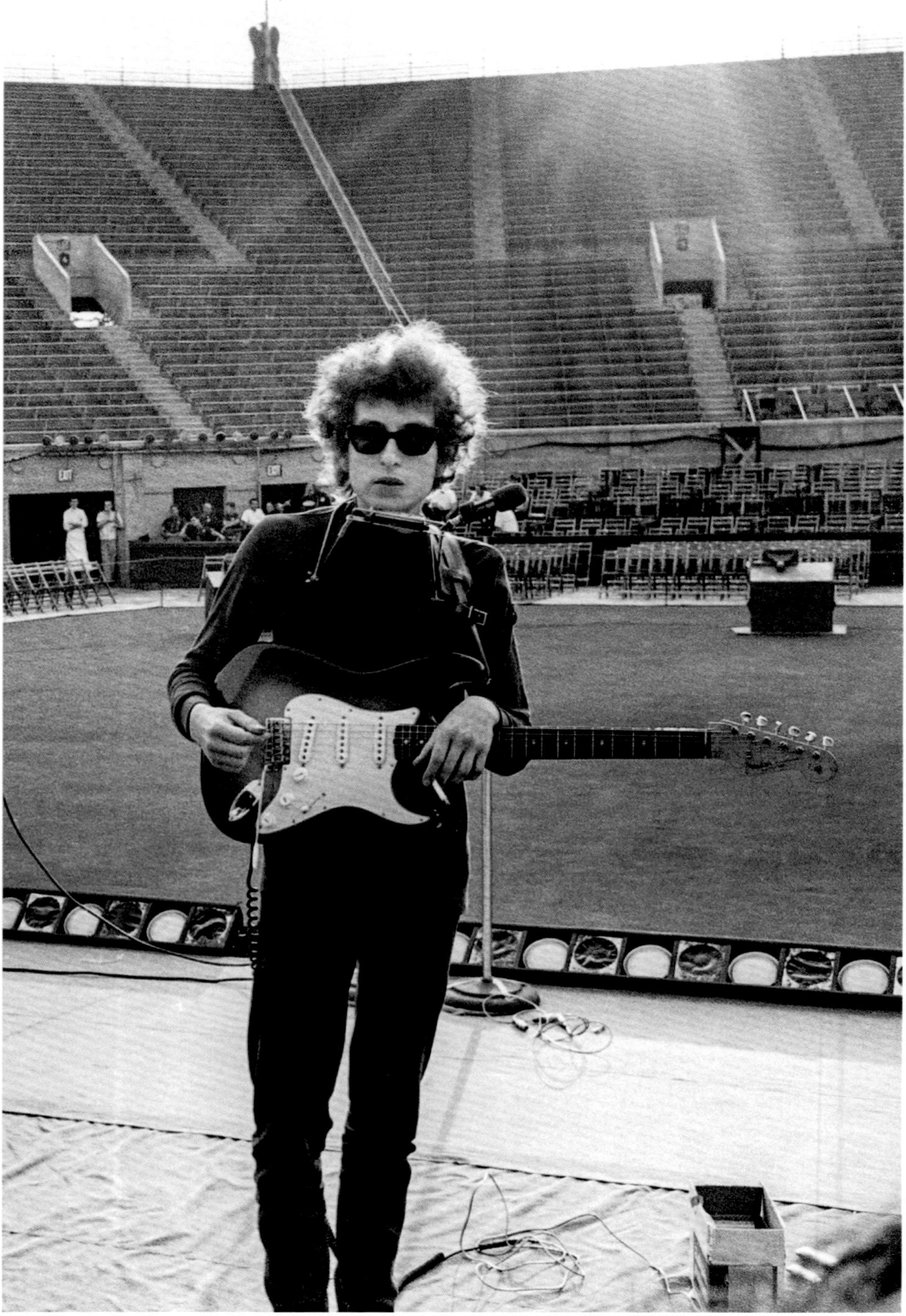
EXIT
EXIT

The stands were packed. Spotlights pierced the windy night. Bob emerged, beams of light following him to the microphone. There was a roar of applause as he began to sing. For the first part of the concert he performed as he always had--alone. It ended with overwhelming applause.

During the intermission Bob held a conference with his band. He told them, probably remembering the unruly crowd at Newport a month earlier, to expect that anything could happen. Their job, he said, was to make the best music they were capable of and what happens happens.

When Bob appeared for the second half of the concert with an electric guitar, followed by musicians, there was a sound of disapproval that rumbled from the stands. The twang of the electrified instruments shattered the night. The electric guitars, the pounding of the drums, and Bob's wail rode the wind that swept across the open stadium, penetrating its farthest reaches.

When the music started, the audience grew quiet. When it stopped, they would cry out, "We want Dylan! We want Dylan!" But Bob Dylan never stopped singing; he never broke his stride. He was doing just what he had told his quartet to do: Make the best music you can and don't be intimidated. This was certainly the man who wrote and sang "The Lonesome Death of Hattie Carroll" the first time I saw him.

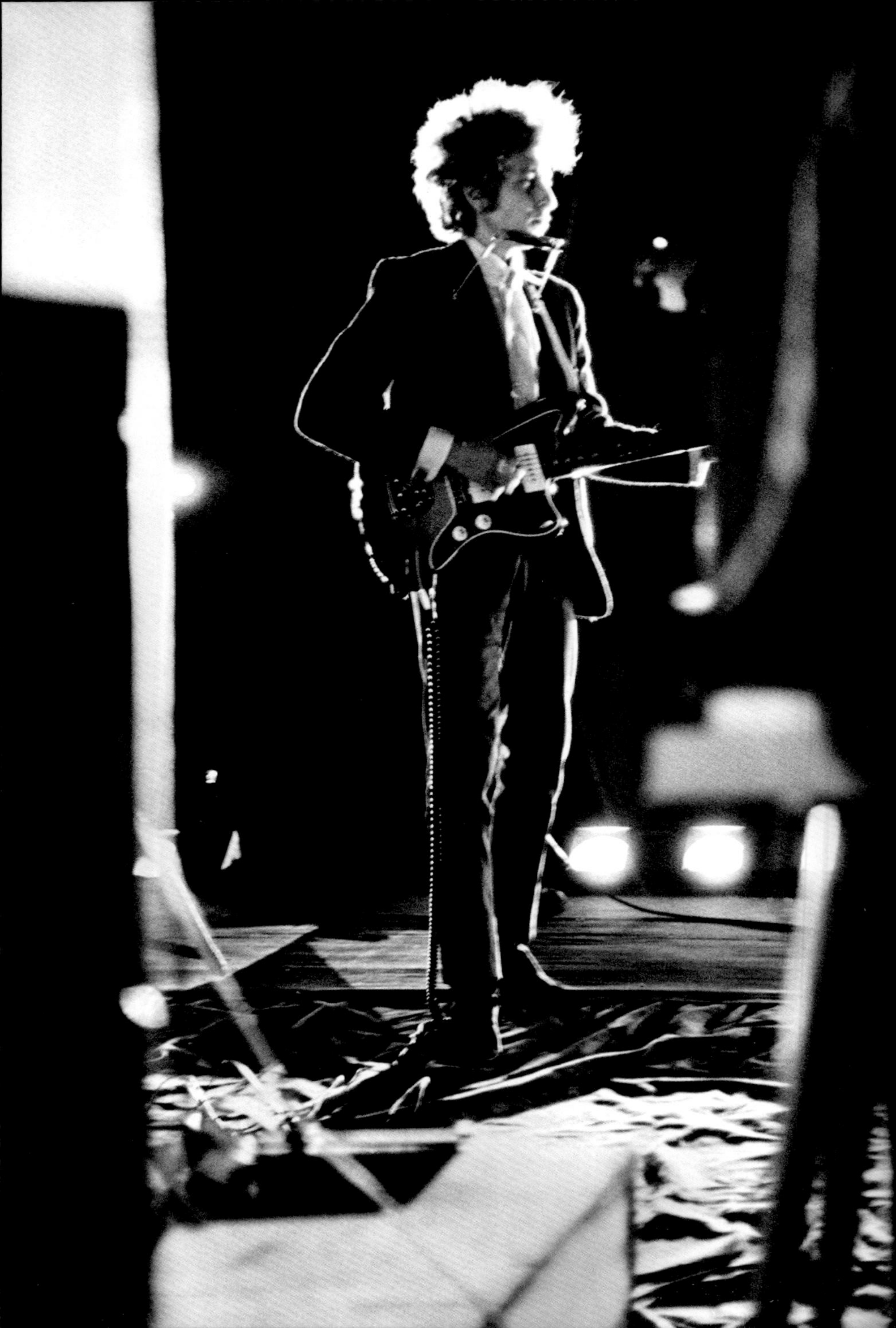

I don’t want to fake you out
Take or shake or forsake you out
I ain’t lookin’ for you to feel like me
See like me or be like me
All I really want to do
Is, baby, be friends with you

ALL I REALLY WANT TO DO

Post-
script

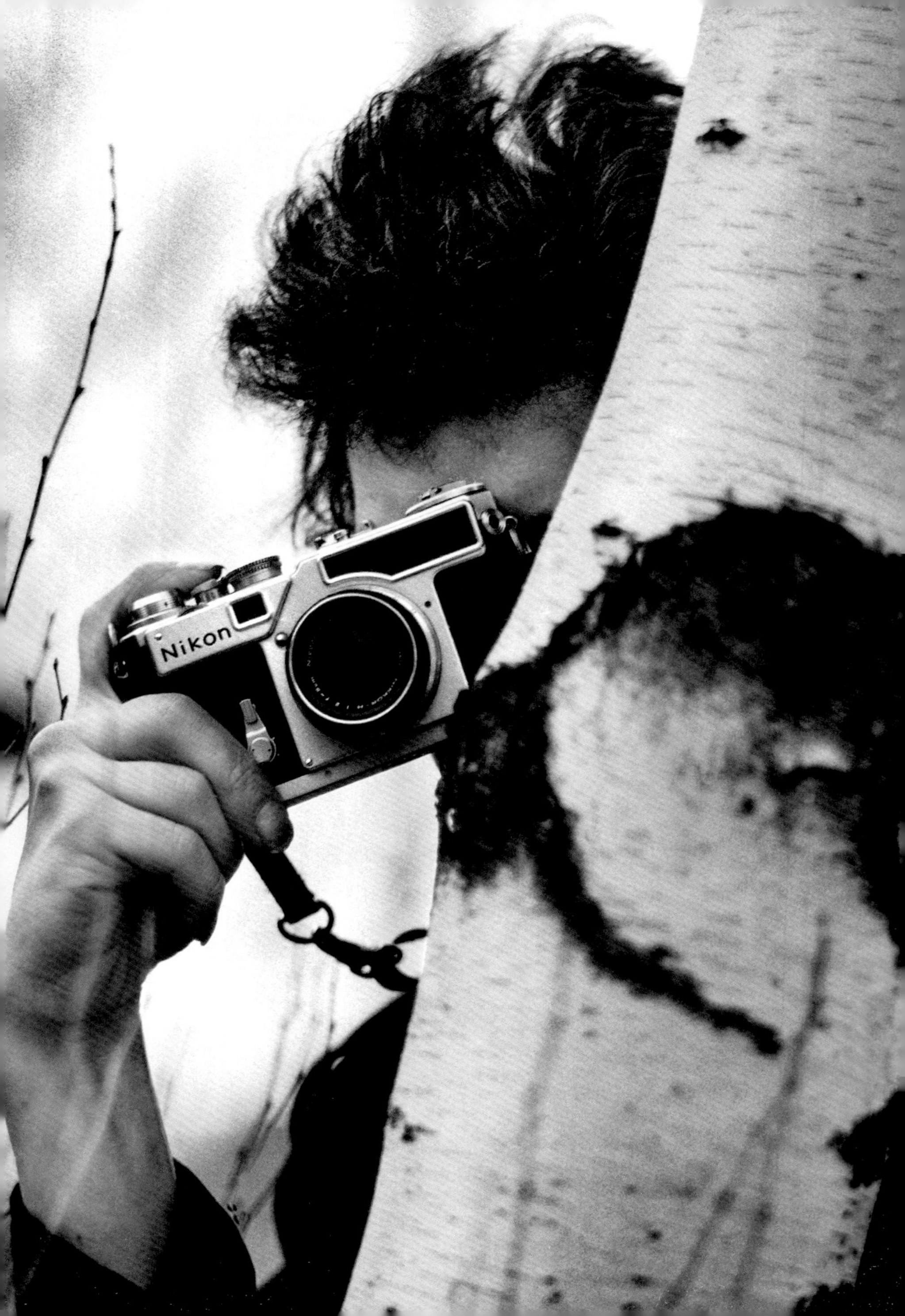
Nikon

I read an account of that night in Forest Hills that described objects being thrown onto the stage and half of the audience becoming a mob. It would have taken a major-league ballplayer to throw any object onto the stage, considering the distance that separated it from the stands. A few people in the audience did make a run for the stage; one or two actually succeeded in mounting the platform. When they did, they seemed content just to run across. I asked one boy why he did it and he replied, "I just wanted to touch him."

The thing I remember most about the show was that when Bob started a new number, there was quiet. The audience had the right to disapprove, and they did, but at the same time they listened to the material. They were willing to give Dylan his chance. They respected him . . .

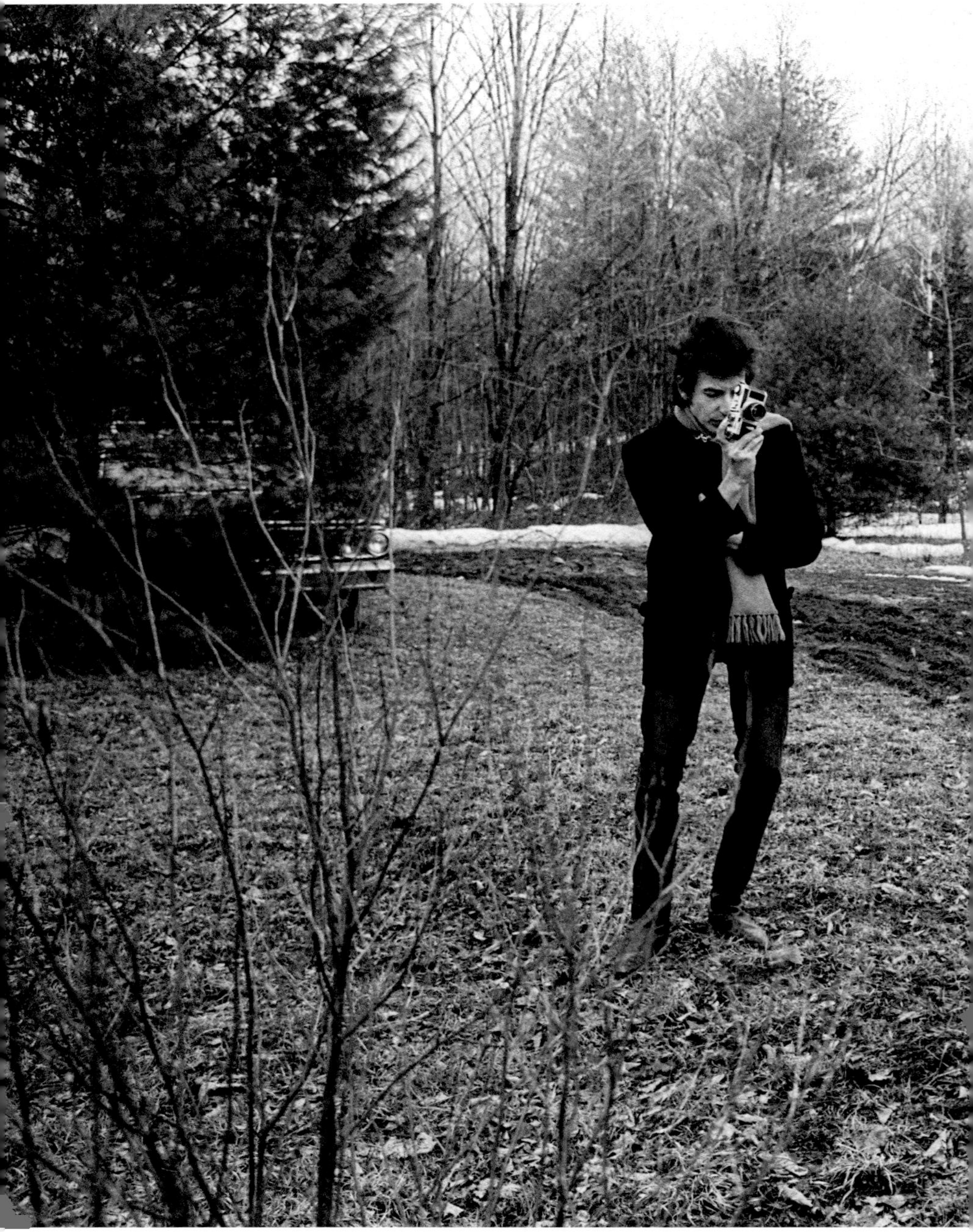

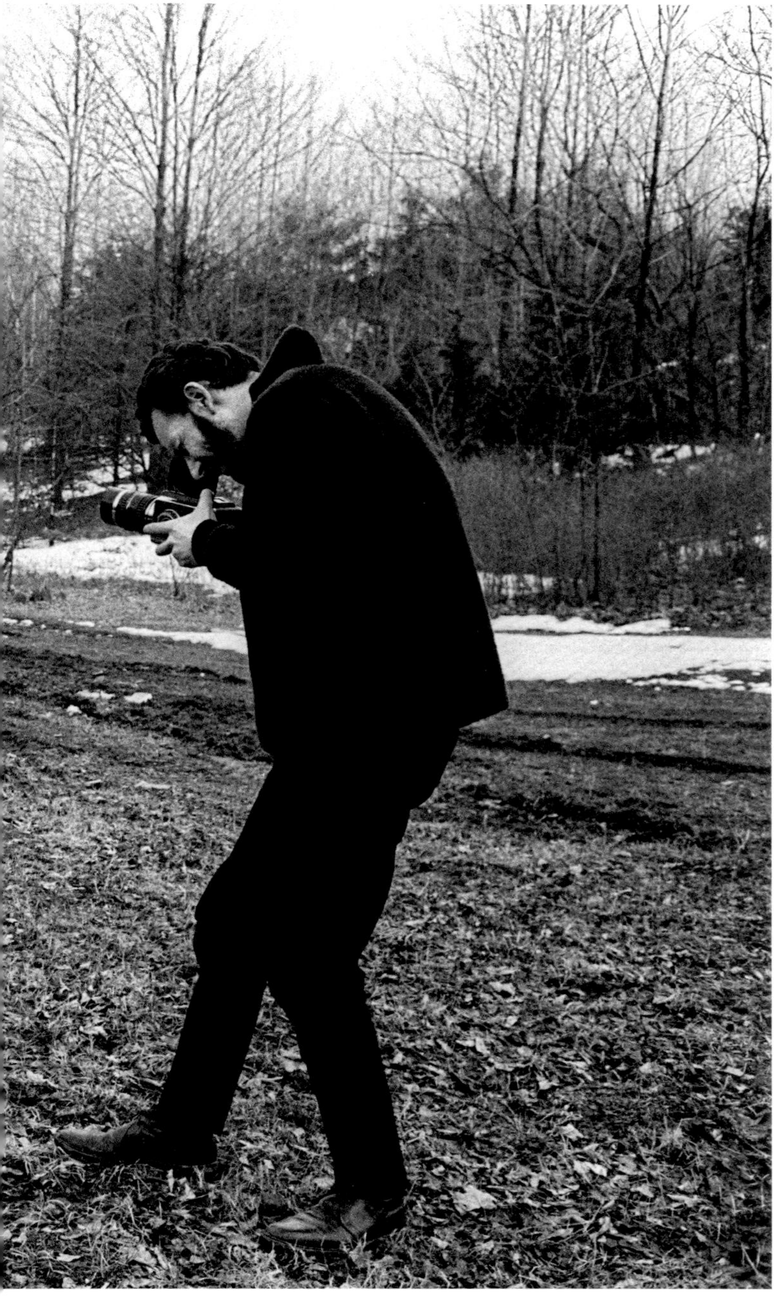

Through a Looking Glass

The first person who looked into a pool of still water and made the connection that the image in the water and himself were one and the same began to make it possible for us to understand ourselves and place ourselves in time and space. With the ability of the painter and the sculptor, early people created images of those around them, of special people who were to be known, revered, and remembered. Combined with language it enabled humanity to form a history of itself and to preserve it.

During the nineteenth century we produced a means of mirroring the image of people, things, and places so that we had an incredibly accurate record we could preserve. Using a number of already known entities, the camera was born, with the means to fix and preserve a mirror-like image of its subject in a permanent way--and that changed everything. Imagine our world and our body of knowledge without the ability of a camera-like device and a lens to bend and transfer the light of the images it sees in such a way so that millions upon millions of others could share the moment, the information and the beauty it can find. Just look around and remove all of the lens-made pictures you might connect with in a single day, one 24-hour period.

The lens, like the pool of water, is now the way we see and transfer very much of what we know. It is our "looking glass" through which we can recognize ourselves and learn where we've been and who, what, and where we are.

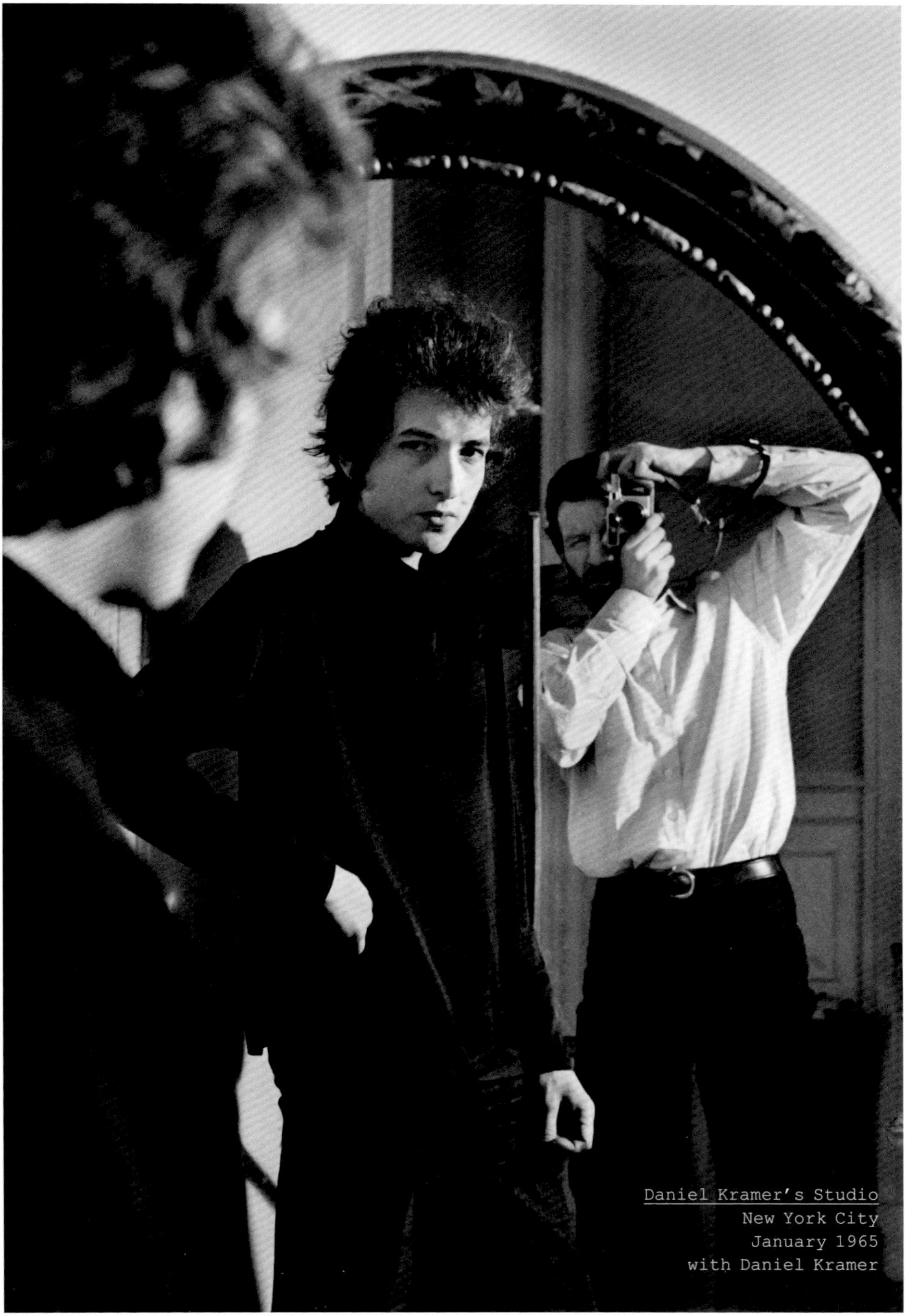

Daniel Kramer's Studio
New York City
January 1965
with Daniel Kramer

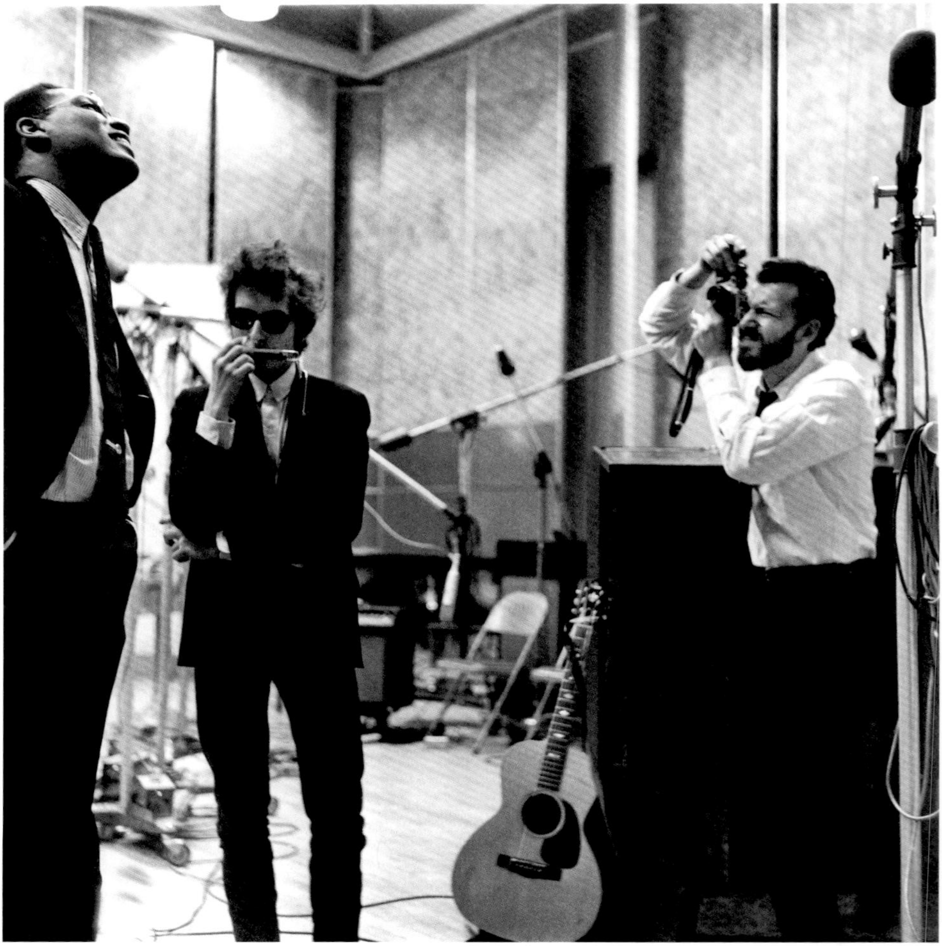

Bob Dylan is as iconic now as he's ever been. He still brings us music with the same vigor and prolific creativity as ever. His love of music, his admiration of the songwriters who came before him, is still intact. He's been touring near relentlessly since 1988, still putting everything into his live performances. He releases new albums on a fairly regular basis, and surprised his audience with a collection of classic standards, _Shadows in the Night_, an album he said he's wanted to make since the 1970s but "waited for the right time." It does what Bob Dylan has always done best, which is surprise us while pushing his own boundaries. He's never let us put him in a box, never allowed us to categorize him. As an artist, he's in constant flux and the result is that he is continually compelling, inspiring, and wonderfully infuriating. He remains, eternally, the young man who couldn't sit still for a portrait, the man who wants to do what feels right for him--not what is expected of him--and he has become our man for all seasons.

--_Daniel Kramer, NYC, 2015_

Daniel Kramer (1933-2024) was a New York City-based photographer and film director whose portraits and picture stories have been published worldwide in major national and international magazines, books, corporate reports, and on numerous album covers. His film work encompasses documentaries, commercials, and educational films. Kramer's subjects include artists, writers, musicians, athletes, political figures, and captains of industry. His photographs have been widely collected and exhibited in venues such as the George Eastman House, the National Portrait Gallery, the Brooklyn Museum, the Rock and Roll Hall of Fame Museum, the Morgan Library and Museum, the International Center of Photography, the Whitney Museum of American Art, the Museum of Photographic Arts, the Musée de la musique (France), the Kunsthal (Netherlands), and Museum Folkwang (Germany).

Kramer's 1967 book, Bob Dylan: A Portrait of the Artist's Early Years, with 140 photographs, recounted his long association with Bob Dylan and was the first major work about the young artist.

Born in Brooklyn, New York, and self-educated in photography, Kramer worked with Philippe Halsman, and Allan and Diane Arbus, and was mentored by his friend W. Eugene Smith. He lectured or conducted workshops at the School of Visual Arts, the International Center of Photography, the Center for Documentary Studies at Duke University, and the Columbia Journalism School. He was a longtime member of the Directors Guild of America, and a past vice president of the American Society of Media Photographers.

FRONT COVER Dylan in Daniel Kramer's studio, New York City, January 1965
PAGES 2, 188 AND 192 Bringing It All Back Home recording session, New York City, January 1965
PAGE 8 Woodstock, March 14, 1965
PAGE 13 On the way to Philadelphia, October 10, 1964
PAGE 14 Rehearsal, Forest Hills, Queens, August 28, 1965
PAGE 17 Town Hall, Philadelphia, October 10, 1964
PAGES 182 AND 184-185 Dylan and Kramer, Woodstock, March 14, 1965
BACK COVER McCarter Theatre, Princeton, New Jersey, November 7, 1964

 Some text adapted and updated from the book Bob Dylan by Daniel Kramer (1967). Daniel Kramer's prints are represented by Staley-Wise Gallery in New York, Fahey/Klein Gallery in Los Angeles, Govinda Gallery in Washington, D.C., and Snap Galleries in London. Daniel Kramer's vintage and estate prints are available upon request through Morrison Hotel Gallery-www.morrisonhotelgallery.com

EACH AND EVERY TASCHEN BOOK PLANTS A SEED!
Each year, we offset our annual carbon emissions with carbon credits at the Instituto Terra, a reforestation program in Minas Gerais, Brazil, founded by Lélia and Sebastião Salgado. To find out more about this ecological partnership, please check: www.taschen.com/institutoterra.
Inspiration: unlimited.
Carbon footprint: (almost) zero.

Want to see more? Visit taschen.com to view our current publications, browse our latest magazine, and subscribe to our newsletter.

Hohenzollernring 53
50672 Köln, Germany
www.taschen.com

ORIGINAL EDITION © 2016 TASCHEN GmbH
EDITOR Nina Wiener, New York
ART DIRECTION Josh Baker, Oakland

ISBN 978-3-7544-0400-3
Printed in Italy

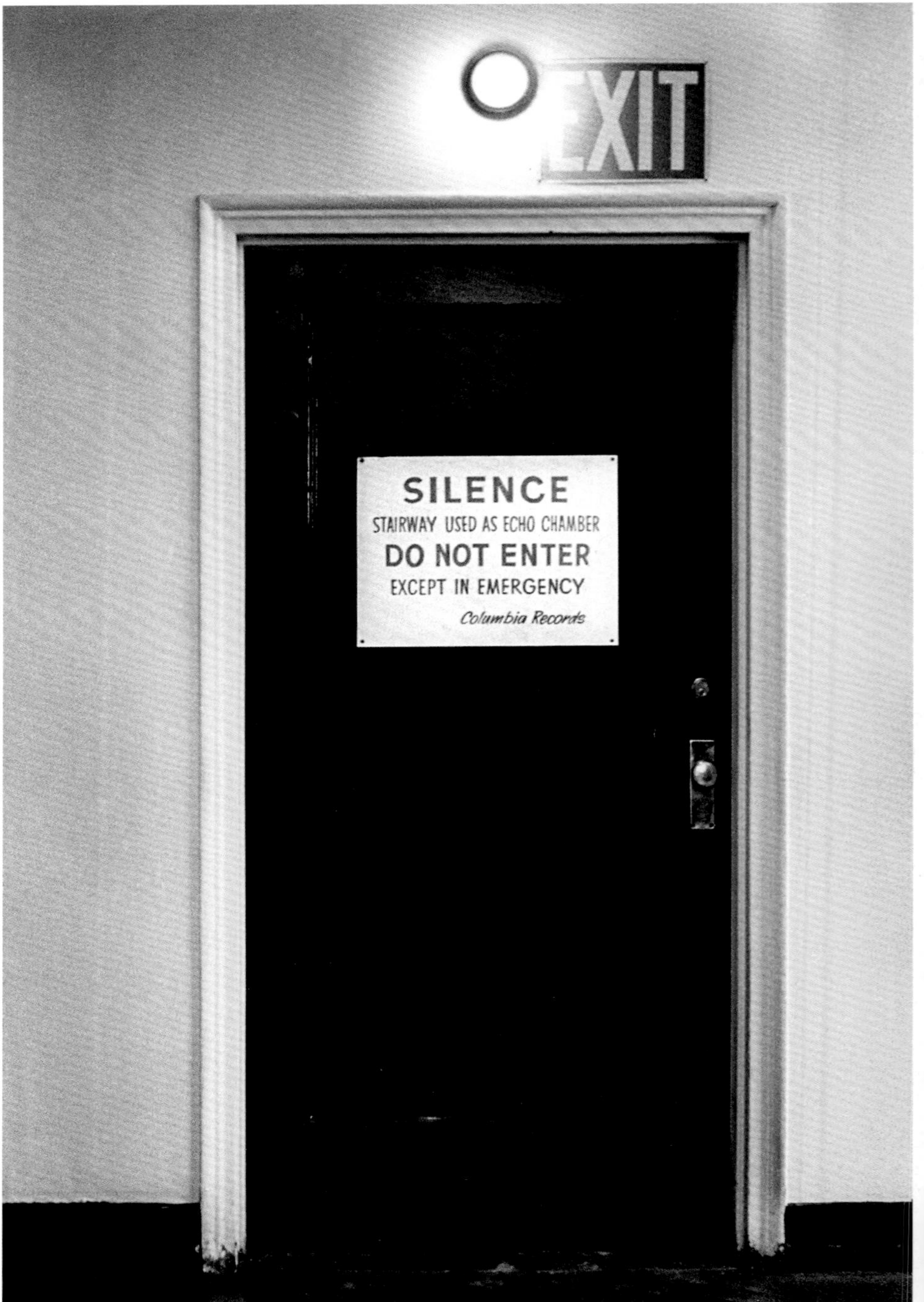
EXIT
SILENCE
STAIRWAY USED AS ECHO CHAMBER
DO NOT ENTER
EXCEPT IN EMERGENCY
Columbia Records